D1208735

Exploration Warehousing

Exploration Warehousing
Turning Business Information into Business Opportunity

W. H. Inmon
R. H. Terdeman
Claudia Imhoff

Wiley Computer Publishing

John Wiley & Sons, Inc.

NEW YORK • CHICHESTER • WEINHEIM • BRISBANE • SINGAPORE • TORONTO

Publisher: Robert Ipsen

Editor: Robert M. Elliott

Managing Editor: Micheline Frederick

Text Design & Composition: North Market Street Graphics

Library of Congress Cataloging-in-Publication Data:
Inmon, William H.
    Exploration warehousing : turning business information into business opportunity /
  W. H. Inmon, R. H. Terdeman, Claudia Imhoff.
      p.   cm.
    Includes index.
    ISBN 0-471-37473-3 (cloth : alk. paper)
    1. Marketing.   2. Consumer behavior.   3. Data warehousing.   4. Database management.   I. Terdeman, R. H. (Robert H.)   II. Imhoff, Claudia.   III. Title.

HF5415.I518 2000
658.4'038'0285574—dc21   00-027525

Printed in the United States of America.

10 9 8 7 6 5 4 3 2 1

CONTENTS

The authors are deeply indebted to Bob Elliott, our editor, for his forbearance in the production of this work. Busy, diverse schedules of authors working in very different segments of the industry make a cooperative effort particularly challenging.

Special thanks to Emilie Herman, who coordinated much of the effort with a cheerful disposition and retained her sense of humor throughout. This task was made more difficult by the need to guide a relatively new author through the production process.

Michael Berry also must be acknowledged for his superb effort in bringing to the attention of the authors the definition of data mining as seen through the eyes of working data miners. Michael is a joy to work with. His humor and his own sense of humility overshadow his huge expertise. Michael has the joy that comes with a true sense of the fun that knowledge discovery can bring.

Special thanks to Florence and Michael Terdeman, who created the social space to complete the writing process. Thanks also to the Bandit Boy for providing company and entertainment, and to fellow workers Eric Mann and Malcolm de Mayo, who provided the freedom to help translate innovation into action.

Bill Inmon, the father of the data warehouse concept, has written 40 books on data management, data warehouse, design review, and management of data processing. Bill has had his books translated into Russian, German, French, Japanese, Portuguese, Chinese, Korean, and Dutch. Bill has published over 250 articles in many trade journals. Bill founded and took public Prism Solutions. Bill's latest company—Pine Cone Systems—builds software for the management of the data warehouse/data mart environment. Bill holds two software patents. Articles, white papers, presentations, and much more material can be found on his web site, www.billinmon.com.

R. H. Terdeman is Chief Data Warehousing Architect at EMC, The Enterprise Storage company. Bob has over 30 years of experience and has advised and consulted on over a hundred data warehousing projects. He has authored papers and articles on data warehousing technology with Bill Inmon and PWC. Bob is one of EMC's most requested speakers.

Claudia Imhoff, Ph. D., teaches courses about the Corporate Information Factory architecture, including the construction of data warehouses and operational data stores, and the development of Customer Relationship Management applications. She is a popular speaker for national and international events on these topics. Dr. Imhoff has coauthored three books dealing with different aspects of the Corporate Information Factory and is a columnist for *DM Review*. She was recently elected to the Board of Advisors for DAMA International, and she recently won the 1999 Individual Achievement Award from DAMA International. She is an advisor for several corporations as well as for The Data Warehousing Institute.

Most Americans are taught as children that all people are created equal. This is of course an idealistic statement and is meant to define rights in the legal process. In the real world, not all people are equal; some are small and some are tall, some are rich and some are poor, and finally, each has a unique set of different talents. In this book we use the terms *farmer, businessperson, explorer, data miner,* and *analyst* to define sets of activities, known as *roles*, rather than people. In the everyday world each individual human being has a matrix of roles, many of which are engaged in simultaneously. Thus during a typical day an individual can be parent, spouse, sibling, child, friend, and businessperson. What makes this possible is that people are trained from early childhood to accept the multitude of roles that need to exist simultaneously.

In business it has become clear, particularly in the last decade, that successful enterprises are often characterized by the ability to define a common strategic objective across all the jobs or business roles. In this book we have defined the exploration process and tool set, and the data mining process and tool set. In both roles the set of tools defined by example in this work is used only to illustrate the nature of the activities. There are new exploration and data mining techniques and tools evolving every day. In the course of any given business day, any individual may perform one or more of the roles and use one or more of these tools. The blurring of the lines between these many roles as a rule is a good thing. It makes the acquisition of knowledge a holistic act and assures that business opportunity is seized from information.

It is the purpose of this work to provide the business user enough conceptual information about tools, roles, and processes so the entire value chain can be understood and utilized. The starting point in the value chain is the obtaining of information from many sources, but most important is the data warehouse, which has become the pivotal point for information coalescence within the Corporate Information Factory.

Data warehousing has come in a short decade from taunted theory to conventional wisdom. Perhaps the simplest and most eloquent testimony to the success of data warehousing is the organization's ability to simply access and analyze data. With a data warehouse, the end user can do the following:

- Access data easily
- Access data quickly

- Access data cheaply
- Access data and be confident that it is accurate

Prior to data warehousing, none of these capabilities were feasible.

However, data warehousing has also brought with it a new opportunity that a few companies are just now starting to take advantage of. In a way, the opportunity that is in front of us is greater than anything that has preceded it. The opportunity is to turn data and information—truly—into competitive advantage.

This book will show that from the study and analysis of data alone, properly applied, it is possible to identify business patterns that in turn can be exploited in the marketplace. The business opportunities come in many forms:

- Introduction of new products and services
- Packaging of old products and services differently
- Discontinuity of products and services
- Discovery and stimulation of new market places
- Tightening of the grip of existing marketplaces
- Streamlining of operations

This book shows the businessperson what infrastructure must be in place and what steps must be followed to turn data into competitive advantage. The analysis begins with the simple proposition: How do you identify business patterns of data that are potentially so important? The patterns are identified through the process of exploration. Once identified in the exploration process, assumptions and hypotheses are formed, and are posited in a form useful to a data miner. Data mining examines these assumptions and hypotheses to discover the truth about the patterns being investigated. Only then can we turn these patterns into ideas that we can exploit for competitive advantage.

What is the process of exploration? The process of exploration begins with the gathering of integrated and relevant detailed data. The detailed data is gathered for a lengthy period of time—in some cases, up to 10 years. Then the detailed data is analyzed—in toto, by subset, randomly, by marketplace division, and so forth—to new insights into patterns of customer behavior. Once the customers' patterns of behavior are discovered, they are analyzed from the following perspectives:

- How prevalent is the pattern?
- How strong is the pattern?
- How predictable is the pattern?

As a rule, a pattern of activity or a habit will lend itself to many business interpretations. Each interpretation will form the basis of a business opportunity.

Usually, business opportunities are measured in terms of enhanced market share or increased profitability. The potential business opportunities are gathered and evaluated, and the ones that appear to be viable are brought to the surface for further investigation.

There is a significant difference between data exploration and data mining, although the two are very closely related. In many regards, data mining and exploration are like the Chinese symbols of yin and yang. One exists in a perfectly complementary state with the other to form a holistic entity. Exploration assumes only that there is some data that may be hiding some interesting and useful patterns of behavior. From those patterns hypotheses are drawn. Data mining assumes only that there is a hypothesis; its purpose is to test the validity and strength of the hypothesis. Exploration needs data mining to test the hypotheses that have been discovered. Data mining needs exploration to identify hypotheses to be tested.

The process of exploration is significantly different from other processes found in the data processing environment in that exploration *must be* a joint effort of the businessperson and the technician. If exploration is done without the businessperson, then the chance of business relevance is greatly minimized. If exploration is done without the technician, then exploration is usually inefficient and the results obtained may well be incorrect. Therefore, the *only way* that exploration is done effectively is through a joint effort of the technician and the businessperson.

In every organization, there exist two kinds of analysts: farmers and explorers. Farmers are predictable; they know what they want before they set out to find it. Farmers submit small requests that may yield small flakes of gold but that seldom find huge nuggets.

Explorers are the corporation's out-of-the-box thinkers. Explorers are unpredictable, taking different perspectives than anyone else has taken before. Explorers submit huge queries. Explorers may go six months submitting nothing, then in one week's time submit 10 different requests. The reason why explorers' requests are so huge is that they look at both detail and history. When you multiply history times detail, the result is always very large requests. Often, the explorer finds nothing; occasionally, however, the explorer finds huge nuggets.

This book is written for the explorers. The farmers of data warehousing have had their share of books written about their needs. The world of data marts exists solely for farmers. Now, it is the explorers' turn.

Upon reading this book, you will understand:

- The process of exploration
- The infrastructure of exploration

- The roles of farmers and explorers in the organization
- The way to form a basis of data that can be used for analysis
- The way that patterns can be turned into business opportunity
- The occasions when patterns should not be turned into business opportunity
- The role of data mining

The audience for this book differs from other audiences whom the author has addressed in previous books. This book is for both the technician and the businessperson. (It was written to ensure that each understands the needs of the other.) Managers or designers of the exploration environment and/or the data warehouse will find this book to be essential reading. Business analysts and decision makers will find this book useful as well; this includes financial analysts, marketing analysts, sales analysts, accountants, and others.

This book is the latest in a series of books that began with *Building the Data Warehouse*. That series includes books about operational data stores, the corporate information factory, data warehouse performance, and so on.

CHAPTER 1

The Information Infrastructure

It is the function of creative men to perceive the relations between thoughts, or things, or forms of expression that may seem utterly different, and to be able to combine them into some new forms—the power to connect the seemingly unconnected.

—WILLIAM PLOMER

When you have a second, sit down at your personal computer and look at a screen that you use in your everyday affairs. Now, ask yourself as you look at the screen—what do you see? If you are like most people, your response will be, "I see some numbers, some letters, and some symbols." In other words, you see the screen presentation (Figure 1.1).

Look again, though, at the screen and imagine the work that it took to get the numbers and the graphical images there. Do you see the infrastructure—the trail of processing—that was required to get those numbers and images to you? By a long shot, the hardest part of the screen creation is the infrastructure and background processing that was needed to create those numbers and images in the first place. The screen display is, in fact, the final product of a massive system, a massive chain of events in which the production of a number is the final act.

This chapter is about the infrastructure that is required to bring numbers onto your screen for analysis. The information infrastructure that is at the heart of corporate information is known as the *corporate information factory* (sometimes abbreviated as CIF). The general structure and components of the CIF are described in Figure 1.2.

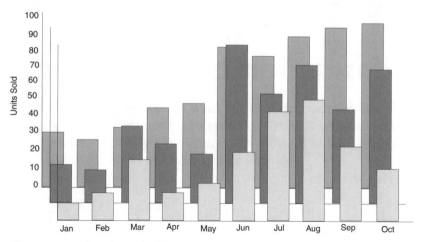

Figure 1.1 Screens are the lifeblood of communications.

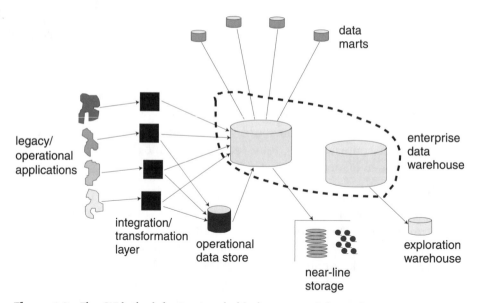

Figure 1.2 The CIF is the infrastructure behind corporate information.

The Corporate Information Factory Architecture

The components of the CIF, shown in Figure 1.2, are as follows:

- The legacy/operational application environment
- The integration and transformation layer
- The enterprise data warehouse

- The multiple data marts
- The exploration warehouse
- The near-line storage component

The information infrastructure architecture is very much like a central hub with a set of spokes. The enterprise data warehouse forms the central hub and the outlying components form the spokes. The following sections of this chapter describe each of the components of the CIF.

The Legacy/Operational Application Environment

The *legacy/operational application environment* is the environment where detailed data enters the information factory. This is the operational environment where applications exist and customers have direct interaction with business systems. Some well-known transaction-processing applications include airline reservation systems, ATM machines, bank teller systems, and insurance claims systems.

The operational application environment is so called because it is directly related to the day-to-day business operations of the corporation. Clerks, data personnel, and customers directly interact with the corporation in the operational applications environment.

The operational environment is often called the legacy environment because, in many cases, it includes the first systems and applications that the corporation had.

The operational application environment is famous for its complexity. There are many legacy applications as well as many interfaces between these applications. These systems and their interfaces have grown up over a long period of time. Figure 1.3 shows a typically complex workflow through the operational/legacy environment. As shown in Figure 1.3, the staple activity in the operational application environment is the transaction. In a transaction, some unit of business is conducted between the customer and the corporation. The transaction rigidly defines and constrains the work accomplished by the transaction. Once the transaction is complete, a record of the transaction appears in the information system that governs the transaction.

In many operational environments, applications are not well integrated. Each application focuses on its immediate requirements; as a result, applications may not agree on such basic things as the following:

- Who is a customer?
- What is a transaction?
- What is a product?

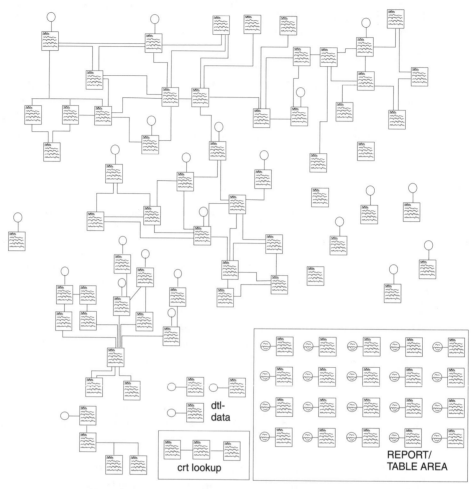

Figure 1.3 The operational environment is famous for its complexity: a flow of data from one system to the next for a large insurance company.

The lack of integration across different applications can be seen in a simple example. Separate financial applications scattered around the world transact business in dollars, pounds, and yen. To achieve a consolidated corporate picture, the results must be converted into a single currency. The lack of integration in this example is minuscule compared with the serious and consequential lack of integration that is found in most companies.

The Integration and Transformation Layer

In the *integration and transformation layer* of the CIF, unintegrated data from legacy applications is converted to an integrated structure that is compatible with data coming from other legacy applications. Data passes from the operational/legacy application environment into the integration and transformation layer, where it undergoes a severe transformation. Different types of conversions are done to the data simultaneously. Figure 1.4 illustrates some of the conversions that occur in the integration and transformation layer.

The interesting aspect of the integration and transformation layer is that *all* of these conversions happen at once. In a normal data warehouse environment, many other types of conversions occur as well. Some of these conversions include standardization of units (as illustrated), standardization of domains (state values), and standardization of data types (numbers for values instead of characters).

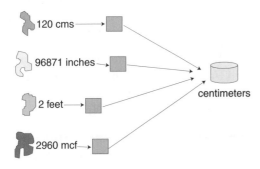

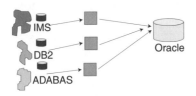

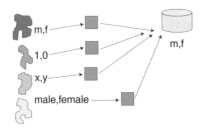

Figure 1.4 Some common examples of the kinds of integration that occur as data passes from the operation environment to the data warehouse environment.

The good news is that there is no need to manually create the interface code between the legacy application environment and the data warehouse environment; this process can be automated. There is software that allows transformation specifications to be entered into the system, and then it generates the code in whatever language the system analyst desires. This software also automates the code maintenance and makes the documentation describing the transformation available as part of the data warehouse infrastructure.

The Enterprise Data Warehouse

At the center of the CIF universe is the *enterprise data warehouse*, which is sometimes simply called the *data warehouse*. The enterprise data warehouse contains the integrated, granular data that forms the foundation of the data warehouse environment. This integration simply refers to the coming together of data from disparate sources. Normalization is the ideal state of affairs. However, data can be centralized and not normalized and still be valuable.

Normalized data is extremely flexible, so it can be shaped and reshaped, or one unit of data can be easily attached to another, depending on the database analyst's wishes. Also, granular data in the enterprise data warehouse can be summarized or otherwise aggregated to create new forms of the data.

It is useful to think of the enterprise data warehouse as an unstructured pile of Legos. (Here, we're referring to the toy building blocks made of plastic bricks.) Figure 1.5 illustrates this metaphor.

The basic building unit with Legos is a small plastic block. Each block has bumps on the top and holes on the bottom that are used to connect it to other blocks. With imagination and enough blocks, you can fashion almost any type

Enterprise
Data
Warehouse

=

Legos

Figure 1.5   One way to think of an enterprise data warehouse is as a large pile of unstructured Legos.

of toy with Legos. The granular, normalized data blocks that reside in an enterprise data warehouse are similar to piles of unjoined Legos. The pile itself has no particular structure. It requires a builder who will take the blocks and shape them into a toy.

One of the important elements of the enterprise data warehouse is that it stores and manages data over a period of time. In most organizations, historical data is collected for reuse. In most other environments, historical data is collected and stored in a manner that is unsuitable for future usage.

Data Marts

Data marts are structures shaped by the granular data that is found in the enterprise data warehouse (see Figure 1.6). Data marts belong to specific departments within a company—usually finance, accounting, sales, or marketing—and are shaped by the requirements of the departments. Consequently, the design of each data mart is unique.

The data structures that are found inside the data mart are less granular than those that are found in the enterprise data warehouse. They are called *star*, or *snow flake schemata*, because when different types of data are gathered by end users, they form unusual and elaborately shaped structures. To extend our earlier Lego analogy, the data mart is composed of the different toys that can be shaped from the Legos, as shown in Figure 1.7.

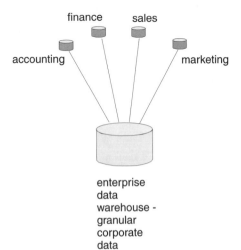

finance   sales

accounting   marketing

enterprise
data
warehouse -
granular
corporate
data

Figure 1.6 Data marts are designed to match the specific requirements of a company's departments.

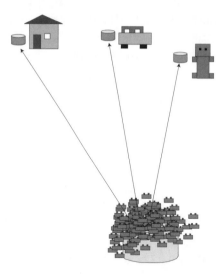

Figure 1.7 If the enterprise data warehouse consists of an unstructured pile of Legos, then data marts contain the small toys that are made from these Legos.

The Exploration Warehouse

The *exploration warehouse* exists solely for the purpose of satisfying the needs for exploration in the CIF environment. Figure 1.8 demonstrates how the exploration warehouse is a direct product of the enterprise data warehouse.

To explain the role of the exploration warehouse, consider what happens when an explorer wishes to approach the enterprise data warehouse. Typically, the queries that the explorer wishes to submit are very large. The query is submitted against the enterprise data warehouse, but almost immediately the data warehouse administrator throws the query off. The explorer approaches the data warehouse administrator and is told that if the explorer's query is allowed to execute, it will ruin performance for all of the other users of the enterprise data warehouse. The explorer now has no place to go to run his or her query.

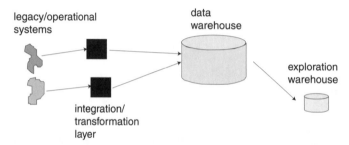

Figure 1.8 The exploration warehouse is fed from the enterprise data warehouse.

The exploration warehouse is the ideal place to go when there is heavy and uncharted analysis to be done, as it contains a wide array of historical and detailed data that is drawn from the enterprise data warehouse.

Near-Line Storage

Near-line storage complements disk storage in the enterprise data warehouse by housing rarely accessed data on photo optical or siloed tape storage. This way, it can still be accessed, albeit at a slower pace than data that is stored on disk.

There are several reasons why near-line storage makes a lot of sense for the mature CIF. They include the following:

- Using near-line storage brings the cost of data warehousing down dramatically. Robust warehouses are more affordable when the data is spread over multiple storage media.

- Storing the enterprise data warehouse only on disk forces the designer to compact and to aggregate data, and this cannot satisfy the corporation's functionality requirements. With near-line storage, however, he or she can design the data warehouse at the lowest levels of granularity.

- Moving unused data out of actively used disk storage greatly enhances the efficiency of query processing.

Near-line storage also plays the important role of feeding data to the exploration warehouse. The near-line storage component contains a wealth of detailed historical data, which is exactly what the exploration warehouse needs. Data is fed directly to the exploration warehouse on an as-needed basis.

These, then, are the components of the CIF. The CIF forms the basis of all Decision Support System (DSS) processing. Different parts of the CIF support various exploration-processing activities.

Do I Have to Build All of the Corporate Information Factory?

One of the most pleasing aspects of the CIF infrastructure is that it does not have to be built in its entirety to be useful. Indeed, most corporations do not have the entire CIF up and running as described in the previous section of this book. For a variety of reasons, the CIF is instead built one piece at a time, using only the parts that are needed at that time. This piecemeal approach doesn't affect the usefulness of the parts that are in existence, however.

Exploration Processing

Exploration processing is the process of looking for information that will yield significant business advantage from data that is gathered by the corporation into the CIF. Exploration processing is an inherently heuristic activity: Each step's focus depends on the results obtained from the previous step. In heuristic processing, you can plan the first step of analysis, but that is about as far as you can go until you actually execute that step.

As an example of a simple heuristic analytical process, consider snow shovel sales for a particular winter. The analyst notes that snow shovel sales generally were down from previous years and wishes to know why. The first step is to gather several previous years' worth of sales data to see if a trend has been building. If this analysis does reveal a trend, it is possible that this year's sales were predictable. If, on the other hand, the analyst determines that there has been no long-term downward trend in sales, this year's drop would appear to be a one-time event.

The next thing the analyst looks at is annual snowfall. Was this year's snowfall significantly lower than that of previous years? The analyst discovers that, indeed, this year's total snowfall was lower than the average year's snowfall. However, the average snowfall was only 15 percent higher than this year's, whereas snow shovel sales were 56 percent lower than the average. The analyst concludes that, although the drop in snow shovel sales may be influenced by the drop in snow levels, there were still other factors at work.

The analyst then looks at the snowfall activity pattern. Even though there was only a small 15 percent drop in snowfall this year, most of the snow fell in the late winter and the early spring. When snow falls at that time, people pay less attention to the snow because they feel it will melt faster in the spring; consequently, people are less likely to shovel snow during those times. The analyst discovers that 48 percent more snow fell in the spring than normal, and that 65 percent less snow fell during the traditional winter months. Now, the analyst feels that the explanation for the drop in snow shovels is coming into focus.

The simple analysis described here is a classical heuristic analysis. One step of analysis leads to another. There is no prescribed plan for analysis that can be preplanned at the outset.

Because exploration processing is heuristic, there are occasions when the explorer will go looking for things and will never find them. There are many reasons why the explorer may not discover a basis for behavior:

- The explorer may not have access to all of the relevant data.
- The relevant data, even if available, may be so complex that analysis won't be able to decipher it.
- The volume of data is so large that the explorer is overwhelmed.
- The tools with which the explorer has to work are limited.
- The behavior occurs under such unusual conditions that the explorer is unable to identify the conditions.

In short, exploration processing is much more of an art than a science, and there are many conditions that work to defeat the efforts of even the best explorer.

What Is the Explorer Looking For?

Explorers look for behavior patterns, unusual occurrences, and relationships between activities and data that have promise for enhancing business position. The world of the business explorer/analyst is one of the here and now. Current and relevant business behavior patterns can do a business some good today, or at the latest tomorrow. Some examples of patterns that business explorers look at include the following:

- Are customers buying more or less alcoholic goods today than they were a year ago?
- How has the mix of alcoholic beverages changed in terms of sales this year from the last?
- What is the effect of promotions on alcoholic beverage sales?
- What is the effect of advertising on alcoholic beverage sales?
- What local geographical tendencies are there in alcoholic beverage sales?

What Does the Explorer Need?

It is a mistake for explorers to attempt analysis using summary data, which can mask detailed data. The explorer *must* operate at the detailed level to find nuggets of wisdom that can give his or her company a competitive advantage.

Consider the analyst who is looking at corporate oil sales. The analyst can simply state what total quarterly sales were for the oil company, but that information isn't particularly useful on its own. Instead, the analyst needs to go down a level or two and discuss West Texas crude and Arabian light so management can begin to find trends in the types of sales made. It may even be necessary to go down to the specific shipment level to see trends occurring. There is a point after which detail becomes a hindrance, and there is such a thing as too low a level of detail. When the volume of detailed data is not useful and distinctions between units of measurement are not meaningful, then detail starts to become detrimental to exploration. In the oil sales example, tracking the movement of individual barrels of oil is simply too low a level of detail to be useful for most processing and analysis.

Detailed data, however, is not all that the explorer needs to use. The explorer needs to use historical data as well, because the conditions that trigger an event do not occur frequently. Therefore, the explorer must look at many instances of data over a long time period to capture the necessary information.

Suppose an analyst is studying the habits of bank loan customers as they take out loans and repay them. Looking at one or two months' worth of transactions does not provide a proper foundation for making statements about the customers' borrowing and repayment habits. Instead, it is necessary to look at the customers' habits over a longer period of time, sometimes years, to find patterns of behavior.

Social scientists have long understood that behavioral patterns are seasonally affected. Thus, to understand changes in demand for perennial products, multiple points of observation must be obtained. This translates to at least two consecutive seasons of data. Two seasons of data, however, will only yield a linear plot. Linear plots do reflect trends, which in most cases are reflected better by a curve than a straight line. To obtain curvilinear behavior, at least three points are required; for this reason, most data warehouses that deal with perennial behavior contain at least 27 months of detailed data.

Analyzing Patterns

Why is it that patterns are of such interest and such value to the corporation? It is because they are the start of a sequence of activities that ultimately leads to corporate opportunity—and not just ordinary corporate opportunity, but new and innovative corporate opportunity. This chain of events is depicted in Figure 1.9.

This figure shows that the gathering of patterns is the start of an interesting sequence of events. Once data has been gathered and patterns have been analyzed, patterns are identified and are used as a basis for understanding behavior. Once behavior is understood, it can be predicted. Once behavior can be predicted, corporate positioning is possible. There are many forms that corporate positioning can take, including the following:

- Introduction of new products
- Introduction of new services
- Packaging of old or new products in a new form
- Marketing of products and services in a novel manner

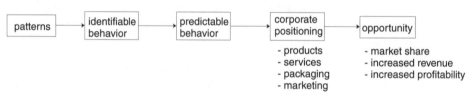

Figure 1.9 The path to opportunity.

Corporate positioning helps open up opportunities that can be measured by revenue. Corporate opportunities take the form of increased market share, protected existing market share, increased revenue, increased profitability, and so forth. This sequence of events is at the heart of a company's ability to grow and remain sensitive to opportunity. At the start of the chain of events is the recognition, and in some cases the anticipation, of patterns of activity.

Pattern-based analysis can be applied practically anywhere. Consider a movie studio that wishes to improve its profitability posture. Prior to pattern-based opportunity analysis, the movie studio relied on intuition. Decisions like what pictures were made, when they were released, and how they were promoted were made by a few executives, based on their intuition and their position in the hierarchy of management. In recent years, the studio has not produced enough hits and the number of viewers for the few hits that the studio did produce was relatively small.

Then, the corporate chief information officer (CIO) decides pattern-based analysis is necessary to make predictions about future films. The first job of the CIO is to gather a large amount of information about already released movies and how well they have done. In particular, the CIO gathers the following:

- Movie title
- Date of release
- Total number of viewers
- Length of run
- Genre (e.g., action, thriller, romance, drama, etc.)
- Stars

The CIO collects as many units of information as possible, from all studios and sources where such information is available. This information collection goes back as much as 20 years. Most information collections, however, go back no more than 10 years. Once the base information is collected, the CIO sets out to analyze the information to find if there are interesting patterns. The CIO looks at many variables, including:

- Do action films do better during Christmas time than in the summer?
- Do drama films that open early in the Christmas season last the entire season?
- Which stars have the most drawing power?
- Are there "summer stars" and "Christmas stars"?
- Do romance films have longer drawing power than action films?

Once the patterns are detected, the CIO creates a chart that predicts what kinds of films featuring certain stars should be released for optimum impact.

There are as many different types of pattern analyses as there are patterns. Following are discussions of two types of pattern analysis: simple and complex.

Simple Pattern Analysis

The most basic type of pattern analysis is simple counts of single events. The simple counts can be broken up in any number of ways, and the counts that are obtained can then be correlated with other events. For example, a simple count can be made of every loaf of bread that is sold in a metropolitan area. A bread company goes to the market basket level and finds out what sales are made. The counts can be made daily, weekly, monthly, or on any other basis desired. In addition, counts can be made by city section. By comparing the different sales counts, the bread company can start to get a feel for the consumption habits of its customers. Other events can be correlated to the simple counts, such as:

- Do the counts reflect the rise or fall of sales with the seasons?
- Do the simple counts reflect the rise or fall of sales with the advent of bad weather? Good weather?
- Do the simple counts reflect the appeal of the bread to single shoppers? Married shoppers?

Although a corporation is far better off making decisions that are based on simple counts than on nothing at all, a simple raw count cannot be stretched very far. The truth is that only a limited amount of analysis can be done with simple counts, making it necessary for analysts to use more complex forms of analysis.

Complex Pattern Analysis

In complex pattern analysis, one event can be related directly to another and indirectly to any number of other events. The outcome may be a probabilistic affair with any number of entry events and multiple outcomes. Results obtained through complex pattern analysis are often questionable. Following are some reasons why pattern analysis of complex events can lead to questionable results:

- The relevant variables and events may not be identified.
- The variables and events that are identified may not be properly understood.
- The variables that are identified are understood, but only in a limited context. In other contexts, the variables are not understood at all.
- The variables and events that make up the network have been assigned incorrect probabilities of event outcome.

In short, the more complex the network for accomplishing pattern analysis, the less sure the conclusions become. As an example of a complex model for pattern analysis, consider the sequence of events that are shown in Figure 1.10.

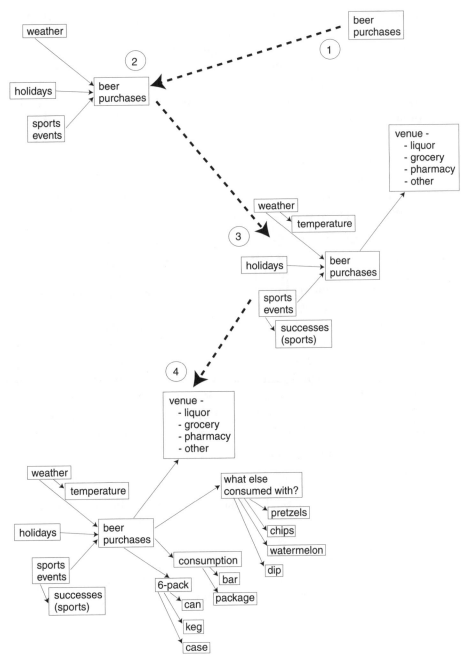

Figure 1.10 Analytical activity grows in size and sophistication from a simple start.

The analysis starts off simply enough: A company is analyzing the purchase of beer. As is the case for most complex analyses, it begins as a simple count analysis. Soon, however, management wants to know more. In the second phase of analysis, the organization analyzes the purchase of beer in the face of holidays, weather, and sports events. To no one's surprise, beer sales rise in hot weather. Holidays spark beer sales as well. Fourth of July weekend causes a consistent spike in beer sales. Baseball games and football games appear to cause a spike in sales.

The next phase includes an analysis of the effect of temperature, as well as of the local sports team's success, on the sale of beer. It is noted that making the playoffs stimulates sales. In addition, the analysis starts to include where sales are made—liquor stores, bars, grocery stores, or other venues.

Management, never satisfied by the results, thirsts for more information. In the next phase of analysis, there is an analysis of what types of beer are sold, what container the beer is in (e.g., keg, six-pack, individual bottle, case, etc.), where the beer is consumed, and what other products are bought with the beer. In short, there is a wealth of information that is now being analyzed. The model, however, is complex. For example, it is doubtful if the model can be used to determine whether temperature makes a difference in the sale of one type of beer over another, whether certain types of beer are bought by the six-pack and other types are bought by the case, or whether the World Series stimulates beer sales in a bottle. All the patterns in the world may not lead the analyst to valid and correct conclusions in this complex model. In addition, there are many omitted variables that may well be relevant to the analysis:

- Are purchases being made by males or by females?
- Are purchases being made by people in their 20s? 30s? 40s?

In short, the complex model may spur as many questions as it answers.

Pattern Processing and Data

Pattern analysis is only as good as the data on which it operates. However, not just any data will do for pattern analysis. Data needs to possess certain characteristics to serve as an effective basis for pattern analysis, including:

Integration.   The data residing in the base of data needs to have consistent definition, structure, and meaning.

Flexible structure.   The data residing at the foundation of pattern processing must be able to be shaped differently for each individual analysis.

Robust breadth.   The data that serves as a basis for pattern analysis must cover a wide breadth of subjects to be useful.

Historical content.   The data must cover an extended duration of time.

Easily accessible.   The pattern analyst needs to be able to get to the data easily.

Documented.   Data must be recognizable and understandable; otherwise, the analyst will make many assumptions that are not true. In short, the data serving as a basis for pattern processing must be rigorously defined and designed to meet the pattern analyst's needs.

The data that will serve as a basis for pattern analysis must also be granular. There is no way that each of the requirements can be met if the data is anything other than at a fine level of granularity.

Each of these data characteristics that serves as a basis for pattern processing is important enough to merit its own explanation.

Data Must Be Integrated

Integration refers to having consistent structures and definitions. If data has different meanings, then the pattern analyst is severely handicapped. Key structures, attribute definitions, and entity definitions must be consistent for the pattern analyst to access the data with confidence and efficiency.

Consider an analyst who is looking at a pool of data that contains inconsistencies. In one place, the key structure for customer is 15 bytes. In another place, customer is represented in 10 bytes. In yet another place, there is no customer key. Before bringing the data from these different places together, the analyst must expend considerable resources simply integrating it. Time that should be spent analyzing and understanding data is instead spent conditioning data. The data itself presents a barrier to analysis when it is unintegrated.

Data Should Be Structurally Flexible

Data that is used in pattern analysis must also be structurally flexible, as suggested by Figure 1.11. One day, finance wants to look at the data one way. The next day, marketing wants to look at the same data another way. On the third day, sales wants to look at the same data in yet another way. The data must be versatile to be useful to many people who want to use the same data for very different purposes. The only way that this can be accomplished is for the data to be structured in as granular a manner as is feasible.

Robust Breadth of Data

The data that is used in pattern analysis must cover a breadth of subjects to be effective. Figure 1.12 shows that there are many different types of data supporting pattern analysis: sales, customer, product, and vendor data. The pattern analyst needs to be able to roam freely among the different data bins using intuition and insight. When the pattern analyst has only a few types of data with

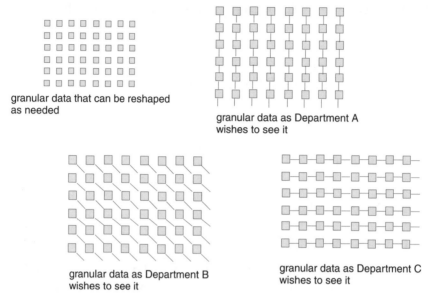

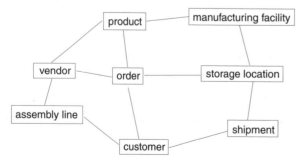

Figure 1.11 Granular data is structurally flexible.

which to work, he or she is restricted in what kinds of observations can be made. The more types of data there are, the greater the chances that the pattern analyst will be able to find patterns that are useful.

Historical Content

The pattern analyst needs to look at a number of years' worth of data to find valuable patterns. Often, patterns of interest occur only over small units of time and under stringent conditions. If the pattern analyst looks only at a small slice of data, it is a good bet that these patterns will be missed. Therefore, a lot of historical data is necessary for the pattern analyst to be most effective.

Figure 1.12 A robust amount of subject areas.

Data Must Be Easily Accessible

It does the pattern analyst no good to be able to have a lot of data if it cannot be accessed readily. Data may be inaccessible because of any or all of the following:

- It is serving the online system and cannot service the kinds of queries submitted by the pattern analyst.
- Another department "owns" the data that is needed.
- The necessary data resides on technology that is different than that available to the pattern analyst.
- Other analytical processing is occurring that preempts the pattern analyst.

There are, then, a whole host of reasons why data may not be available. *All* of these reasons must be mitigated for the pattern analyst to be effective.

Data Must Be Well Documented

It does little good for there to be an otherwise excellent source of data for the pattern analyst to work on unless the data is well documented. The minimal set of documentation needs to include:

- Definitions of the tables and columns
- Description of the structure of the data
- Description of the relationships between tables and columns
- Identification of the source of the data
- Description of how much data there is
- Description of the structure of the tables and attributes
- Description of the frequency of refreshment

There can, of course, be documentation of other more unique aspects of the data as well.

The pattern analyst simply cannot be effective if he or she is locked into looking at data as it has always been looked at previously. To be effective, the pattern analyst must be able to visualize and imagine data in a form and structure seldom, if ever, perceived before. In many cases, the pattern analyst will find nothing useful or positive in the "imagination" analyses. Imagination analysis is somewhat like looking at clouds in an attempt to find recognizable objects. To be successful, the analyst must have the ability to take known facts and rotate them into a new context. This type of "imagineering" often leads to conceptual breakthroughs. Walt Disney brought the term *imagineering* into common usage in conjunction with the products of his company. In some cases, there is nothing to be found. In other cases, the pattern analyst simply is approaching the data improperly. However, every now and then, the pattern analyst is able to discover a previously unknown perspective in the data that is of great use to the corporation.

Acquiring Data for Pattern Analysis

All of our previous discussions assumed that data is available for pattern analysis. Is it safe, however, to assume that data for pattern analysis simply appears out of nowhere? The answer is, of course not.

Perhaps the biggest obstacle and challenge to pattern analysis is the gathering, organization, and structuring of data. In many instances, the greatest cost and challenge of doing pattern analysis is that of collecting the data to be analyzed. Figure 1.13 shows that gathering data is its own important activity.

Data can be collected from internal, external, or multiple internal systems. As the data is collected, it can be integrated or converted so that it arrives at the collection point in an integrated, cohesive state. Once the data arrives at the common collection point, it must be united with data that has already been collected.

The collection, integration, and conversion processes are extremely important; yet, organizations that are just entering the pattern analysis realm are always shocked at just how much work and resources are required to prepare for pattern analysis. (It is unheard-of for an organization to allocate a proper amount of resources for this aspect of pattern analysis the first time around.)

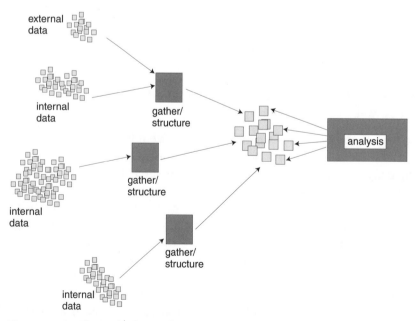

Figure 1.13 The gathering and structuring of data for analysis is a big job.

Data Quality and Pattern Processing

Because so much effort is required for data acquisition before pattern processing, it can be tempting to take shortcuts. Under pressure to get results, steps may be omitted that should not be. For example, there is the temptation to merely input available data into the pattern-processing experience without properly editing or scrubbing the data. The haste causes data to be entered into the system that is inaccurate and unintegrated. What happens when "dirty data" enters the system? The answer is a time-honored truism: Garbage in, garbage out.

The pattern analysis that results from operating on incorrect and incomplete data cannot be satisfactory, regardless of the best and most inspired efforts of the pattern analyst. Bypassing essential data integration and editing steps negates the entire pattern-processing effort.

There are many ways that data must be scrubbed, including:

- Verification that there is compatibility at the key level
- Domain checking of attributes
- Verification of data relationships, where applicable
- Commonsense analysis of data attributes
- Verification of the meaning and usage of data attributes

The Corporate Information Factory and Pattern Processing

The CIF forms a very convenient foundation for supporting pattern analysis. It is tempting to think that pattern analysis can be done anywhere in the CIF; however, pattern analysis can be done only in certain places.

Figure 1.14 shows that the proper places to do pattern analysis are the exploration warehouse, the enterprise data warehouse, and the near-line storage component. It is *not* appropriate to do pattern analysis at the following levels:

- *At the operational systems level.* Because data is unintegrated and performance constraints prohibit access.
- *At the operational data store (ODS) level.* Because of performance constraints and because data in the ODS is constantly changing. If data in the ODS is constantly changing, the analyst can never be sure whether the differences between two analyses are due to changing data, changing assumptions, or both.
- *At the data mart level.* Because data is not at a low level of granularity. Data is summarized and aggregated according to end users' needs, and the data is not fit for the kind of analysis that the pattern analyst needs to perform.

The enterprise data warehouse, the exploration warehouse, and near-line storage all have unique considerations when it comes to pattern analysis.

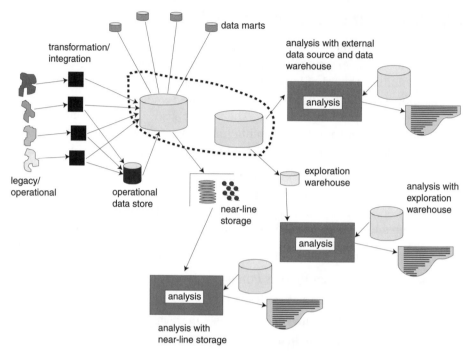

Figure 1.14 The places in the CIF where exploratory processing can be done.

Near-Line Storage and Pattern Analysis

The advantages of doing pattern analysis from near-line storage are that it contains a wealth of historical data, a great deal of detailed data, and data that is structured at a very fine level of granularity. The main disadvantage centers around the fact that near-line storage is not based on a standard database management system (DBMS). Consequently, many analysis tools will not operate in the near-line environment, or, if the tools will operate in the near-line environment, they will not operate efficiently.

A better alternative to pattern analysis from near-line storage is moving data to an exploration warehouse for analysis.

The Enterprise Data Warehouse and Pattern Analysis

One advantage of using the enterprise data warehouse as a basis for pattern analysis is that the data can be structured exactly as the pattern analyst wishes. The other advantage is that the enterprise data warehouse already exists. The pattern analyst can just start to dig in and do analysis with little or no fanfare.

There is a major disadvantage to using the enterprise data warehouse as a basis for pattern analysis. One minor disadvantage is that if pattern analysis is done on a frequent basis, it becomes a serious drain on computer resources. Other users may suffer as a result of constant pattern analysis. As long as the enterprise data warehouse is used infrequently for pattern analysis, there is no problem. Once pattern analysis starts to become a regular activity, however, it is time to move that activity off onto a separate exploration warehouse.

Exploration Warehouse and Pattern Analysis

The biggest advantage of the exploration warehouse is that the underlying technology is perfectly suited for pattern analysis. The underlying technology is equipped to handle large amounts of data and to perform the necessary kinds of analysis. Furthermore, the processing efficiency that can be achieved is significantly greater than the standard relational technology.

The disadvantages of exploration processing are that it requires its own separate environment and getting the data into that environment can be a complex task.

Exploration Warehouse—Permanent or Temporary?

One of the major issues of the exploration warehouse environment is whether an exploration warehouse should be a permanent or a temporary part of the infrastructure. In truth, an exploration warehouse can be either. There are advantages and disadvantages to both.

The advantage of having a permanent exploration warehouse is that it is immediately available should the need arise for a quick analysis. The convenience and the immediacy of the permanent exploration warehouse make it very attractive. However, there are some disadvantages, including:

- The permanent cost of the infrastructure, whether it's being used or not.
- The permanent exploration warehouse is unlikely to have all of the data needed for any given analysis. In the best of circumstances, some new data may have to be added to the exploration warehouse when it comes time for a new analysis.

The advantage of a temporary exploration warehouse is that there is no cost when it is not being used. The disadvantage is that setup time will be required every time an analysis must be done.

Whether the exploration warehouse is permanent or temporary, there must be an easy way to refresh data inside the exploration warehouse. It is unacceptable to have to reload the exploration warehouse in its entirety every time a change needs to be made.

The exploration warehouse is refreshed from either the enterprise data warehouse or near-line storage. Two types of data refreshment into the exploration warehouse need to be done (Figure 1.15):

different subsets of the same type of data

different types of data

Figure 1.15 The exploration warehouse can be broken into component pieces in more than one way.

1. Incremental loads of the same type of data.

2. Entirely new types of data to be added to the exploration warehouse.

The issues here revolve around the ability to create accurate relationships between the data that is being added and the data that already resides in the exploration warehouse.

In Summary

The infrastructure of information, or the CIF, belies the simplicity and elegance of information as presented on a screen. Many different components make up this CIF, including legacy online transactional processing (OLTP) systems, ODSes, data marts, data warehouses, customer relationship management (CRM) systems, and e-commerce systems. An easy way to think about the CIF is in terms of what can be called a hub-and-spoke architecture. The center of the hub-and-spoke architecture is the data warehouse, where granular, integrated data resides and can be reused for many forms of decision support processing.

The exploration warehouse is fed from the enterprise data warehouse, external data, or near-line storage. It is where the different out-of-the-box queries are run. Exploration processing can be done in many places in the CIF. The common places are:

- Enterprise data warehouse
- Exploration warehouse
- Near-line storage

We will cover the exploration warehouse in more detail in Chapter 2 ("The Exploration Warehouse").

The Exploration Warehouse

In a few minutes, a computer can make a mistake so great that it would take many men many months to equal it.

—MERLE MEACHEM

The exploration warehouse is exclusively dedicated to exploration processing, allowing explorers to do the following:

- Execute very large queries
- Hold large amounts of detailed data
- Restructure stored data in many ways
- Compact data
- Compress data as it enters the exploration warehouse

Exploration Warehouse Sources

The exploration warehouse is fed by three separate sources, as seen in Figure 2.1:

1. The enterprise data warehouse.
2. The near-line storage component.
3. External data.

Each of the three sources has its own set of considerations.

Enterprise Data Warehouse Feeds

Feeding data from the enterprise data warehouse into the exploration warehouse is most natural because the data needs little or no restructuring when it

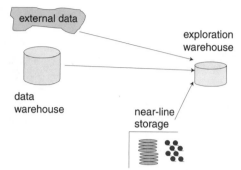

Figure 2.1 The architectural positioning of the exploration warehouse.

is moved from one to the other. Also, the enterprise data warehouse contains a robust amount of history that the exploration warehouse often needs for exploration processing.

The enterprise data warehouse is not (normally) replicated in its entirety in the exploration warehouse. Rather, subsets of data are moved from the enterprise data warehouse to the exploration warehouse by the explorer.

The data subsets can be created at the table, column, or row level. The explorer may choose an entire table to be placed into the exploration warehouse, or he may select one or two columns or rows from the enterprise data warehouse. In addition, the explorer may want to condition and alter the data as it is moved into the exploration warehouse. New columns can be created, rows can be merged, and so forth, as data is loaded into the exploration warehouse.

The enterprise data warehouse may contain several fields—for example, sales amount, tax, commission, and shipping charges. It may be convenient for the exploration analyst to create a new field—net sales—as the enterprise data is being read. Net sales equals sales amount minus (tax + commission + shipping). The intent of the new field is to create a convenience for the purpose of future analysis.

Near-Line Storage Feeds

Most of the same design considerations for the enterprise data warehouse hold true for near-line storage. However, data coming from near-line storage must be handled a little bit more carefully because so much data resides there and it is more difficult to access than data that is in the enterprise data warehouse. Near-line data is stored in a bulk, sequential format. Accessing it often requires more processing than accessing data residing on disk. Explorers shouldn't underestimate the resources required or the awkwardness of accessing huge amounts of data in near-line storage in search of a few rows. Nevertheless, the detailed, historical data that resides in the near-line storage environment makes a very attractive source for the exploration warehouse.

It is worth noting that a fair amount of conditioning of near-line storage data is necessary as the data moves into the exploration warehouse. Whereas data in the enterprise data warehouse is integrated before it enters the architectural component, the variety of data that flows into near-line storage requires careful editing and selection.

External Data Feeds

With external data, the analyst can create a contrast of data values that leads to important insights into patterns. However, acquisition and integration of data into the exploration warehouse is not nearly as controllable as data residing in a company's internal systems, and it must be conditioned (see Figure 2.2).

The act of conditioning external data includes:

- Altering the key structure of the external data
- Removing attributes
- Converting or reformatting attributes
- Calculating and creating new attributes
- Combining external data with other external data
- Resequencing external data

However, there are some important cautions to note.

The main issue is compatibility: on a key and attribute level and in terms of granularity. Key and attribute compatibility refers to the cohesiveness between the exploration warehouse data and external data.

Consider the exploration warehouse, where there is a *net sales* column. In the exploration warehouse, net sales is calculated by taking the gross sales amount and subtracting all levies, taxes, commissions, and so forth. In the external sales data, *net sales amount* is calculated by subtracting local taxes from gross sales amount. Net sales in external data is for American sales only, not European sales. There is an entirely different formula for the calculation of European net sales. Simply throwing exploration warehouse net sales with external net sales into the same exploration warehouse will produce misleading results.

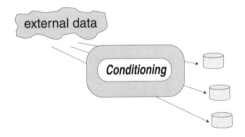

Figure 2.2 Before external data can be used effectively, it must be conditioned.

Where there are different interpretations of data, it must be rationalized so there is a single meaning of data or so the differences are understood. Otherwise, there is no way to meaningfully compare, contrast, add, or subtract different types of data.

In addition to requiring cohesiveness between the exploration warehouse data and external data, both sources must also have the same level of granularity. Suppose data in the exploration warehouse represents point-of-sale (POS, otherwise known as market basket sales) purchases by individuals. Market basket sales are at a very low level of detail, showing that Mrs. Jones bought bread, tomatoes, salmon steaks, lemons, and pound cake. The sale was made in Englewood, Colorado, at King Soopers on July 11, 1999. Point-of-sale data by store by week shows that King Soopers in Englewood, for the week of July 10 through July 18, 1999, sold 209 salmon steaks, 178 loaves of bread, 27 lemons, 197 tomatoes, and 13 pound cakes.

We can see that external data is at a much higher level of granularity than the exploration warehouse data. The only way these two types of data can be used together is if the lowest-level data is summarized or aggregated higher to be compatible with other data. In this example, the explorer would need to add the individual market basket sales together. Trying to lower the level of granularity of data is not possible. The aggregation process is always in the upward direction. Attempts to take aggregated value and force it to a lower level of granularity are made occasionally with financials; this is referred to as *allocation* or *prorating*. This allocation is done by model and is usually arbitrary. It is a substitution for the recording of actual costs and, incidentally, is the source of endless ill will in many organizations.

Another issue with using external data in the exploration warehouse is alteration of the external data. When a company using internal data for analysis finds something wrong with the data, there is always the option of going back and correcting or editing the internal data. With external data, however, there are fewer opportunities for returning and modifying data. The explorer has scant opportunity to affect the data at its source simply because by definition, the explorer cannot get to the external data at its source. With external data, it is pretty much "what you see is what you get."

Evolution of the Exploration Warehouse

As previously detailed, exploration processing can be done directly in the enterprise data warehouse and the near-line storage component (see Figure 2.3). A predictable evolution occurs in the enterprise data warehouse or near-line storage component (Figure 2.4). Once exploration processes run with regularity, processing naturally migrates to the exploration warehouse.

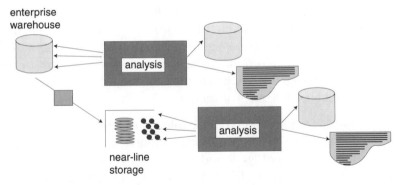

Figure 2.3 Exploration processing can be done out of the enterprise data warehouse or the near-line storage component.

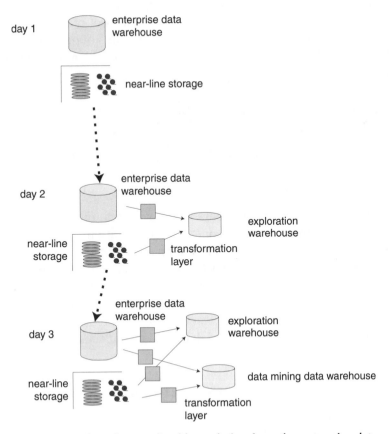

Figure 2.4 There is a predictable evolution from the enterprise data warehouse to the combination of an exploration warehouse and a data mining warehouse.

There are two reasons for the migration. The first reason has to do with performance considerations. If a few exploration processes are to be run in the enterprise data warehouse, there is no significant performance problem. However, when there are a lot of exploration processes to be run, they start to consume considerable resources if they remain in the enterprise data warehouse, and the exploration warehouse becomes attractive.

The second reason for migration to the exploration warehouse is that the technology found in the exploration warehouse is much more suited to exploration processing than the technology found in the enterprise data warehouse. The database management system (DBMS) technology found in the enterprise data warehouse is suitable for a wide variety of tasks, but is not optimized for specific tasks. However, the technology found in the exploration warehouse environment is not designed specifically for exploration processing.

There are other forces of evolution at work, though. One of those forces is the need to move exploration processing away from near-line storage. As long as there is only a small amount of processing being done out of near-line storage, there is no problem. However, doing significant amounts of processing in near-line storage is difficult and time-consuming. It is much more expedient to process in the exploration warehouse.

Creating the Exploration Warehouse

After the exploration analyst becomes proficient, he or she discovers that the exploration warehouse itself can be its own best source of information for creating the next iteration of the exploration warehouse.

There is a peculiar problem that occurs when one iteration of the exploration warehouse feeds another, and that is one of documentation. As one exploration warehouse feeds another, there is a temptation simply to create the new exploration warehouse in place. As the old warehouse melts into the new, no documentation of what the old warehouse looked like is kept. As long as there is never a need for that knowledge, there is no problem. If, however, you ever need a disciplined audit trail of how one data element relates to another, then allowing an undocumented melting of data throughout the different iterations of the analytical process is counterproductive.

Creating a Permanent or Temporary Structure

The exploration warehouse can be built as either a permanent structure or a temporary structure. When the exploration warehouse is built as a permanent structure, the explorer can plow right into the exploration warehouse without having to wait. The disadvantages to building the exploration warehouse as a permanent structure include the following:

- There is no guarantee that the explorer will want to see the data currently residing in the exploration warehouse. The explorer may well want to access other data. In this case, the exploration warehouse serves little purpose.

- There is a cost involved in creating a permanent infrastructure. The explorer must be willing to pay for an exploration warehouse even when it is not being used.

- The exploration warehouse must be refreshed and revised periodically. There is a cost to the maintenance of a permanent infrastructure, especially the exploration warehouse.

The advantages of creating the exploration warehouse as a temporary structure include the following:

- There are no permanent infrastructure costs incurred.

- No ongoing maintenance costs accrue when the exploration warehouse is not being used.

- The exploration warehouse always is suited to the needs of the analysis being done.

The disadvantages of a temporary exploration warehouse are the following:

- The exploration warehouse must be created from scratch each time a new analysis is done. This creation takes time and other resources.

- The exploration warehouse that is created on a temporary basis may become permanent without anyone realizing it.

Different circumstances fit different companies, and you'll need to weigh the pros and cons of temporary and permanent exploration warehouses before determining which is right for you.

Subdividing Data in the Exploration Warehouse

Because of the volume of data that resides in the exploration warehouse, another useful technique for creating your exploration warehouse is to subdivide the data that resides in it. There are two ways to subdivide data: (1) using different subsets of the same type of data or (2) using different types of data (refer back to Figure 1.15).

In the second type of subdivision, the explorer can access types A and B independently from other types. There is a great deal of flexibility to be gained by creating data structures in the exploration warehouse that can be separated and handled independently. The explorer can do the following:

- Move data types A, B, and C to another platform.

- Optimize A, B, and C for access that is independent of other data types.

- Index A, B, and C independently of other data.

Another aspect of the ability to create and manage independent components of the exploration warehouse is that new types of data can be added gracefully. Figure 2.5 shows this aspect of the properly designed exploration warehouse.

New types of data are added by simply creating the data type, populating the data, and ensuring that the proper data relationships are in place. For example, suppose an analyst has created a table for parts where the key is partno. The table consists of such basic information as description, unit of measure, unit of storage, and color. The table is created and populated. At a later point in time, the analyst creates another table containing the historical manufacturing resource planning (MRP) projections for a part. The MRP history table contains a key: partno. The data that is contained in the table includes attributes such as date of projection, MRP amount projected, and actual amount consumed. The MRP history table is created independently from the original base table; however, both tables can be joined by using partno or partno and date.

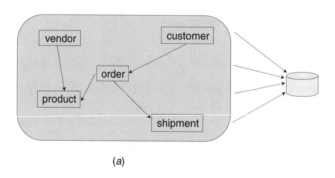

(a)

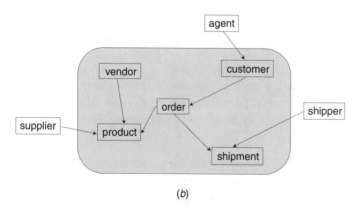

(b)

Figure 2.5 New subject areas are added to the design of the exploration warehouse. (a) Day 1: The basis of the exploration warehouse design is a normalized model. (b) Day 2: New subject areas are added to the exploration warehouse design.

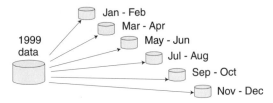

Figure 2.6 A large block of data that has been subdivided.

Partitioning Data in the Exploration Warehouse

The best technique for handling large amounts of data is that of creating segments of data that can be partitioned physically. Certain types of data found in the exploration warehouse are voluminous. For example, a bank may have a lot of transactions to store in the exploration warehouse. One approach is to store the bank transactions into separate tables that are segmented by time. One table is for the transactions that have occurred in January–February 1999; the next table is for transactions that have occurred in March–April 1999; and so forth. Figure 2.6 illustrates this approach.

The great benefit in partitioning data according to its time occurrence is that the analyst can easily move data in and out of the exploration warehouse and quickly determine which data is needed for a particular query.

Incremental Loading of the Exploration Warehouse

Of course, the first load of the exploration warehouse must include all of the data that resides in the exploration warehouse. Subsequent loads of data into the exploration warehouse should be incremental. The loads of data that are done into the exploration warehouse are nonreplacement loads. In other words, when data is loaded, it is added to other data that is already in the exploration warehouse. Loading data over existing exploration warehouse data or altering data that already exists in the exploration warehouse is not good policy. Figure 2.7 shows the incremental loading of data after the initial load.

Incremental loads of data can be done at the row level or at the column/table level. When the row-level loading option is used, more data of the types that already exist in the exploration warehouse are loaded. For example, the explorer may have data for 1998 in the exploration warehouse and decide to load data for 1999. In this case, more rows of the same type are loaded into the exploration warehouse.

Also, the explorer could decide that corporate customer reference tables need to be added to the exploration warehouse. In this case, he or she would define a new table or expand the definition of an existing table and then load the new data into the exploration warehouse.

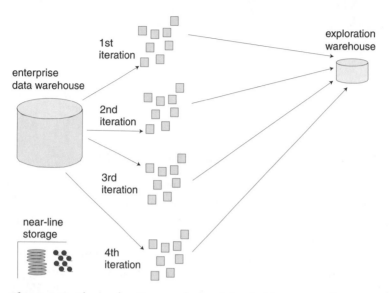

Figure 2.7 The exploration warehouse is loaded incrementally.

One of the considerations of adding new tables or new columns to the exploration warehouse is that of compatibility with existing data. Often, the explorer will load the data into the exploration warehouse and then execute a utility that determines the quality of the relationship. For example, if an analyst decides to load in a country reference table, he should first run a utility to verify that the country codes used in the exploration warehouse table are the same country codes as those in the reference table. If England is UK in the exploration warehouse table and is GB in the reference tables, then the analyst must make amends and cause the data to be compatible. Furthermore, how are Scotland and Wales coded? They too must carry the GB code in the reference table.

Normalizing Data

When data is normalized, it is in its most flexible state. Normalized data exists in small, numerous tables. Each table represents one small unique aspect of the business, and each table has key/foreign key relationships with other tables. Using these key/foreign key relationships, the data that is found in the exploration warehouse can be shaped and reshaped in many ways. The data that is found in the exploration warehouse is normalized (see Figure 2.8).

In this example, the exploration warehouse contains a record for customer. The customer record contains customer identification, customer name, customer address, customer type, and other related customer fields. There is another record for order. The order record contains such data as order number, date of

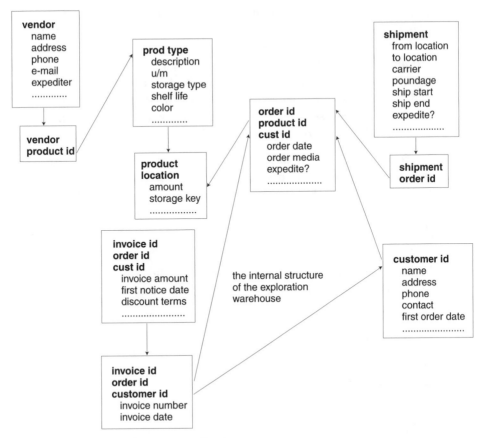

Figure 2.8 The base data is normalized.

order, order amount, cost of order, part(s) ordered, and so forth. In addition, the order field contains such information as which customer placed the order, whether the order should be expedited, and so forth.

There are many ways in which this relationship between data types can be exploited. Some of the questions you may want to look at are the following:

- Are there orders that have been placed where there are no customers?
- Are there customers who have placed no orders?
- Are there orders that have been placed by foreign customers?
- Are there customers placing multiple orders?

Although customer information is interesting and order information is also interesting, the intersection of customer and order is even more interesting. The key/foreign key relationship gives the exploration analyst the opportunity to examine aspects of data that would not otherwise be possible.

The normalization that is found in the exploration warehouse is not perfect. Some amount of denormalization makes sense; otherwise, the normalized structure becomes very inefficient to access. The kinds of denormalization that are allowed are related to the common usage of the data in the exploration warehouse. For example, if a year's worth of data is kept by monthly snapshot, and if the monthly snapshots are then commonly and regularly accessed together, it makes sense to store the monthly snapshots as elements in an array of data, rather than to store the monthly snapshots separately.

There are many other examples of light denormalization that are possible and that make sense in the design of the exploration warehouse. The common thread is whether the data is used regularly in the form that is stored in the exploration warehouse. If only one department looks at the data in the way that it is stored in the exploration warehouse, then the design is most likely not correct.

Figure 2.9 shows that normalized data is at the core of the exploration warehouse. From this core, many different types of tables can be created.

The kinds of tables that can be created include the following:

- Material requirements planning
- Expedited order
- Product order
- Quarterly order
- Weekly invoice
- Shipment
- Product status
- Bill of material summary change

There is inherent flexibility in the ability to take granular data and reshape that data to suit the needs of a particular analysis.

Cost Justifying the Exploration Warehouse

One of the interesting aspects of the exploration warehouse is that it can almost never be cost justified before construction. The very nature of exploration processing is that unknown results will occur. Therefore, doing an a priori analysis of an exploration warehouse's benefits before it is built is creating a work of fiction.

For this reason, most exploration warehouses are built as a *skunk works* project. In a skunk works project, the budget for the project is taken from some

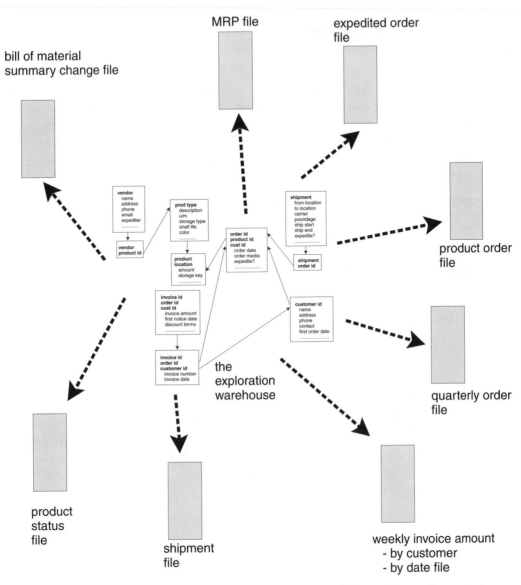

Figure 2.9 From the detailed normalized data, many different files can be created.

larger justification. Resources are siphoned off onto the skunk works project. The budget for exploration is small, because any large expenditure will raise a red flag and the exploration development may be discovered. Of course, once the exploration warehouse is built and proves its value, then it is easy to get funding for it. By this time, all risk has passed and the exploration warehouse has probably already paid for itself.

Exploration Processing

The essence of exploration processing is: "Give me what I say I want, then I can tell you what I really want." The explorer cannot tell anyone what her or his requirements are until she or he sees what the possibilities are. Requirements—or at least the hypotheses that will lead to well-formulated requirements—can be stated as a result of diving in and doing exploration. Exactly what kind of processing, though, occurs inside the exploration warehouse? Figure 2.10 shows a high-level overview of exploration processing.

Common exploration warehouse processes include the following:

- Simple browsing
- Set processing
- Statistical analysis
- Subset selection and analysis
- Correlative analysis

Later chapters will go in depth into these kinds of processing.

Data Stabilization

Data stabilization is the act of not allowing data to be updated or altered in any way during analysis. The exploration warehouse, and indeed the entire corporate information factory (CIF), requires data stabilization during analysis. Figure 2.5 illustrates the need for data stabilization.

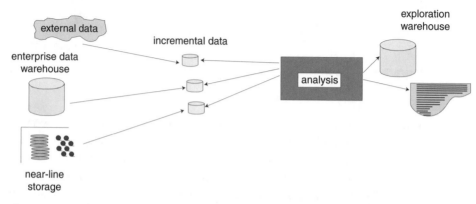

Figure 2.10 The kinds of processing that occur inside the exploration warehouse.

To understand the need for data stabilization, consider an analyst who is working on a financial analysis. The analyst creates the first iteration of analysis. The first set of results is studied, and it is decided to do another iteration of analysis—a very normal thing to do! In the second iteration of analysis, the assumptions of analysis are changed, but the data on which analysis has been done has also been updated. The analyst is stumped because he or she does not know whether the changes in results are due to the changes in their assumptions or changes in the data. In many regards, doing exploratory analysis is like doing a carefully controlled laboratory experiment. Variables must be held constant to understand the effect of the change of a few control variables.

Restoring Previous Analyses

One of the more important and yet overlooked aspects of the exploration warehouse environment is the ability to restore a previous analysis. Figure 2.11 shows that occasionally an analysis needs to be restored and resumed after it has been thought that the analysis has reached completion.

The sorts of information and processes that are stored as a result of completion of an analysis include the following:

- Reports
- Queries
- Extract programs
- Editing/scrubbing programs

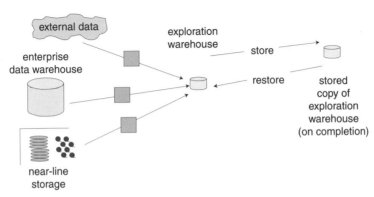

Figure 2.11 At the completion of an analysis, data needs to be stored so that it can be restored at a later point in time.

- Assumptions of analysis
- Descriptions of iterations

Consider the analyst who throws an entire analysis away, thinking that everything is completed. Three months later, management asks the analyst to change a few factors and reanalyze the variables. If the analyst has to start from scratch, this can be a time-consuming and expensive process. This is likely to make top management think that the analytical department is unresponsive. If on the other hand, at the end of the analysis, the analyst has carefully stored data and queries, she or he can quickly restore the project and reanalyze based on management's new requirements.

Which to Build First?

The normal pattern of creation is to build the enterprise data warehouse first, then build the exploration warehouse. For a variety of reasons, this sequence of events is most natural. It is possible, however, to build the exploration warehouse first, and then to build the enterprise data warehouse later. The circumstances in which the exploration warehouse is built first are as follows:

- The amount of data that is involved is relatively small.
- The data to be loaded into the exploration warehouse is reasonably clean, accessible, and integrated.

There are both advantages and disadvantages to this approach. The disadvantages of building the exploration warehouse first are as follows:

- Gathering data to populate the exploration warehouse is a painful and tedious process. The data must be scrubbed and integrated, and this usually means a great deal of labor.
- It slows down the iterative process enormously to accommodate the iterative gathering and cleansing of data. The sources of detailed data for new iterations of the exploration warehouse require further capture and integration of data.

There are, surprisingly, some very real advantages to building the exploration warehouse first. They include the following:

- A minimal investment is required.
- The exploration warehouse can serve as a basis for the design of the first iteration of the enterprise data warehouse. In this case, very quick iterative design of the enterprise data warehouse can be accomplished.

If there is a preferred sequence for building, it is to build the enterprise data warehouse first. However, there are circumstances where the building of the exploration warehouse first is a possibility.

Exploration Warehouse Categories

Exploration warehouses can be divided into two categories: dynamic and static. *Static exploration warehouses* are never updated. They are useful for analysis where the explorer needs to hold values constant while assumptions and hypotheses change. Typically, static exploration warehouses include older, historical data.

A *dynamic exploration warehouse* is constantly updated. Updates may occur hourly, daily, weekly, or on another time schedule. Dynamic exploration warehouses are useful for analysis that depends on up-to-the-second (or as close to up-to-the-second as possible) values. In this type of processing, assumptions are already established. The data needs to be monitored, sometimes over many occurrences of data, to determine when a state of change has occurred. Dynamic exploration warehouses always include very current data.

An interesting matrix can be made when comparing static and dynamic exploration warehouses and temporary and permanent exploration warehouses. Figure 2.12 shows such a matrix.

There are four segments to the matrix shown in Figure 2.12:

1. Static temporary exploration warehouses.
2. Static permanent exploration warehouses.
3. Dynamic temporary exploration warehouses.
4. Dynamic permanent exploration warehouses.

In theory, any of these exploration warehouses can exist. In practice, however, there are only static temporary exploration warehouses and dynamic permanent exploration warehouses. A static permanent exploration warehouse is an anomaly because a static exploration warehouse needs to be updated at some point if its data is to be useful. A dynamic temporary exploration warehouse is likewise an anomaly because there is a considerable infrastructure required to

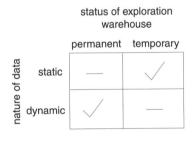

Figure 2.12   A matrix for the different categories of exploration warehouses.

make an exploration warehouse dynamic. Building a large and complex infrastructure for a temporary database does not make sense in most environments.

In Summary

Once an organization tires of doing exploration processing in the enterprise data warehouse, they begin building the exploration warehouse. Data is fed from the enterprise warehouse, external data, and/or near-line storage. Data is fed from the enterprise data warehouse in subsets and is often manipulated to limit the rows and columns to whatever is anticipated to be needed. By limiting the volume and extent of the data, each subsequent pass over the exploration data is made faster and requires fewer processing cycles, thus speeding up the mechanical phase of the analysis. Data fed from external sources must be integrated with existing data. When data is fed from near-line storage, the explorer must be careful not to overwhelm exploration resources. The exploration warehouse is processed iteratively, meaning that it can become its own source for future exploration warehouses.

The data structures that are inside the exploration warehouse are normalized, consisting of tables, attributes, keys, and foreign keys. In general, there are quite a few normalized tables in an exploration warehouse, each representing an entity or a subset of an entity of the corporation. One of the advantages of the normalized structure is that it can be modified easily, having new tables connect to older tables through key/foreign key relationships.

One of the most valuable aspects of the exploration warehouse is that external data can be mixed with internal data inside the exploration warehouse. The comparison of external data with internal data can lead to valuable and profound observations. External data, however, must be conditioned properly before it can be used effectively inside the exploration warehouse.

CHAPTER 3

The Exploration Warehouse and the Chain of Beneficence

One of the greatest failings of today's executive is his inability to do what he's supposed to do.

—MALCOLM KENT

Most data warehouses start with a group of people called *farmers*, experienced analysts who know what they want out of a data warehouse. They can tell you what their requirements are. When the time comes to justify the expenditures for a data warehouse, in almost every case the justification is done on the basis of the farmer's requirements. After the initial iterations of the data warehouse are completed, an entirely new infrastructure is built to suit the farmer's needs.

Explorers are a different breed altogether. Explorers cannot tell you what their requirements are; they operate on hunches and intuition; they are often wrong. Trying to cost justify the expense of a data warehouse based on explorers is close to impossible. If data warehousing were baseball, farmers would be singles hitters with high batting averages, and explorers would be home run hitters with a lot of strikeouts.

Because explorers are so unpredictable, it is very difficult to build an infrastructure for them. Corporations require a good reason for making large investments, and the explorer having a hunch is not generally considered a good reason. Therefore, little or no corporate infrastructure grows up with the explorer.

It is of interest that the two places where explorers have become institutionalized is in the actuarial offices of the insurance companies of the world and in certain process control engineering environments. Almost everywhere else the explorer is an outcast.

Part of the infrastructure of corporate operations is a methodology that describes how work flows. Methodologies have long been common in many parts of the information processing world. Farmers have long had methodologies. There is little or nothing for the explorer, however, in the way of a methodology. The explorer operates in a world where there are, practically speaking, no formalized procedures and no infrastructure.

The chain of beneficence describes a chain of both intellectual and business processes necessary to general business value. There are no hard and fast rules about the chain, and often steps are bypassed. However, businesses that are aware of the chain tend to understand that by more or less consistently following the chain, innovation becomes institutionalized in the organization. For an example of this process, look at Lucent, the former AT&T Bell Laboratories, where technology innovation has been institutionalized in the very structure of the organization.

From Numbers to Competitive Advantage

The path to competitive advantage is ill defined and it differs for every company. For as many successes in achieving competitive advantage, there are at least an equal number of failures. Of course, even these failures can lead to a tremendous amount of learning—about the corporation, the marketplace, and competition. It is necessary (and normal) for a company to experience failure before the final success, because failure teaches corporations to ask the right questions. Even if no immediate benefits are apparent, initial failure exploratory analysis can be extremely valuable to a corporation in the long-term quest for competitive advantage.

The Start of the Quest

The start of the path to competitive advantage is clear—it begins with an idea. Typically, the idea comes from observation, discovery, or insight, or from all of the above. However it appears, the idea becomes the embryonic basis for competitive advantage.

It is fair to say that most ideas—even very good ones—will never result in genuine competitive advantage for a corporation. For every 100 ideas, perhaps one will reach fruition. There are many reasons why an idea may not lead to competitive advantage:

- The idea may simply be wrong.
- The idea may be impractical.
- It may not be the right time for the idea.

- The idea may already be implemented in a different form.
- The idea may not be possible with existing technology.

In short, the odds are highly stacked against any one idea becoming the basis of corporate competitive advantage. Like baby turtles dodging predators to reach the safety of the open sea, newborn ideas struggle to reach maturity, but only relatively few succeed. Those two or three ideas that do make it successfully through the gauntlet of the corporation, the marketplace, and other competing ideas make it worthwhile for all of the immature ideas that never come to fruition.

Once an idea starts down the path to maturity, the idea turns into a hypothesis. It is the hypothesis that formalizes and gives structure to the idea. If the idea is an infant, the hypothesis is a toddler. To achieve even toddlerhood, a fledgling idea must run the gauntlet of several corporate tests, each entailing a measurement of worthiness and validity. The gauntlet is based on more than one criterion of worthiness. Ultimately, the gauntlet renders ideas that are fit for prime time. Those ideas then grow up and turn into products, services, and market share, and indeed, they do turn into corporate advantage.

Different Types of Data Bases

To prove or disprove an idea, there is usually an analysis of data underlying the idea. That data is usually found in a data base.

To anyone involved in information technology (IT) over the past decade or two, it comes as no astonishment that there are many types of data bases. In the beginning, data base theoreticians called for a single data base to serve all purposes. This was no surprise as the theoreticians were—at that time—focusing on cleaning up a world where there was nothing but applications built for very immediate requirements. However, when you look around today, you see all sorts of data bases that do not fit the original theory of a unified data base. We have transaction-processing data bases and high-performance data bases. There are data warehouse data bases and exploration data bases. We even have archival data bases and data mining data bases.

How exactly do these data bases fit together? What framework brings these very different types of data bases and their associated disciplines together to form a cohesive whole? How is it that competitive advantage can be reaped from these many types of data bases?

Figure 3.1 shows that there is a cycle that is created as the different data bases interact with each other. The application data base provides data for the data warehouse. The data warehouse in turn provides data for both the data mining

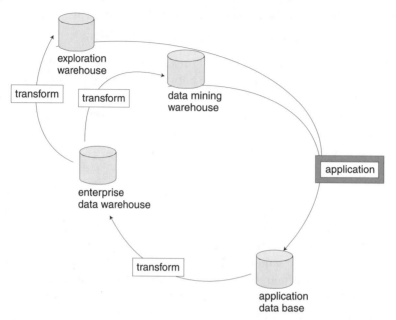

Figure 3.1 The cycle of analysis that occurs as an analytical project passes through different phases.

data warehouse and the exploration warehouse. In between the different types of data bases is a transformation process. Each of the transformation processes is fundamentally different; however, each transformation process indeed results in the passage of data from one environment to another and makes a fundamental transformation of the data. Note that the data bases form a cycle in which data is repeatedly transformed and recycled. Of course, the cycle of transformation operates in sync with activities that are occurring in the chain of beneficence.

The Chain of Beneficence

To understand how the different kinds of data bases fit together to produce competitive advantage, consider a sequence of events that can be called the *chain of beneficence*. The chain of beneficence provides a high-level perspective of how different parts the corporation relate in the process of going from insight to competitive advantage. The chain is shown in Figure 3.2.

The chain of beneficence describes how ideas are turned into competitive advantage. The chain of beneficence connects several related activities. The major activities are as follows:

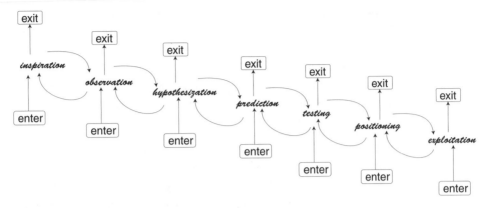

Figure 3.2 The chain of beneficence.

Inspiration. Inspiration is the act of creating or being able to first articulate an idea. Inspiration can occur in many ways—through intuition, insight, a lucky guess, and so forth.

Observation. Most inspirations come in a very unrefined form. Observation is the way that very rough ideas become a lot more accurate or focused.

Hypothesization. Hypothesization is the process of reducing an inspiration down to the form of "if we did . . . then the result would be . . ." Ideas are reshaped into postulates about how the world would react based on one or more stimuli.

Prediction. Prediction takes the hypothesis and estimates and quantifies the expected result. It is during prediction that many other factors enter the equation. Prediction of necessity must be able to be stated in terms of fact or in relevant real-world variables.

Testing. The results of the hypothesis and the prediction need to be measured and quantified for the testing to be most effective. Testing can be done on a small or grand scale, against a limited audience or large audience, and so forth.

Positioning. Positioning occurs when the corporation creates new products and services, packages existing products and services, or alters existing packaging to capitalize on the hypothesis and predictions. It involves both internal products and services, as well as setting the external message and tone that are external to the corporation.

Exploitation. Exploitation involves the capture and protection of market share, as well as the maximization of profitability, both long term and short term. These activities flow from one link of the chain of beneficence to another. Note that these activities touch different types of data bases as they flow through the chain, as shown in Figure 3.1. At first glance, the chain of beneficence may appear to be similar to a waterfall development methodology (i.e., the old structured-analysis-and-design approach to the development of information systems). Although there may indeed be some similarities, there are some very distinct differences as well. These differences include:

- In the chain of beneficence, movement can be in any direction. For example, an analyst may observe some data, which in turn triggers an inspiration. The inspiration may lead to more observations, at which point the analyst may create a hypothesis. The hypothesis is examined and rejected. The analyst returns to observation and rehypothesizes the observations. Now, the hypothesis is examined and predictions are made. In such a manner, the chain of beneficence is traversed backward and forward.

- The chain of beneficence can be entered or exited at any activity. In other words, any project that passes through the chain of beneficence can start anywhere and can end anywhere. This describes the reality of projects that sound like a good idea but simply do not pan out. The same phenomenon describes projects that are created with no theoretical foundation.

The waterfall development methodology is very inflexible in terms of flow of activities—first, one activity occurs, then another, and so forth. The chain of beneficence shows that activities flow from one step to another, but there is very little if any structure to the flow. Furthermore, there is no precise timing to this flow.

How formal should the chain of beneficence and the cycle of transformation be? In some places the chain is very formal—for example, between the application data base and the data warehouse, there is a set of extremely formal transformation procedures. Between observation and inspiration, however, there is only the flimsiest of formal interfaces. Obviously, the chain of beneficence runs the gamut when it comes to formalization of interfaces.

The exploration warehouse becomes the incubator for many early activities in the chain of beneficence. Inspiration can occur in the processing that takes place in the exploration warehouse. Certainly, observation occurs in the exploration warehouse, and even testing and formalization of the hypothesis occur in there.

It is true that applications can be created without passing through the activities outlined in the chain of beneficence. Applications have been created over the years with no knowledge whatsoever of the chain. However, the odds of achieving an important business payoff are mightily increased by passing through one or more iterations of the chain of beneficence.

Examples of the Chain

As a simple example of a short-lived path through the chain of beneficence, suppose that a manager has the inspiration that there is an opportunity to sell more cars in Denver—the manager just "feels it in his bones." The inspiration leads the manager to believe that he could sell more cars if he could open a new dealership in Highlands Ranch. For several years, Highlands Ranch has been one of the fastest growing areas in the United States. The inspiration, however, does not blossom into a plan of action for a variety of reasons, including a lack of capital, zoning laws, competition that has already claimed the high ground, and available space. The idea enters and exits the chain of beneficence at the same place.

As another example, a newly minted MBA out of the University of Colorado has the idea that there is a hidden market for upscale children's Halloween costumes. She observes that the baby boomer generation is now creating a second wave of boomers and that the baby boomers of today are more affluent than their parents were. The inspiration is supported by observation, but the idea goes nowhere for a variety of reasons:

- Lack of capital.
- Lack of distribution.
- Lack of advertising.
- Halloween is an annual event and would only generate cash flow for a limited time each year.

This time, inspiration has passed into observation but has stopped there.

Now, consider a third case. A Stanford MBA has the inspiration that people like fresh, warm chocolate chip cookies. Indeed, it is hypothesized that people will smell cookies and buy them spontaneously, and at a premium. He also observes that getting cookies is not particularly easy. Therefore, the original inspiration is enhanced by stating that people will pay a premium for fresh-baked cookies if the cookies are easy to get to and easy to acquire. He hypothesizes that if there were easy and convenient access to cookies and if the smell of the cookies enticed people who were doing otherwise normal activities, then people would pay a premium. Thus, Mrs. Field's cookies were born.

Now, consider an excursion through the chain of beneficence that begins with a prediction. The prediction is that the Internet will fundamentally alter the course of retail sales, and that in the year 2000, retail malls will have 10 percent of their sales volume diminish because of the Internet. To determine the truth of this prediction, it is necessary to examine the hypotheses on which the prediction is made. The fundamental hypothesis is that people will do more and more shopping over the Internet in years to come. Although this observation is probably true, the question then becomes, based on observation, just how many people will do their shopping over the Internet in years to come? A survey is taken and it is estimated that only 2 percent of shoppers will actually be using the Internet actively in 2000. Furthermore, only a subset of businesses will be using the Internet, thereby shrinking the volume of potential sales made over the Internet. Based on these revised observations, a new prediction is made: Retail mall sales will be diminished by only 1 percent in the year 2000. In this case, the chain of beneficence has been entered at the point of prediction and several jumps have been made up and down the chain.

Suppose a bank has the inspiration that it could make more money by making loans. The bank observes that it is more profitable to make loans to its largest customers. The bank could avoid much administrative overhead and risk by concentrating on potential customers who are likely to bring the largest profits. Not surprisingly, the hypothesis is made that if the bank catered to a wealthier crowd, it would make more money. Based on observations about the distribution of wealth, the bank predicts that if it could attract residents of two zip codes—80104 and 80106—it would be positioned to make profitable loans. The prediction is tested by sending a promotional mailing to people in those zip codes offering free banking services. The prediction is that if the resident can be enticed to join a bank by using free banking services, a relationship with the bank will ensue. Based on the relationship that is formed, the resident will look to the bank when it is time to take out a loan. The hypothesis is tested and sure enough, residents of those zip codes respond well to the offer for free services. In this case, the chain of beneficence is traversed from inspiration to positioning.

The 72-Hour Query

Why are queries that are found in the exploration environment so large? Large queries require the following:

- Detailed data be accessed.
- Processing be done against historical data. Exploration cannot be done properly when only a short amount of time is available for analysis.
- Data be reshaped. This process drains energy from a standard DBMS that thinks that data should be shaped in a static manner. The reshaping of data often requires that a single value be substituted for a group of values. A DBMS must pause, look up the alternative value, and then continue the processing stream. This recoding cycle, when multiplied by many columns and millions of rows, leads to long runtimes.

In short, large queries result when detail is multiplied by history, which is multiplied by reshaped data.

Heuristic Processing

The analytical processing that results from the chain of beneficence is called *heuristic analysis*. In a heuristic analysis, the first step is planned, then executed. The results of the first step are analyzed, and the next step is based on these results. The second step is executed and its results are analyzed. Those results are obtained and analyzed and the planning begins for the next iteration. This explains why heuristic analysis is sometimes called *iterative analysis*.

Heuristic analysis is fundamentally different from other kinds of analysis, which are designed and refined before any work is done. The requirements for heuristic analysis are not specified beyond the first iteration.

The heuristic style of analysis fits the needs of explorers, who start out with vague ideas, and it refines those ideas through analysis. Each step of the analytical process allows the explorer to better understand the problem.

Samples and Heuristic Analysis

One of the biggest challenges facing the explorer is coping with the huge volumes of data that are needed for doing heuristic processing and analysis. There are many ways that the explorer can cope with large volumes of data:

- Buy lots of hardware.
- Design the data bases cleverly.
- Use proper architecture.

These approaches are all valid and should all be used. However, there is another approach that should be considered in conjunction with these approaches—executing heuristic analysis against samples of data rather than the entire data base. A sample of data can be as small as 5 or 10 percent of the original data base, depending on the statistical significance needed. Operating against samples of data can save huge amounts of time and resources. The technique of using sample data bases for the first few heuristic analytical efforts is especially appropriate.

The following example demonstrates the use of sampling techniques for heuristic analysis. In this example, an airline wants to do a better job of marketing to women. To understand just who the female flyers are, the airline selects a subset of their flight historical data—the past three months' worth of general flight history data. A separate sample data base is created for the purpose of sampling-based heuristic analysis.

The primary objective of the exercise is to determine whether female flyers are pleasure and vacation travelers or business travelers. There are probably other categories into which women flyers fit, but these two are of primary interest. Once the airline understands the fundamental motivations of female flyers, it can undertake initiatives that are designed to attract and cater to this particular niche.

The analyst in charge of the project first runs an analysis against the sample data base to determine how many female travelers there are. This is accomplished by looking for designations of *Ms.* or *Mrs.* on the tickets.

However, on many tickets, the designation does not appear at all. Failing to find a designation, a secondary analysis of gender is made to determine gender by first name. Names like Mary, Jane, and Elizabeth are designated as female; names like Bill, Mike, Donald, and Joseph are designated as male. Certain names—such as Chris, Terry, and Pat—are discarded because the name can be male or female. Based on designation and/or name, it is observed from the sample data base that 17 percent of flyers are female.

The first pass at determining whether a woman is a companion flyer or an independent flyer is to see if there is someone on the same flight with the same last name. This technique works well in some cases but not in others. Some of the cases in which the technique does not work well are:

- The last name is a common one, such as Smith or Johnson.
- A wife has not taken her husband's last name.
- A mother is traveling with a son.
- The reservation agent has spelled one name incorrectly.

This inexact approach to telling whether a woman is traveling with her spouse yields the result that .874 percent of flights that women take are with their spouses. This finding is deemed to be statistically insignificant.

Because estimates of whether a woman is traveling with her spouse proved to be unhelpful, another approach is attempted. An assessment is made of how many women are weekday flyers versus how many women are weekend flyers. The theory is that business flyers are primarily traveling on weekdays and vacation flyers travel on weekends. Using this criterion in the sample data base, the airline determines that 86 percent of women are weekday flyers and that 14 percent are weekend flyers.

It is also hypothesized that most business travelers take trips of one week or less. Based on this assumption, the question is then asked: How many female flyers are traveling on trips that are greater than one week? The sample data base yields the answer that 7 percent of trips made by women last more than one week. This result is combined with the previous result to create an increasingly accurate picture of the female flyer.

The next tack taken by the analyst is to look at how many women's trips are tied to vacation packages. The analysis against the sample data base shows that 26 percent of the trips that women make are tied to a package. Combined with the results of previous analyses, we now have an even better picture of female flyers.

Another way to try to profile the female customer base is to look at female tickets sold to vacation cities versus tickets sold to nonvacation cities. It is determined that Orlando, Orange County, and San Francisco are vacation destinations. Cities that are not designated as vacation cities include New York, Dallas, and St. Louis. However, there appear to be too many variables to allow the results to be used in the final analysis. For example, it is pointed out that many businesswomen travel to Silicon Valley out of San Francisco airport.

Analysis further sorts women by frequency of travel. Of those women who are designated as business travelers, how frequently do they travel? The categories of travel include two or three trips per year, one trip per year, four or five trips per year, and so forth.

After all of the analysis is done against the sample data base, it is decided to use the criterion of weekday travel versus weekend travel as the distinguishing criterion for female business travelers versus female pleasure flyers. A full-scale analysis of three years' worth of data is executed against the large transaction activity data base of the airline. The first pass through the data base identifies women who are designated as business travelers. The next pass determines how many trips have been made. Then, the women's records are passed against the frequent flyer file and the determination is made of which women are frequent flyers and which are not. At this point in time, the airlines have a good grip on exactly who composes their female customer base of business flyers.

There are many ways that the airlines can use this information: direct mail promotions, telesales, and focus groups, to name a few. Once the airline starts to cater to its female business flyers, then the airline can repeat the analysis in a much more sophisticated manner. One future question to be asked is how the female business traveler customer base is growing? Shrinking?

The cycle of activity in the chain of beneficence is open ended. The airline may choose to do more analysis; it may choose to take action; or it may simply decide that now is not the time for any new initiatives and delay action until a later time. In short, the airline adapts the chain of beneficence to its own particular needs and timetable. There is no rigid order to be followed.

Once the airline does take specific actions, results can be measured. For example, placing an ad in a magazine may be good for company exposure, but it is difficult to determine whether the ad led directly to increased sales or other factors. On the other hand, with a direct mail campaign or a telesales campaign, results can be quantified immediately.

Sampling Techniques

There is then a real place for sampling techniques in the world of exploration processing. Sampling techniques are very convenient for handling large volumes of data found in the decision support/data warehouse environment. They are also blended with heuristic analysis very beneficially.

When using sampling data bases, it is necessary to determine the appropriate samples size. Depending on the specifics of the data base being built and the ultimate use of the samples, the sample data base may be as small as 1 percent or as large as 10 percent of the original data base.

Two types of samples can be placed into a sampling data base—*random samples* and *judgment samples*. A random sample is just that—a set of records chosen at random. A simple way to get a random sample is simply to march sequentially through a large data base and select every 10th record.

The other type of sample is a judgment sample. A judgment sample is one in which every record that qualifies under a certain criterion is selected. For example, in a sales data base, every sale between $5 and $50 is selected for the sample data base. Any sale below $5 and any sale above $50 are excluded from the sample data base. Depending on the usage of the sample data base, either the random sampling approach or the judgment sample approach is appropriate.

However sampling is done, bias is created in the data. For example, the original data base may contain 51.2 percent males and 49.8 percent females. The sample data base may contain 50.6 percent males and 49.4 percent females. Such a small difference will not matter for most analyses; however, if by chance the sample data base ends up having 76.9 percent males and 20.4 percent females, then the bias of the sample data base will be such that the analysis done against the sampling data base will be invalid. The elimination of bias is not a possibility in a sampling data base. Instead, understanding and managing the bias inherent to a sampling data base should be the goal of the exploration analyst. If heuristic, iterative analysis is done against the sampling data base and final analysis is done against the full data base, most effects of a biased sampling data base can be eliminated.

The exploration analyst also needs to be aware that there *are* some limitations of sampling techniques. Suppose that an analysis is made of how many females get new driver's licenses versus how many males get them. Using a sampling data base, the analyst determines that 51.76 percent of applicants are female. To make that determination, the analyst had to access 5000 records. Now, suppose that the analyst operated against the state motor vehicles data base. The analysis against the full data base yields the calculation that 52.01 percent of the applicants are female. To arrive at this more accurate answer, the analyst had to execute against 2 million records. Just how much is accuracy worth? This is ultimately a business decision.

Other limitations of a sampling data base include:

- A sampling data base cannot be used for examination of the existence of individual records.
- Samples grow old over time. Periodically, the sampling data base needs to be refreshed to keep the analysis that is done against it fresh and accurate.

Reuse of Analysis

Once an analysis is complete, what does the analyst do with the work products that have been created? One approach is to call the analysis a success and throw everything except the reports away. What if management wants to revisit the analysis later on, though? If ever there is a need to restart the analysis, it will be much easier to regenerate the reports if some basic information is stored for the long haul:

- The data that was selected for the analysis
- The source of the data
- The time when the data was selected
- The queries that were run
- The syntax of the queries
- The reports that were generated
- The copies of the reports

Many other facets of the analysis can also be saved. Ironically, the data that was used for the analysis is not saved. It is usually cumbersome and awkward to save the actual detailed data that was used in analysis. Of course, if there is a chance that later analysis will need to return to the data and analyze variables that have not yet been analyzed, then it would behoove the analyst to save the detailed data as well.

In Summary

The approach to exploration processing can be called, at a very high level, the chain of beneficence. The chain of beneficence specifies how the different activities of exploration occur. The steps in the chain of beneficence include:

- Inspiration
- Observation

- Hypothesization
- Prediction
- Testing
- Positioning
- Exploitation

Unlike a methodology, the chain of beneficence can be entered anywhere and can be exited anywhere. Furthermore, there is free flow from any one activity to another. There is no specified order of activities, and many may lead nowhere; however, some activities lead to unique and effective business advantages.

The chain of beneficence is supported by an infrastructure of data bases, including the following:

- Exploration warehouse
- Data mining warehouse
- Application data bases
- Enterprise data warehouse

CHAPTER 4

Exploration Processing

Trend is not destiny.

—LEWIS MUMFORD

A t a high level, exploration processing is depicted by the chain of beneficence, as described in Chapter 3. Figure 4.1 shows the chain of beneficence at the 50,000-foot level as well as at the 10,000-foot level, which depicts a more detailed cycle of analysis.

Exploration analysis is a process of evaluating data that is found in the data warehouse, exploration warehouse, or other source, and arriving at a business decision. The steps of the exploration cycle of analysis are as follows:

- Gather data and find patterns.
- Determine the influence of external forces and assess causality and correlation.
- Translate the relationships that have been discovered into business strategies and tactics.

Figure 4.2 shows the steps in the exploration process as they relate to the chain of beneficence. As noted earlier, the exploration cycle of analysis is iterative. Once analysis has begun, there is flow of activity from one node to the next until either the activity of exploratory analysis is abandoned or a successful completion is achieved.

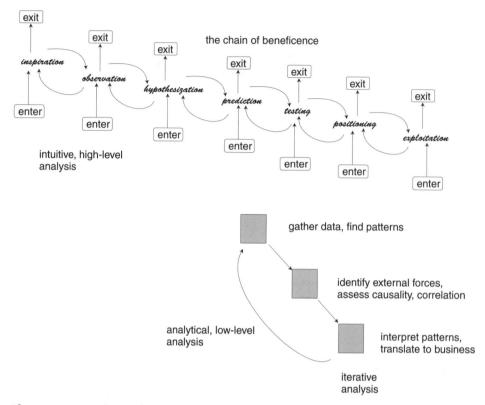

Figure 4.1   Iterative analysis at a high level and a low level.

Gathering Data and Finding Patterns

The first step in exploration processing is gathering data. Data can come from many sources—the enterprise data warehouse, near-line storage, or other external sources. If the data is not cleansed and integrated, then it needs to be before it can be used for exploration analysis. As discussed earlier, the process of gathering and cleansing data can consume huge resources and must be carefully considered by the explorer.

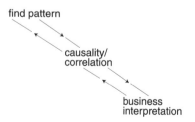

Figure 4.2   The exploratory analytical process.

Once the data base is ready for analysis, iterative analysis in search of meaningful patterns can begin. Patterns show up in transactions, customer lists, and elsewhere. Some patterns are of vital interest, whereas others are only of passing interest. (Some patterns may appear to be of passing interest but, in actuality, should be of vital business interest. The explorer must learn to distinguish subtle differences in patterns over many occurrences of data from a large mixture of observations.)

Usually (but not always) vital business patterns focus on the customer. There may also be significant interest in patterns that involve the following:

- The efficiency of manufacturing
- The efficiency of shipping and logistics
- The effectiveness of promotions and advertising
- The effectiveness of research and development

The customer, however, holds the primary attention of most analyses.

Focus on the Customer

To run at maximum profitability, a retailer must understand the interaction and dynamics of such variables as pricing, item elasticity, and physical positioning. Then the explorer must take those findings and interpret them to help the retailer achieve the greatest business impact.

Of course, the business patterns of interest will differ from industry to industry. The manufacturer will be interested in different patterns than the retailer. The retailer will be interested in different patterns than the telecommunications analyst, and so on. Some examples of customer patterns of vital interest include:

- Why do some customers buy more expensive items than other customers?
- Why do some customers buy more frequently than other customers?
- Why are some items more attractive than other items?
- Why are some items more profitably placed in one part of the store than in other parts?

Determining Causality of Behavior and Correlation between Variables

Once the relevant patterns are discovered, it becomes necessary to identify the circumstances that cause the pattern to occur. Ideally, when a business can say what factors caused an activity, then it can start to accurately predict customer behavior and its marketplace position. This enables the company to optimize its position with respect to market share and profitability.

Finding causality of behavior is a rare thing, though. The more normal case is to find *factors of correlation* among different variables. A factor of correlation is one in which other conditions and activities are correlated with the activity of interest, but are not necessarily caused by the activity. In some cases of correlation there is indirect causality, which may or may not be identified.

The movement of correlated variables with each other can be in any direction. Two (or more) variables can move up and down in lockstep with each other. One variable can move in one direction while another variable moves in another direction. One variable can move one step in the same direction as another variable that is moving at the rate of two steps to one, and so forth. The direction in which the variables move is not the point; that they move consistently with each other in whatever directions at the same rate is the point.

The weakest correlation between two variables is *random correlation*. A random correlation between variables or events indicates that, on occasion, one event or activity moves in coordination with another. On other occasions, the variables and activities do not move in coordination with each other.

The Spectrum of Relationships: Identifying External Forces

As we have seen, the spectrum of relationships between variables can be summarized as follows:

Causal relationship.   This is the strongest type of relationship between variables.

- Hot weather causes beer sales to rise.
- The approach of Christmas causes retail sales to rise.

Correlative/indirect causal relationships.   These are potentially strong relationships.

- Men tend to have better golf scores than women.
- As individual IQ rises, the propensity to have a larger income rises.

Random relationship.   This is a nonrelationship.

- As the United States makes more gold medals in the Olympics, the Dow Jones industrial average rises.
- Pork belly futures rise along with the sale of firecrackers for the Fourth of July.

The stronger the correlation between variables, the greater the business opportunity. There is effectively no business opportunity for random correlations of data.

To take advantage of causal or correlative variables, the explorer needs first to identify and investigate the external forces that influence variables. Examples of external forces include:

- Temperature influences the type of clothes we wear.
- Economic climate influences the disposable income of a household.
- Annual snowfall of a region influences the slope of the roof.
- Competitive environment influences the pricing of a product.
- Cost of manufacturing influences the list price of a product.
- Unfulfilled demand for a product influences the sales price of a product.

In short, every business point of interest is influenced by multiple external forces, ranging from strong to weak. The movement that the corporation makes as a result of external forces is a function of two factors:

1. The will and force of factors that are internal to the corporation.
2. The sum of the external factors that affect the corporation.

External forces can be measured, just as the point of interest can be measured. For example, if the external force is the economy, typical measurements include:

- The inflation rate
- The stock market averages
- The unemployment rate
- The number of new housing starts

If the external force is competition, the measurements might be as follows:

- The number of products that the competition is offering
- The number of units that the products have sold
- The sales force size of the competition
- The market share that is enjoyed by the competition
- The number of competitors

In some cases, the point of interest is moved *because* of these external forces (Figure 4.3). The explorer relishes finding cases in which the external forces cause movement of the point of interest because it is easy to determine predictability in such cases.

True movement of the point of interest caused by an external force is rare. Much more common is the case in which external forces move in tandem in correlation with the point of interest (Figure 4.4). There may be hidden causal factors that are locking the movement of the point of interest to the movement of the external force, but because these factors are hidden, they cannot be found. In this case, the explorer must be content with noting the movement that occurs and the strength of the coincidental relationship.

The third type of relationship between the point of interest and the external forces is a random relationship. In this case, sometimes the external force moves in tandem with the point of interest, and sometimes it moves contrary to the point

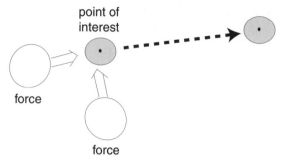

Figure 4.3   Some movement is causal.

of interest (Figure 4.5). The explorer discards a random relationship in which the point of interest and the external force have no relationship. (Note that the explorer is not just interested in simply observing the direction of movement, but also the rate of movement.)

Direct Causal Relationships

There are many different types of relationships among the external forces and the point of interest. The simplest type of relationship is that of *direct causal*. Figure 4.6 shows the direct causal relationship.

Figure 4.6 shows that when the external force moves, it causes the point of interest to move as well. The movement can be in any direction. For example, when the external force moves upward, the point of interest moves upward as well. When the external force moves downward, the point of interest moves upward. When the external force moves upward, the point of interest moves upward at half the rate. The direct causal relationship can manifest itself in many ways.

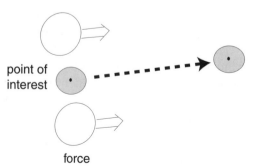

Figure 4.4   Some movement is merely correlative.

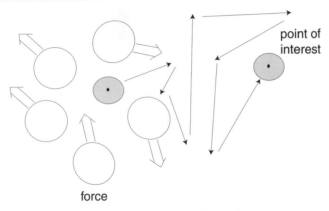

force

Figure 4.5 Some movement is purely random.

Indirect Relationships

Although direct causal relationships are interesting and useful, they are in fact quite rare. Much more common are *indirect relationships*. Figure 4.7 shows a simple indirect relationship.

Figure 4.7 shows that an external force has changed. The external force has caused another external force to change, which in turn has had an influence on the point of interest. In this simple case, it is probable that the relationship between the external force and the point of interest can be measured and quantified. However, usually the relationship between the external force and the point of interest is not so simple. Usually, there are any number of external forces that operate in conjunction with each other to form a web of forces that influence the point of interest.

When the relationship between an external force and the point of interest becomes very complex, the explorer should aim to relate the external force to the

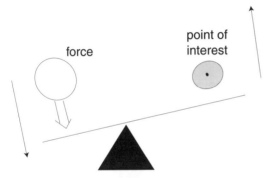

Figure 4.6 A direct causal relationship.

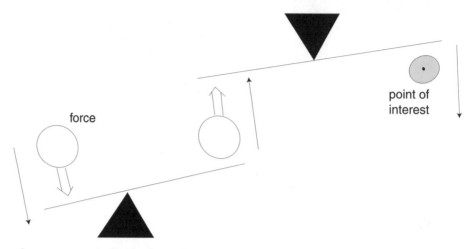

Figure 4.7 An indirect relationship.

point of interest by simple correlative measures. Figure 4.8 shows that the relationship between an external force and the point of interest has become so indirect and so complex that it is best measured in a correlative manner. At some point, the relationship between the point of interest and an external force is so far fetched that it is best described as random.

After the external force(s) and the point of interest have been selected, the next step is to select which of the variables are representative of the external force(s) and the point of interest. Figure 4.9 shows that the variables are selected.

Only one set of variables may be selected, or multiple variables may be selected. The variables are, of course, most representative of the movement of the point of interest or the external force(s).

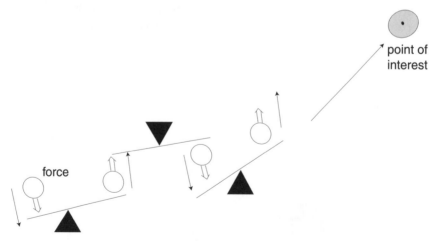

Figure 4.8 A correlative and complex relationship.

force   point of interest

Figure 4.9 Different variables that directly measure either the point of interest or the external force can be traced.

Once the representative variables have been selected, then the interval of time for exploratory analysis is also selected. Once the interval of time is selected, then the movement and the pattern of the variables are captured and measured. Figure 4.10 shows the different variables as they are captured and measured.

Another single-variable measurement over time is shown in Figure 4.11. It is difficult to draw many conclusions from this measurement. Interpretation of data requires an indication of causality to obtain maximum value. Without multiple variables, interpretation is reduced to simple description. While description can be useful, description alone cannot lead to predictive assertion, which is the highest state of value. When predictive factors are known, then, for example, product can be shipped to retail locations ahead of demand. This leads to maximization of profit and collaterally minimization of waste. In short, the highest value of the chain of beneficence comes when as many predictive variables as possible are known. However, this measurement may still prove valuable, as the data included is homogeneous. If the interval of time has been chosen properly, this measurement can be quite elucidating. For example, it is not unusual in sales reporting to report hard goods sales in a retail chain weekly. In many chains this is standard practice and is adequate. However, when the capability is there to report sales hourly, a new phenomenon is often discovered. This phenomenon may indicate that departments within a store show differential activity by the hour and that by using dynamic staffing—shifting of personnel from department to department based upon a known pattern—sales revenue can be

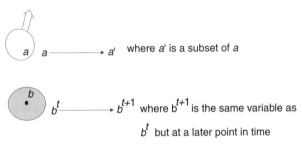

$a \longrightarrow a'$ where a' is a subset of a

$b^t \longrightarrow b^{t+1}$ where b^{t+1} is the same variable as b^t but at a later point in time

Figure 4.10   Measuring variables as they are captured.

Figure 4.11 A simple measurement over time.

greatly improved. The choice of the time unit of analysis is critical to the discovery of the business value.

A more robust measurement is depicted by Figure 4.12 where multiple variables are measured. The conclusions that can be drawn from the third type of measurement (Figure 4.12) are the most interesting because it is here that the relationship between the external force(s) and the point of interest can be measured. Likely conclusions include:

There is no relationship between the external force(s) and the point of interest.

There is a simple and direct relationship between the external force(s) and the point of interest.

There is a complex relationship between the external force(s) and the point of interest, such as:

- The external force(s) and the point of interest have a ripple effect in which the external force leads or trails the point of interest.
- The external force(s) have an inversely proportional relationship to the point of interest (i.e., the external force rises while the point of interest falls).
- The external force(s) have a relationship that is in a ratio to the point of interest (i.e., when the external force(s) rise one unit the point of interest rises two units).
- There is a relationship between the external forces and the point of interest at some points in time and not at other points in time.

Each of these relationships must be investigated. The sorts of things that the explorer looks for include:

- The strength of the relationship
- The precise nature of the relationship
- The interrelationship of more than one factor

After the relationship that is described in Figure 4.12 is quantified, the businessperson must determine the nature of the relationship. In particular, is the relationship causal or correlative? If there is a causal relationship, the businessperson needs to identify the exact nature of the business relationship. If the relationship is correlative, then the businessperson needs to see if:

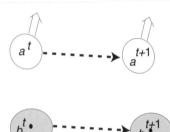

Figure 4.12 Measuring multiple variables.

- There is an underlying hidden relationship.
- There is no obvious underlying hidden relationship.
- What is the strength of the correlative relationship (if any)?

To determine the nature of the relationships, there are some underlying assumptions that the businessperson can make use of. The first assumption is that if the interval of time has been chosen properly, the forces that act on a are the same external forces that act on a'. Figure 4.13 illustrates this assumption.

The second assumption is that if there is a hidden (or previously undiscovered) relationship between a and b, the behavior of the external force and the point of interest will be the same for the interval of time (technically speaking, the behavior of the external force and the point of interest will be governed by the hidden relationship for the interval of time). Figure 4.14 shows this assumption.

A third assumption is that the forces that are acting on a may or may not be the same as the forces that are acting on b.

The sorts of things that the businessperson and the technician look for are patterns of movement of the point of interest and the external forces. In general, the

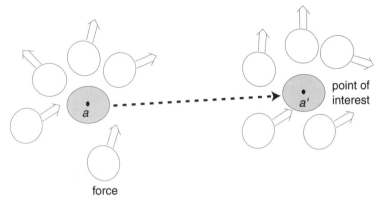

Figure 4.13 The assumption is that the forces that are acting on a are very similar to the forces that are acting on a'.

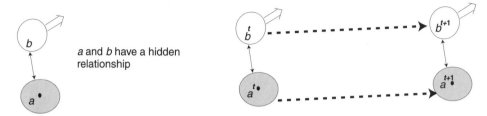

Figure 4.14 The assumption is that if *a* and *b* have a hidden relationship, they will move in tandem.

businessperson and the technician pay little attention to a single occurrence of data. Any single occurrence of data may be a once-in-a-lifetime anomaly; there may or may not be a relationship. Merely looking at the behavior of two variables, *a* and *b*, is weak evidence of a hidden relationship. The explorer needs to look at lots of variables.

The single occurrence of the relationship is independent of whether the relationship is rising, falling, or anything else. Figure 4.15 shows different types of relationships.

The recurrence of a pattern of behavior, repeatedly and consistently over a lengthy period of time, is what is indicative of a relationship.

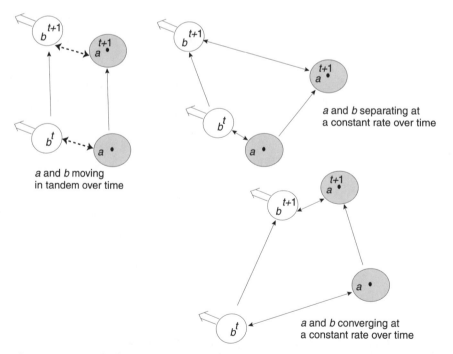

Figure 4.15 A single occurrence of a correlation is useful only if the correlation is measured over a lengthy period of time.

The consistent repetition of a pattern of rises and falls of two or more variables is indicative of a causal or a very strong correlative relationship. Once the explorer has found such a pattern, then there are many business possibilities.

Of course, there is the case in which there is one long-term relationship between an external force and the point of interest with no intervening lapse in the relationship. The pattern that is displayed over time is a constant one. The point is that there are no intervening behavioral patterns interrupting the pattern. However, even more likely is that there is a relationship between the point of interest and the external force that over time has had interruptions. Figure 4.16 shows such a long-term relationship.

Other Relationships

The explorer expects to find the pattern shown in Figure 4.16. In a way, the recurring nature of the behavior shown in Figure 4.16 indicates that the relationship between the point of interest and the external force is very strong. Before the explorer and the businessperson can start to draw conclusions, they must also determine if any external forces that might exert significant influence on the point of interest have not been identified.

The effects of an external force can show up in many ways:

- As an unexplained dip or alteration of the point of interest
- As a counterforce to an already identified external force
- As a counterforce to an unidentified external force

It should be noted that an identified external force may take an unanticipated change of course, which will then result in an unanticipated effect on the point of interest as well. Unanticipated changes may also occur to the collective external forces that influence the point of interest.

The net effect of considering changes to the external forces and the consequential changes to the point of interest is the definition of the relationship between

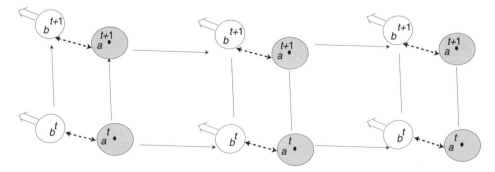

Figure 4.16 Multiple occurrences of correlation over different periods of time.

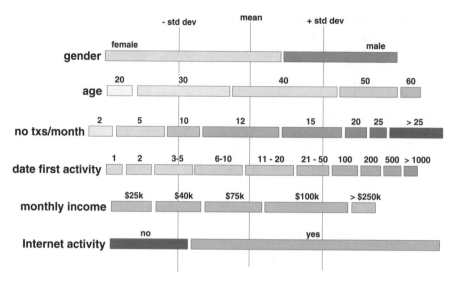

Figure 4.17 A profile for the average bank account.

the external forces and the point of interest. Once the relationship is understood, the business basis of the relationship can then be investigated.

Creating Profiles

Often, the analyst discovers many correlative factors, but no causal factors. In this case, it is normal to create what can be called a *profile* for the point of interest. The profile is a shorthand statistical overview of the correlation of many variables as they relate to a single point of interest. Figure 4.17 shows a simple profile for a point of interest.

Figure 4.17 illustrates several correlating factors for the average bank account of the bank. The average bank account is depicted by the mean, and the upper and lower standard deviations are depicted as well. In a single glance, the analyst can see the correlating factors and how they relate to the point of interest. In the illustrated example, gender, age, income, and Internet activity are all believed to be correlated factors.

Capitalizing on Predictability

Once the external factors that influence a business point of interest are discovered and the strength of correlation is assessed, the corporation can start to predict behavior. The ability to predict future behavior allows a corporation to proactively prescribe business policy and practices. Some of the ways that a corporation can capitalize on the predictability of customer behavior include:

- Aligning the business with new allies
- Introducing new products and services
- Repackaging existing products and services
- Repositioning existing products and services

Once the corporation has acted, results are gathered and measured, and the analytical process begins anew.

A Simple Methodology for Exploration Analysis

Figure 4.18 shows the methodology for exploration analysis. This methodology corresponds to the cycle of analysis described in Figures 4.1 and 4.2. The individual activities and opportunities for detailed analysis that are referenced in the methodology will be described later in this chapter.

NOTE The exploration methodology described in this chapter is very rudimentary. This simple methodology focuses on the high-level activities that need to be performed, the order in which they need to be completed, and the decisions that need to be made at each point.

The methodology outlined in Figure 4.18 is best executed by a joint effort of a businessperson *and* a technician as equal partners. If only the businessperson is allowed to do exploration processing, the process may be conducted inefficiently or without discipline. If only the technician conducts the exploration process, it may be well executed, but it may focus on irrelevant aspects of the business. It therefore behooves the organization to mix—equally—the talents and time commitments of both groups.

The Point of Interest

The focus of the exploration analysis is on a *point of interest*, which is a critical success factor that can be measured. The explorer knows when he or she has selected the right point of interest when business and technical managers agree that its movements reflect on the health of the business. Typical points of business interest include:

- Bill-to-book ratio
- Profitability of the company
- Growth of customers
- Cost of sales
- Length of the sales cycle

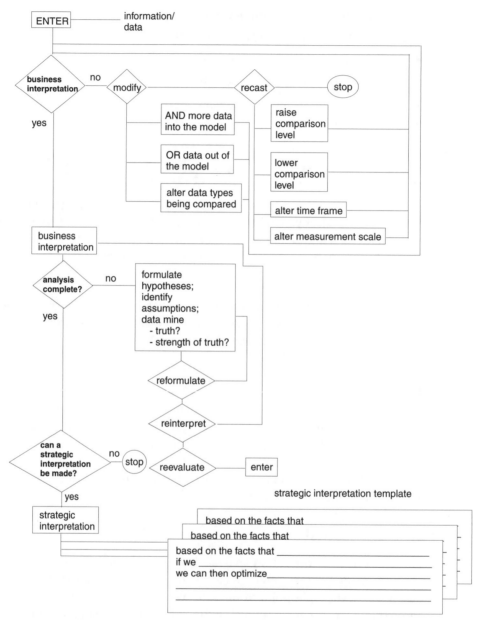

Figure 4.18 The model to data approach: A simple methodology for going from data to business deployment of competitive advantage.

The technician and the businessperson should agree on the point of interest at the outset of exploration analysis. In the name of simplicity and efficiency, it behooves the explorer to limit the points of interest being analyzed.

Units of Measurement

At one extreme, the movement of a point of interest can be measured in seconds. At the other extreme, movement can be measured in decades or even centuries. As a rule of thumb, the larger the summaries of data measured by the point of interest, the larger the unit of measurement of the rate of movement. For example, the Japanese economy can be measured in decades, whereas the sales that occur in an open-air farmers' market can be measured in terms of hours.

There is an interesting implication to the selection of the rate of movement as it relates to the point of interest. When the rate of change is measured in small increments (e.g., days or seconds), it is unlikely that the external forces have changed their relationship to the point of interest to any great extent. Consequently, the comparison of forces that cause the movement is very homogeneous. Over a longer period of time, however, it is very likely that the external forces that influence the point of interest will change, and, in some cases, change dramatically. When movement is measured by the decade, external forces that influence the point of interest are likely to be very different, forming a very heterogeneous basis for analysis. For example, the forces that drive the stock value of IBM Corporation one day are very likely to be the same forces that drive its value the next day; however, the forces that drove IBM stock value in 1960 are very different from the forces that drove its value in 1990.

The Proper Interval of Time

One of the keys to effective exploration is selecting an interval of time that allows changes to be well focused. In the case of IBM stock value, the interval of time that is selected will vary, depending on how the information is used. For example, a day trader may select a short time interval to study the stock, such as a week or even a month, whereas a mutual fund analyst may choose a year or even a decade as the interval of interest. A focused measurement of movement, therefore, is an interval of time that is long enough to have allowed the external forces to have changed and short enough to have made the forces acting on the point of interest to have remained reasonably constant.

Focus is achieved by selecting an interval of time that is long enough to have allowed the external forces to have changed their influence, but not so long that the external forces themselves have changed. In other words, if the explorer has chosen too short of an interval of time to measure change, then the changes in external forces will not have measurably altered their influence on the point of interest. If the explorer selects too long of an interval of time over which to measure change in the point of interest, then many external forces will have influenced the point of interest that will have never been measured throughout the interval.

In summary, one of the most important decisions the explorer makes is that of selecting the interval of time over which to measure changes in the movement of the point of interest.

Conditions of Insight

There are (at least!) three essential conditions of insight—all three conditions must be present for exploration processing to be effective:

1. Analysis must be done with the right level of detail.
2. Analysis must be done on multiple occurrences of multiple variables.
3. Analysis must be done on reasonably homogeneous data.

The Right Level of Detail

The origin of insight starts with the question: When considering the point of interest, is insight found at the level of lowest detail or at the level of highest summarization? In truth, the origin of insight almost always lies somewhere in between. If you operate at too low a level of detail, you can't see the forest for the trees; however, if you operate at only the level of summarization, you can't see the trees for the forest.

Consider an analyst who looks at every sale that a retailer makes. After looking at 10,000 sales, one sale starts to look like every other sale. There are so many sales and so many details that the analyst soon is lost in a sea of detail.

Looking only at summarization is no more enlightening, though. Consider the single summary number shown in Figure 4.19. It shows that monthly sales have been $10,246. The problem is that by itself this summarization says practically nothing. Is $10,246 a good or bad number? Were sales expected to be more? Less? What were last month's sales? The number $10,246 by itself says nothing meaningful.

Figure 4.19 A single observation says nothing meaningful.

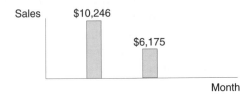

Figure 4.20 Context is established by having more than one observation.

Multiple Variables

For a number—any number—to be useful, there must be something with which a comparison can be made. Figure 4.20 shows that when two numbers stand side by side, there is context for interpretation. We can now say whether a result is "good" or "bad" based on the comparison.

When there is a basis for comparison, there is the foundation for insight. Even better than two numbers for a comparison is a continuum of numbers. With a continuum of numbers, trends can be identified, as seen in Figure 4.21.

WARNING

To properly extrapolate into the future from current trends, it is necessary to understand the underlying business reasons or business causes behind the trends. Once the causality factors and external forces are identified—then and only then is it safe to extrapolate trends based on history.

Homogeneity of Comparative Numbers

Although it is necessary to have more than one number to interpret that number, it is also necessary to examine the heterogeneity and the homogeneity of the

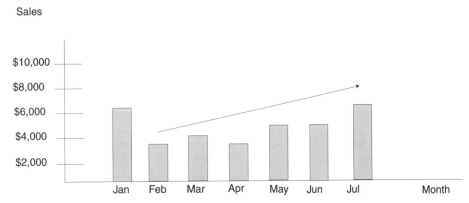

Figure 4.21 With multiple observations, trends can be identified and analyzed.

numbers being compared. When the detailed basis of the items that are being compared is very similar, those items are "homogeneous." When the detailed basis of the items that are being compared is very dissimilar, those items are said to be "heterogeneous." There is a spectrum of homogeneity. Items are not perfectly homogeneous or heterogeneous; instead, items are relatively homogeneous or heterogeneous.

For example, suppose that this month's sales of a product are being compared with last month's sales. Under normal circumstances, this comparison would be considered to be homogeneous. The detailed items being compared are essentially identical. The only factors that have changed are the month itself, bringing marginally cooler or warmer weather, small changes in the marketplace, small changes in the competition, and so forth.

Now, suppose that the sale of beer is being compared with the sale of farm tractors. Although such a comparison could be made, it just doesn't make much sense to do so. The items are simply very different from each other in many ways. This comparison would be very heterogeneous under normal circumstances.

The heterogeneity and the homogeneity of the detailed data being compared must be factored into the comparison equation. The more homogeneous that data is when being compared, the greater the chance of insight. The less homogeneous that data is when being compared, the less the chance of insight.

Examples of Very Homogeneous Variables

The first set of variables that is shown in Figure 4.22a compares predicted sales with actual sales of a product. These variables are almost perfectly homogeneous. The only difference between the two variables is how the calculations were made. The analyst can expect to achieve insight from the differences in the numbers.

The second set of variables, in Figure 4.22b, compares sales made this year with sales made last year. These are very homogeneous variables but may not be perfectly homogeneous. For example, there may be a different product mix this year than the product mix that was available to the salespeople last year. There may have been a new release of products. Prices for unit sales may be different this year from last year. The taxation rate and the foreign exchange rate may not be the same. These environmental differences must be factored into the differences in results to result in a meaningful comparison.

The third homogeneous comparison that is shown, Figure 4.22c, is between sales made in different states. Although most factors are equal, there may be differences in weather, state taxes, demographics, and religious preferences. Nevertheless, there are enough similarities between the states to make this comparison homogeneous and meaningful.

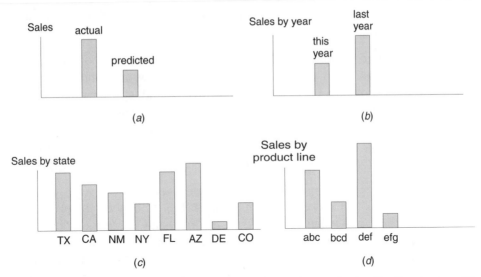

Figure 4.22 Examples of very homogeneous data. (*a*) Actual sales/predicted sales. (*b*) This year's sales/last year's sales. (*c*) Values that differ by geography. (*d*) Values that differ by product line.

The final homogeneous comparison that is shown, Figure 4.22*d*, is that of one product's sales versus another's. Although this comparison is reasonably homogeneous, there are likely some differences that make these variables less than perfectly homogeneous:

- One product line is older than another product line.
- One product line is a loss leader.
- One product line is a cash cow.
- One product line receives more promotion than another product line.

All of these variables are homogeneous enough that comparisons between the variables are meaningful. Even where there is less than perfect homogeneity, the variables are positioned to lend insight.

Examples of Somewhat Homogeneous Data

Homogeneous comparisons of data are very common. However, there are different degrees of homogeneity. A different level of homogeneity among variables is illustrated by Figure 4.23.

The first comparison, in Figure 4.23*a*, is between the dollars that are spent by men and by women on a product. The degree of homogeneity depends on the items whose sales are being measured. For example, if the dollars spent are based on brassieres or shaving cream (i.e., gender-specific items), then most likely the variables are heterogeneous. However, if the dollars spent are based on the measurement of expenditures of some gender-neutral item such as ball-point pens, then the variables are homogeneous.

The second comparison of variables, Figure 4.23b, is for total industry beverage sales versus corporate cola sales. These variables are somewhat homogeneous in that a cola is a beverage. Comparing total industry beverage sales with cola sales may yield some insight. Industry beverage sales, however, include much more than colas; they include beer, wine coolers, canned juices, and other beverages that are not necessarily comparable with colas. The exploration analyst must carefully consider the homogeneity of these figures or risk making the wrong interpretations.

The third comparison, made in Figure 4.23c, is between the prime lending rate and new home loans by a bank. On the one hand, there is no direct relationship between the prime lending rate and the making of a loan. The bank is free to charge whatever rates it wishes, and the consumer is able to take a loan or not. The variables, therefore, are heterogeneous in the strictest sense of the word. There is a very powerful indirect connection, however, between the customer's willingness to take a loan and the prime rate, even if the prime rate is not directly connected to the specific loan rate offered to the customer.

Where variables are somewhat homogeneous lie both opportunity and danger. There is the opportunity to discover a hidden relationship between two seemingly heterogeneous variables. If this is the case, the explorer may well be onto

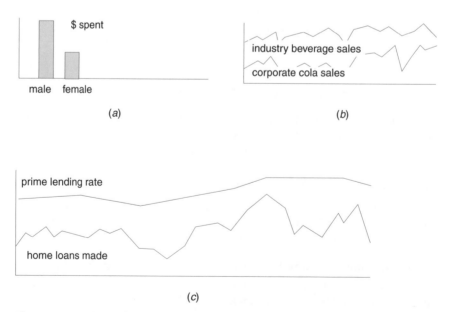

Figure 4.23 Examples of somewhat homogeneous data. (*a*) Dollars spent by gender. (*b*) Industry comparison of industry beverage sales versus corporate cola sales. (*c*) Prime lending rate/home loans made.

a very important discovery for the corporation. However, if there is no hidden relationship between two heterogeneous variables, then the explorer may draw incorrect and even dangerous conclusions.

Examples of Heterogeneous Variables with No Direct Relationship

The first set of variables, shown in Figure 4.24a, compares corporate sales and the rise and fall of the Dow Jones Industrial Average. Unless your company is a stock brokerage, it is highly unlikely that there is any factor—direct or indirect—that correlates the two variables. The variables shown in this comparison are very heterogeneous. Making any kind of inference based on the relationship of these variables is very questionable.

The second comparison, Figure 4.24b, is between the rise and fall of the number of households in the United States versus the number of units of a product produced by your company. In almost every normal circumstance, there is no

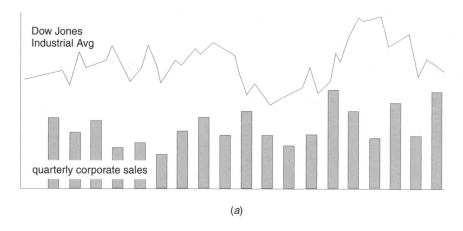

(a)

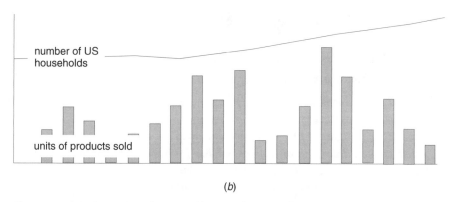

(b)

Figure 4.24   Some examples of nonhomogeneous data. (a) Dow Jones Industrial Average / quarterly corporate sales. (b) Number of U.S. households / product units sold.

factor that relates the behavior of one variable to the behavior of the other variable. As a consequence, the variables shown in Figure 4.24*b* are very heterogeneous and are very unlikely to yield insight.

The previous examples show that there are degrees of homogeneity and heterogeneity of variables. The more homogeneous the variables, the greater the chance that a comparison of the variables will be meaningful and will yield insight.

Examples of Heterogeneous Variables with an Indirect Relationship

There is a powerful case to be made for comparing apparently heterogeneous variables, in the event that there is a relationship—a hidden relationship—that actually interlocks the behavior of the variables. Discovering that hidden relationship is at the heart of the reason why exploration processing should be done. This kind of proposition is exactly what the explorer is looking for in doing exploration processing.

False Positives

What the explorer is not looking for is called a *false positive*. A false positive is a set of numbers that would lead to a conclusion that was not true. A famous false positive is shown in Figure 4.25.

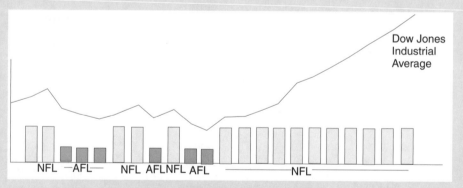

Figure 4.25   A famous false positive: comparing the winner of the Super Bowl with the Dow Jones Industrial Average.

Figure 4.25 shows that for many years, the annual rise or fall in the Dow Jones Industrial Average could be picked by determining the league of the winner of the Super Bowl. Looking at the comparison leads to the conclusion that when the NFL wins the Super Bowl, the Dow Jones will rise for the year; when the AFL wins the Super Bowl, the Dow Jones will fall. Such had been the case for many years until the Denver Broncos won the Super Bowl in 1998 and 1999 and broke the consistency of the rises and falls of the stock market and the league of the Super Bowl winner.

Of course, there is no indirect factor relating the winner of the Super Bowl and the rise and fall of one of the most important indicators of the American economy. Given enough numbers and enough transactions, correlations will start to appear simply because there are so many patterns. Patterns will appear to have strong correlations with other patterns when there is no business basis for them. Given enough numbers and enough patterns, a case can be made for correlation for some of the patterns simply as a result of chance.

Figure 4.26a shows that two heterogeneous variables—the outside temperature and the sale of beer—have a strong indirect relationship. The hotter it gets, the more beer is sold. The two variables are connected by the indirect factor that as the heat rises, people get thirsty, and as people get thirsty, the sale of beer goes up.

The second set of heterogeneous variables, shown in Figure 4.26b, is the relationship between accidents and the age of the male driver. Even though the variables—the accident rate and the age of the driver—are heterogeneous, there is an underlying factor that relates the two variables—the rise of testosterone in young males.

There are then some interesting implications of the heterogeneity and the homogeneity of variables in the exploration process:

- The more homogeneous data is, the likelier it becomes that analysis of the variables will yield important insights.
- In the case of heterogeneous variables being compared, if an indirect factor not previously discovered has been found, important assertions can be made.

Trends over Time

Once homogeneous variables have been collected, they can be placed side by side to create a trend. Figure 4.27 shows a trend that has been created in this manner.

Trends are useful in that they broaden the spectrum of analysis that is possible. The explorer can see a larger picture of what is going on with trend analysis. However, there is a pitfall: trying to use trend development and analysis as a basis for extrapolation. There is a temptation to extrapolate the trend based on four or five points of data. If there is an underlying business basis for continuing the trend, then such an extrapolation may be valid and very useful. If, however, there is no understanding of the underlying business basis for the trend or in fact no business basis for the trend exists, then creating an extrapolation is a very dangerous thing to do and may be flatly incorrect.

For example, suppose the Dow Jones Industrial Average has closed up for six consecutive days. The mapping of the variables shows a real trend here. Because the Dow Jones has closed up for six days, is it safe to draw an extrap-

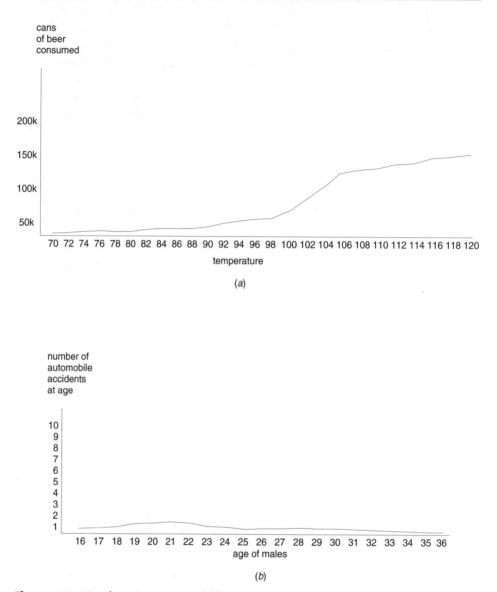

Figure 4.26 Two heterogeneous variables can have a strong indirect relationship. (*a*) Outside temperature and the sale of beer. (*b*) The accident rate and the age of the male driver.

olation projecting that the Dow will close up for the seventh day? The extrapolation of the trend indicates that the market will indeed close up. However, there are so many factors that affect the Dow that there is no reason why the Dow might close upward (or downward) on the seventh day. In this case, the underlying business reasons do not support an extrapolation.

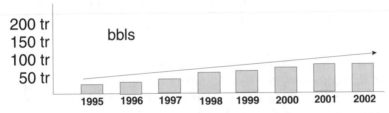

Figure 4.27 Growth of gasoline consumption over time. tr, trillion; bbls, barrels.

On the other hand, suppose that a study is made of the number of Internet business transactions being made. There is a sea change in the pattern of customers making purchases, and that sea change is being driven by the Internet. Given that more people are accessing and doing business on the Internet, is it possible to create an extrapolated trend line of transactions? If the answer is yes, an extrapolation may be in order because the business fundamentals warrant such an action. Even in this case, though, where there is a basis for extrapolation, there is nothing to say that the extrapolation is correct. The extrapolation may be more or less than the actual trend line.

Different Approaches to Exploration Analysis

There are many approaches to finding and understanding important business patterns. Two very different approaches will be described in the remaining portion of this chapter:

1. The *business-model-to-pattern* approach.
2. The *pattern-to-business-model* (i.e., brute-force) approach.

In the business-model-to-pattern approach, a business model is created that consists of a point of interest and the external forces that have an impact on the point of interest. The business model can be as simple or as elaborate as the modeler desires.

Once the business model is created, the explorer hunts for business patterns that will bear fruit in the most likely places. For brick-and-mortar companies these points include physical store location, population density, accessibility to major transportation artery or mass transit, and marketing sphere of influence. In the business-model-to-pattern approach, most of the time is spent in understanding the business, with less time spent in analysis of data reflecting that business. Those who focus primarily on the business only will use data such as sales reporting, inventory control reports, and product pipeline information. All of these reports are operationally useful but are not focused upon factors that may reflect a need for a new or altered business model. A new, emerging business model can often be discovered at the onset of change with the pattern to model approach, which does not make any assumptions about the business model.

The second approach to exploration analysis is that of pattern to business model. In the pattern-to-business-model approach, much analytical processing occurs, from which is derived some part of the larger business model. Once the patterns have been discovered and analyzed, the relevant business model is created. In the pattern-to-business-model approach, much time is spent in analytical processing, with only a small amount of time spent in business modeling.

Both approaches to exploration analysis have their strengths and weaknesses. The business-model-to-pattern approach is useful when there is either very little data on which to do analysis or when there is an overwhelming amount of data. Where there is very little data, the business-model-to-pattern approach can help predict where more data would be useful. When there is an overwhelming amount of data to be analyzed, the business-model-to-pattern approach can help weed out whole sectors of data that will be unproductive to analyze.

The pattern-to-business-model approach to exploration is useful when there is enough data to be meaningful, but not so much as to make analysis overwhelming. Let's now look at the pattern-to-business-model approach in more detail.

The Pattern-to-Business-Model Approach

Often, an explorer will look at a body of data and sense important business correlations or causal factors between data variables, but she or he just can't put her or his finger on the relationship or causal factors. Using the pattern-to-business-model approach, the explorer can identify the business patterns that are of vital interest to the corporation.

The transition between data and business is made by focusing and refocusing the comparisons of variables. Once two or more variables have been properly focused, the business implications seem to "pop out." At this point, the underlying business model is obvious and easy to construct. Until the variables become focused, however, no such business revelations are likely to occur.

There are some basic things that the explorer can do to focus and refocus the analysis, such as:

- Reduce the scope of homogeneity of one or more variables (i.e., *AND* the data).

- Increase the scope of homogeneity of one or more of the variables (i.e., *OR* the data).

- Alter the X-axis measurement.

- Alter the Y-axis measurement.
- Select a different span of focus for the analysis.

Cross-Tabular Analysis

In cross-tabular analysis, the most frequently used technique for exploration, data is usually presented in two-dimensional tables. The *X*- and *Y*-illustrations used in this chapter refer to the horizontal and vertical axes of the two variables in the analysis. Thus, to present all of the possible analytical combinations in a three-variable analysis, at least one *X*-axis/*Y*-axis table must be presented for each category of the third variable in the analysis. This rapidly leads to a very large number of two-dimensional representations. For this reason, complex analysis generally leads to the adoption of higher-level statistical techniques fairly rapidly, for in almost every analysis there are *N* dimensions.

Each of these scenarios is part of the pattern-to-business-model approach. (Note: These steps correspond to the activities shown in the simple methodology seen in Figure 4.18.)

The pattern-to-model approach is much simpler than the model-to-pattern approach, in that no business models have to be created to start to explore data. The pattern-to-model approach, however, requires the ability to do massive analysis on huge amounts of data. In this sense, the pattern-to-model approach is more time consuming and resource consumptive than the model-to-pattern approach. As such, this approach is often called the brute-force approach to exploration.

The data that has been gathered in the exploration warehouse is laid out and the explorer simply starts to examine the data, looking for patterns, in contrast with the model-to-pattern approach. Usually, there is a lot of data at the outset and the explorer must be creative in determining how the patterns are formed. Some patterns will be formed by having different occurrences of data exhibit manifestations of the pattern. For example, the explorer notes that the pattern of interest occurs in records rec(126), rec(178), rec(286), rec(471), rec(512), rec(758), rec(1276), rec(1290), and so forth. It is the job of the explorer to identify the occurrences that are of interest and then to postulate why and under what circumstances they occurred. As another example, the explorer notes that when two record types are joined together, a pattern occurs. The explorer notes that a pattern occurs when records reca(16)/recb(187), reca(1984)/recb(176), reca(19827)/recb(1), reca(2)/recb(28715), reca(76)/recb(7614), reca(2761)/recb(6718), and so forth, all form a pattern. The explorer then sets out to find out what is unique about these combinations of records.

In a large body of data, the explorer will surely find patterns. In a way, finding patterns is itself an issue because:

- Some patterns are simply not relevant.
- Some patterns are false.

An irrelevant pattern is one that is real but that has no application to the business. Upon discovering such a pattern, the reaction is, "So what?"

The other kind of pattern that is discovered is one that is false. A false pattern is one in which there is a genuine statistical relationship between two variables, but there is no business relationship or hidden factor of causality behind the statistical correlation.

After the explorer has identified and established the patterns that are derived out of the body of occurrences, then the next task is to weed out which patterns are irrelevant and which are false. Figure 4.28 shows this weeding-out process.

After the irrelevant and false patterns are weeded out, then the explorer is left with valid and relevant patterns that have been derived from the body of occurrences. From these remaining patterns, the explorer creates a model of the external forces that have an influence on the point of interest. In this sense, the explorer ends up using this approach where the explorer using the model-to-pattern approach has started. Figure 4.29 shows that patterns lead to the creation of a business model.

The explorer who uses the pattern-to-model approach is free to use the symbols developed earlier for the model-to-pattern explorer. From the business model, the explorer is now positioned to start the process of business interpretation.

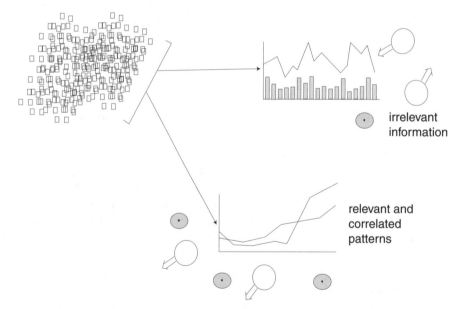

Figure 4.28   The brute-force approach, in which external forces and points of interest are relevant to or correlated to the patterns that emerge from the analysis of data.

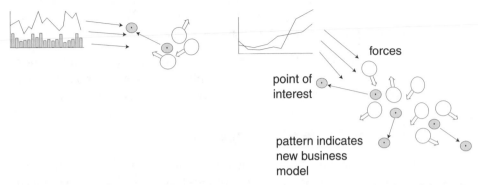

Figure 4.29 What point of interest/external force models can be developed from the brute-force analysis that has been done?

At first glance, it appears that the pattern-to-model process is much simpler and more straightforward than the model-to-pattern process. When the conditions are right, that is very true; however, there are some pitfalls of which the explorer needs to be aware, including:

- Finding patterns of data may not pick up all the patterns that are there. In fact, this process almost never picks up all the processes that are there. This means that, ultimately, there will be unidentified external forces at work against the point of interest. The resulting business model will be incomplete.

- Determining false positives is not necessarily an easy thing to do.

- Determining whether an external force is causal or correlative is not easy.

- Determining whether there are hidden factors linking correlative variables is not particularly easy to do.

Therefore, the explorer needs to give careful attention to which approach—model-to-pattern or pattern-to-model—is the appropriate approach. As a rule, the following circumstances apply:

Model-to-pattern approach

- Used when there is little or no body of occurrences with which to begin
- Used for business analysis at the highest level
- Used for points of interest that are indicative of the corporation's movements at the highest level
- Used for macromodels of the corporation

Pattern-to-model approach

- Used when a body of occurrences already exists
- Used in a bottom-up approach

- Used to analyze very low level patterns
- Used for a micromodel of the corporation

Whether the explorer has chosen to use one approach or the other, the end result is that after this level of analysis, the explorer and his or her business counterpart are now prepared to go into business analysis of the model that has been created.

Reduce the Scope of Homogeneity

If the explorer is unable to focus on two or more variables that are being compared, then one approach to help refocus the comparison is to reduce the scope of one or more of the variables being analyzed. Figure 4.30 shows such a reduction of scope.

In Figure 4.30, the scope is reduced from women to women between the ages of 25 and 50, to women between the ages of 25 and 50 who are married, to women between the ages of 25 and 50 who are married and who have college degrees. Each time the scope is lowered, there is the chance that the explorer will be able to see the underlying business implication. Of course, each time the explorer lowers or reduces the scope of homogeneity, the less general the findings will be. This approach is called *ANDing* the data because it starts with a general scope of data and successively selects only a smaller subset of the original set of data.

> **In Boolean logic, each additional AND condition usually limits the number of cases.**

The reduction of scope is usually an easy process as long as the explorer has enough granular data to begin with. Each time the explorer reduces the size of the scope, fewer occurrences of data remain to be analyzed. Of course, at some point the number of occurrences being analyzed is reduced to the point that the set of data being analyzed is no longer statistically significant. Among the alternatives for focusing data, however, this alternative is usually the easiest to accommodate.

What to do when things don't focus

Women → women from → married women → college-educated married
25 to 50　　　from 25 to 50　　　women from 25 to 50

Figure 4.30　Reduce the scope of homogeneity.

Increase the Scope of Homogeneity

The second alternative that the explorer has in the quest for focus is to increase the scope of homogeneity. In this case, the explorer adds new types of data to the variable(s) being analyzed. Figure 4.31 shows the increase in the scope of homogeneity.

In the example shown in Figure 4.31, the explorer has increased the scope of homogeneity from manufacturers having revenue of less than $50 million to manufacturers of any size to any company, manufacturer or otherwise. The increase in the scope of homogeneity allows the comparison of variables to be expanded considerably.

The process of expanding the scope of homogeneity is called *ORing* the variable. The notion of ORing stems from adding more variable types to the scope. The problem with ORing the scope is that many more observations of data may be added to the scope, and that focus of the scope becomes increasingly blurred as the scope is expanded.

Alter the Measurement of the X Axis

The next technique for bringing the comparison of variables into focus using the pattern-to-business-model approach is that of altering the range of measurement of the X axis. The X axis is the horizontal axis of measurement. The X axis, like the Y axis, is measured by units. The explorer can alter the scale of those units if it will help to focus the comparison of variables. The X scale can be either raised or lowered depending on the data being compared.

As an example of the fitting of the X axis to the variables being compared, the number of transactions that a bank runs during the day could be measured on a minute-by-minute basis or on an hourly basis. It does not make sense to make such measurements and report them on a second-by-second basis. Nor does it make sense to report the transactions run on a weekly basis if the concern is for the purpose of immediate management of response time.

What to do when things don't focus

Small manufacturers ← manufacturers ← all manufacturers ← all companies
< $50 million

Figure 4.31 Expand class of homogeneity.

Alter the Measurement of the Y Axis

Just like the units of measurement of the X axis, the units of measurement of the Y axis can likewise be altered in using the pattern-to-business-model approach. As an example of the importance of choosing the proper Y scale for comparison of variables, consider the measurement of the Dow Jones Industrial Average. If the Y scale is measured in terms of pennies, the display of the rise and fall of the Dow Jones will be massive. If the scale is in terms of units of $10,000, the Dow Jones will appear as if it never moves, even though in fact the Dow is constantly moving. For most measurements of the Dow Jones, a scale of $1 works quite well, unless, of course, the measurement is over a lengthy period of time where the measurement might be in units of $10 or even $100.

Select the Proper Time Span Focus

The time span focus involves selecting an interval of time during which to compare variables. Defining each time span is a start time and a stop time. The comparison of the variables to each other before the start time and after the stop time is irrelevant to the analysis at hand. Figure 4.32 shows that the time span focus is a deliberate choice made by the explorer.

Figure 4.32 shows the time span that has been chosen is for the month of January to the month of December. Such an annual time span might be appropriate for variables such as total corporate revenue, corporate profitability, or GNP. Measuring total corporate revenue from January 1, 10:35 A.M. to January 1, 11:14 A.M. simply does not make sense. The variables will not have meaningfully changed in that time span. Likewise, choosing a time span from 1796 to 2076 for the measurement of IBM's revenue does not make sense, because IBM did not exist in 1796, and it is going to be a while before we know what IBM's revenue for 2076 is going to be.

The time span that is chosen is relevant to the X-axis measurement. If the time span is measured in terms of years, then it does not make sense to choose an X-axis scale of seconds. In addition, the more summarized the variables are, the longer the time span represented. Conversely, the more detailed the variables being considered, the shorter the time span.

The selection of the time span is not a trivial consideration. The time span selection can be used to eliminate variables that were relevant before the time

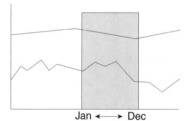

Jan ◄——► Dec

Figure 4.32 Select a span of time on which to focus.

span was selected but not relevant after the start of the time span. The proper selection of a time span goes a long way toward the focusing of two (or more) variables against each other.

The insight that explorers gain by focusing their variable comparison sets the stage for future success. Focusing the exploration process helps the analyst identify where analysis efforts will be most productive. If the explorer does not go through the qualifying process of focusing the exploration when doing the pattern-to-business-model approach, it is possible that exploration processing will lead nowhere. Focusing the exploration effort greatly increases the odds for success and a positive outcome.

The Business-Model-to-Pattern Approach

There is another way to arrive at essentially the same place as the pattern-to-business-model approach, and that is the business-model-to-pattern approach. Using this approach, the explorer creates a simplistic model of the business and then searches the model for patterns that will prove to be productive. In many regards, the business-model-to-pattern approach is the exact opposite of the pattern-to-business-model approach.

This approach is a very good one for the purpose of organizing a lot of seemingly unrelated factors and for dealing with a very grand business and very grand external forces. The problem with the model-to-pattern approach is that it can become very complex very rapidly. Constant discipline is required to maintain an orderly and well-thought-out model. Simplicity is of the essence when using this approach.

Refinement Analysis

The first step in the business-model-to-pattern approach is to create a simple model of the business. This begins with the notion that there is a point of interest. The point of interest can be any variable. Usually it is the following:

- Relevant to the business
- Quantifiable
- Measurable over time

Some sample points of interest might be a company's

- Financial health
- Productivity
- Positioning in the marketplace versus competition
- Market share

In truth, a point of interest for a corporation can be practically anything. Given the emphasis and energy that is placed on the point of interest, it often makes sense to make the point of interest a key performance indicator for the corporation.

Surrounding the point of interest are several measurements—all of which tend to reflect on and measure the point of interest. Suppose a corporation has selected the success of the corporation as its point of interest. The corporation can measure success in many ways:

- Corporate revenue
- Corporate profitability
- Number of customers
- Number of products
- Number of products in the pipeline

Each of these measurements reflects on one or the other aspects of corporate success. The symbol that will be used for showing a point of interest is surrounded by many different measurements.

It is noteworthy that a point of interest may have a few or very many measurements, and that each of the measurements will reflect on a different aspect of the point of interest.

Changes to the Point of Interest— External Forces

Over time, all points of interest change. What changes a point of interest? A point of interest is changed over time by the workings of its own internal forces and by the external forces. Some external forces have a direct influence on the point of interest, and other external forces have an indirect influence. Some external forces have a strong influence on the point of interest and other external forces have a weak influence. Some external forces act like a tugboat and pull the point of interest. Other external forces have a pushing effect, like a bulldozer. Still other external forces have a "suction" effect, like the forces of the sea when a ship sinks, pulling down survivors with the force of the dive.

Again, using a company's financial health as the point of interest, external forces include:

- Competition
- Marketplace demand
- Financial state of the world
- Technological advances
- Legislation
- Growth of the population
- Marketplace penetration

There are an infinite number of external forces. The explorer is only interested in any and all relevant external forces that

- Can be measured
- Influence the point of interest significantly

as well as

- The degree to which influence is felt
- The cumulative effect of *all* of the external forces working at once

Of great interest to the explorer are the movements over time of the point of interest. Is the corporation heading for prosperity? Is the corporation heading for rough times? Is the corporation just treading water? All of these measurements can be taken by looking at the measurements that surround the point of interest and measuring their changes over time.

For example, if the point of interest is the financial health of the corporation, then looking at the changes over time for such things as

- Changes in revenue
- Changes in profitability
- Changes in number of customers
- Changes in number of units of products sold

are all indicators of the movement of the corporate financial picture.

Changes to the Point of Interest—
Different Stances

There are (at least!) three stances that the corporation can take when it comes to understanding external forces and the changes that are wrought by these forces over time:

1. *First stance.* The corporation can be unaware of the influence of external factors at all. The corporation has no idea where it is heading. Each day is a new surprise in life at this corporation. Executives wake up one day and find out that market share has evaporated or that the company is no longer profitable.

2. *Second stance.* The corporation can measure the movement of the corporation. In this case, the corporation may be losing market share, but at least the executives are aware that customers are leaving.

3. *Third stance.* The corporation can understand what the forces are, how strongly they are at work, and the movement that is occurring as a result of the external forces. The result is that the corporation is able to predict where the movement will be in the future and at what rate.

A corporation does not have to do anything to achieve the first stance. Just sitting there and passing the time of day will achieve this. A corporation must have systems of measurement in place to achieve the second stance to periodically measure critical success factors and to record and report on them. To achieve the third stance, the corporation must measure its own progress and also be aware of external forces (and their strength) to measure and anticipate the effect of those external forces.

When a corporation is in the first stance, it operates in a blind reactive mode. When a corporation operates in the second stance, it is in a reactive mode, but at least it is not blind. The corporation is aware of what is happening, but is not yet in a proactive stance. In the third stance, the corporation is proactive. Not only does the corporation know where it is, but it knows the rate at which it is going and what is driving it there.

The opportunity to be proactive is worth an inestimable amount to the corporation. Simply stated, when a corporation is able to understand the future (even the very short term future!), the corporation can count on growing and thriving. When a corporation can only measure where it is, then the corporation can only maintain the status quo. When a corporation has no idea where it is or where it is going, then the corporation will eventually wither and die.

Different Levels of Complexity for This Approach

Figure 4.33 shows the different possibilities of using the model-to-pattern approach, from a very simple model to a very complex model. With simpler models, the corporation can see what is happening, and with more complex models, it can tell not only what is happening but also where the corporation is likely to be heading.

As a general rule, the explorer wishes to keep the model that has been produced as simple as possible. The more complex the model, the more difficult the analysis. It must be admitted, however, that to create a meaningful model, the model itself must come to grips with at least a modicum of complexity. The balance between simplicity and relevancy is one that the explorer must be constantly aware of.

To summarize the worth of the models that are created by using the model-to-pattern approach, when a causal relationship can be found (which is admittedly rare), the explorer can position the corporation in a position of great advantage. When a causal relationship is found, the explorer pays special attention to:

- How much influence does the external force have over the point of interest?
- What does the relationship between the external force and the point of interest actually look like?

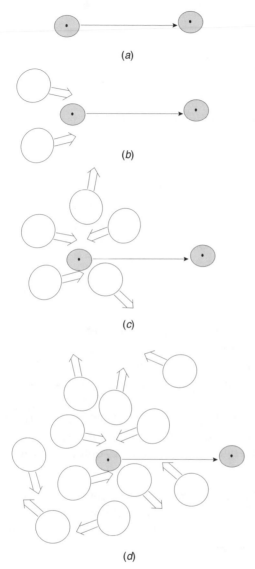

Figure 4.33 The relationship of the model and the corporate stance toward proactivity and reactivity. (*a*) Movement in the abstract with no knowledge of external forces (the corporation must guess where it is going). (*b*) Movement where the point of interest is influenced directly by causal forces (the corporation can at least tell where it has been). (*c*) Complex model of movement where the point of interest is shaped by causal and indirect forces (the corporation has a good idea of where it is heading). (*d*) A very complex model where the point of interest is shaped by a wide variety of forces (the corporation is very sure of where it is heading).

- At what points do the external force and the point of interest come into contact?
- How do changes in the external force affect the point of interest?

For the more common but less powerful correlative relationship, the explorer looks for such things as:

- Which *a/b* are correlated?
- How are *a/b* correlated?

- What is the strength of correlation of *a/b?*
- Is there a ripple effect?
- What other *b*s are correlated to *a/b?*
- For what periods of time are *a/b* correlated?
- Under what conditions are *a/b* correlated?
- Are there hidden factors that explain the correlation?
- What profile of correlated factors can be created?

Examples of Exploration Processing

It is one thing to understand the principles of data mining and exploration; it is another thing to be able to apply those principles. The following examples depict how data exploration is being used by businesses.

Air Bag Manufacturer

An air bag (for automobiles) manufacturer has a quality problem with the mixture of the explosive that detonates upon a crash to fill air bags. The issue of quality of explosive is taken very seriously, and the engineers test the explosive frequently. At random intervals, the explosive fails quality tests. The engineers examine everything they know to try to explain the failure. They question the suppliers of the raw goods that go into the explosive. They question the way the raw goods are mixed and stored. They question the containers in which the raw goods are mixed. However, the engineers are unable to determine why there is problem with quality of mixture.

The engineers therefore turn to an explorer. The explorer first creates an analytical depiction of the quality ratio as it goes up and down over time (Figure 4.34). It shows that quality of the explosive mixture is high for the most part, but the quality turns low at random intervals.

The explorer then uses data analysis to determine what is different about these moments in time when quality turns low. In particular, he looks for what happens immediately before the quality turns low. The explorer looks at every variable

Figure 4.34 Periodically, the quality of the mixture of explosive varies dramatically.

that can be measured to see what has the same pattern of behavior as the low quality of the explosive mixture, but he is still unable to find a similar pattern.

One day the explorer hits on the idea of examining the weather. The explorer looks at temperature, length of day, weather forecast, and humidity. The locale where the air bag company is located is famous for being hot and dry. Occasionally, however, low pressure will pass through and the humidity will rise. When the explorer creates an analytic graph of the rise of the humidity in the air and compares it with the incidences of poor quality of explosive, the result is astounding. Figure 4.35 shows this comparison.

The humidity—unknown to the engineers—has a great effect on the mixing of the explosive. As long as the air is dry, the explosive can be mixed successfully; however, when the humidity rises, the explosive mixture turns bad. The matching of the analytics shown in Figure 4.35 leads the engineers to the conclusion that there is a hidden relationship between the point of interest (the quality of explosive) and the external force (the humidity in the air).

Once the manufacturer discovers this fact, the safety of the plant and the efficiency of the manufacturing process increase dramatically.

Banking Customer Relationship Management

Exploration processing is widely used in banking customer relationship management (CRM), although in a slightly different form than the classical form described in this chapter. Customer relationship management is used to attract and maintain market share in the banking environment.

The first step in CRM is to build a data warehouse where many characteristics about the customer are collected and integrated. In addition, the transactions that the customer has executed are collected and integrated as well in the data warehouse. It is not unusual for the bank to enhance the internally collected informa-

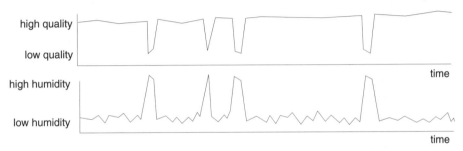

Figure 4.35   The pattern of humidity in the air correlated with the quality of the mixture of explosive.

tion with other information that has been collected externally. The external demographic data can contain any sort of information that can be imagined.

The internal data and the external data are collected and integrated into a data warehouse. The data warehouse becomes the foundation on which analysis is done. The first step is to divide the customer base into one of several categories. Those categories are shown in Figure 4.36.

Figure 4.36 shows that customers are divided into the categories of profitable, marginal, in transition, and unprofitable. The bank uses many criteria to divide its customers into these categories, such as:

- Net worth
- Total number of accounts with the bank
- Number of transactions
- Customer retention level

In addition, attention is paid to the cumulative value of the customer, not necessarily the current worth of the customer.

Once the customers have been divided into these categories, then an extensive analysis is done of many characteristics that relate to the customer. The primary analysis of characteristics centers around information that the bank has immediately available.

A secondary characteristic analysis is done on information that is available for some customers and for information that is available through external sources, including:

- Zip code
- Gender
- Age
- Size of house
- Own/rent
- Credit rating

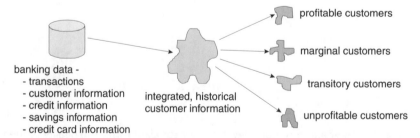

Figure 4.36 Customers can be classified into one of four categories by the bank.

- Income
- Income type
- Number of accounts

Still another level of analysis is done for tertiary data that is occasionally available for customers:

- College education
- Type of job
- Past financial history
- Vacation destination
- Cost of home
- Married/single
- Airline trips taken

The primary, secondary, and tertiary analyses of characteristics of customers attempt to understand how customers fit into each category. In other words, how do profitable customers differ from marginal customers, and how do marginal customers differ from in-transit customers, and so forth. The bank finds that it generates the vast amount of its profits from a relatively small number of customers. Conversely, the bank loses money on another class of customers. To maximize profitability, the bank wishes to concentrate its affection on those customers who have been its top producers.

The net effect of the segmentation analysis that is done by the explorers is to produce a profile for each of the categories, as seen in Figure 4.37. The profile shown in Figure 4.37 shows that many different characteristics are used to describe the category that is being analyzed.

After the primary, secondary, and tertiary information is collected and attributed to the categories, the result is a description of the different categories of customers of the bank. Figure 4.38 shows the different profiles that match the customers' categories.

One of the interesting outcomes of this profile creation for each of the categories of the bank's customer analysis profiles is the ability to see how a customer changes categories over time. In other words, as a customer ages, how does a customer fit into one category or another.

Indeed, the bank notices that customers do not fit into a category in a static manner. Customers are constantly moving from one category to the next. Sometimes, a customer moves from a position of marginality to profitability. In other cases, the customer moves from profitability to marginality. In any case, whenever a customer moves from one category to another, the customer either represents a loss of money or a gain of money for the bank. To maximize profits, the bank

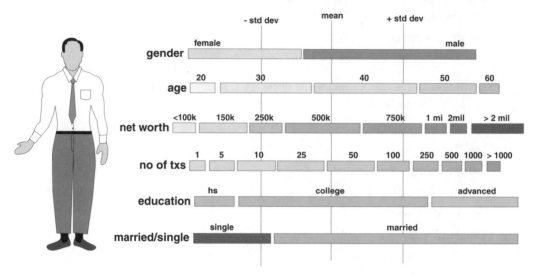

Figure 4.37 A profile is created for the average profitable customer.

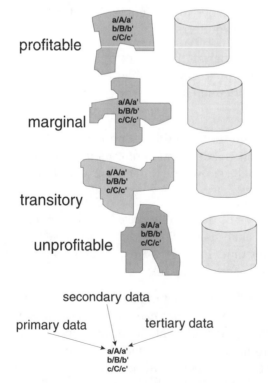

Figure 4.38 The different categories are fully attributed and populated.

wishes to minimize the movement of a customer down the chain and wishes to maximize the movement of a customer up the chain. Figure 4.39 shows the movement of customers up and down the chain of categories.

At every level of categorization, there is a core of customers that are unlikely to change categories anytime soon. These core customers are surrounded by transitory customers who are likely to change in either direction. To maximize profits, banks focus on the customers who move between categories. Profiles are created for customers who move up and down the chain. Once those profiles are created, the bank designs specific programs aimed at moving the customer segment up the chain or preventing or slowing the customer segment from moving down the chain. In addition, the bank aims at removing unprofitable customers from the chain altogether. The profiles are created over time for each category and subcategory.

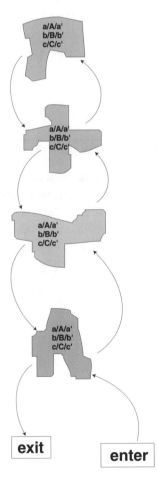

exit

enter

Figure 4.39 It is noticed that there is movement of customers from one class to the next.

Once profiles are gathered over a period of time, an analytic depiction is created. Over time, a set of profiles changes. These changes help the bank become sensitive to the changes in its customer base. Another depiction of the use of profiling for the analysis of customers is shown in Figure 4.40.

Customer Churn in the Telephone Environment

The term *churn* refers to the customer turnover. When measured on a 12-month basis, the number of customers who have dropped out in the past year are considered a company's churn. The smaller the churn, the larger and the more stable the customer base.

One day, a telephone company that had developed an extensive data warehouse found that it needed to address its corporate churn problem. The data warehouse seemed to be a good place to start. The telephone company's data warehouse contained the normal things that would be found in a data warehouse:

- Detailed data
- Integrated data
- Historical data
- Customer data
- Transaction data

In short, the telephone company had a normal data warehouse.

The telephone company decided to pick the records out of the data warehouse for those customers who had left the company. Because the data warehouse contained historical data, finding these customers was easy to do. The next step was to demographically characterize these customers, which was done on three levels. Once the customers were characterized, a profile for these customers was created, as shown in Figure 4.41. Over time, a moving profile analytic was created.

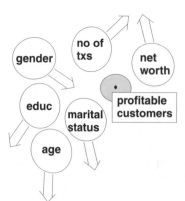

Figure 4.40 An essentially correlative model is created for customer profitability.

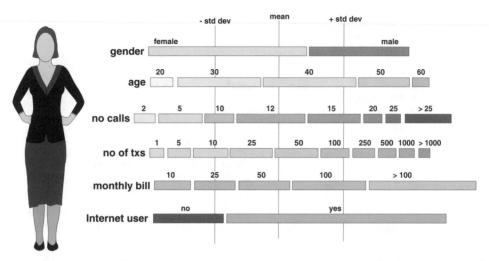

Figure 4.41   A profile is created for customers who frequently leave the telephone company.

Once the telephone company was satisfied that it understood who the customers were that were leaving, it began to look at its active customers. Each current customer record was analyzed, and if the current customer fit the profile created, then the current customer's record was marked.

The current customer's record was not marked in a binary manner. There were many criteria that determined if an individual was likely to leave. No one record was likely to be a perfect fit. Therefore, many factors were analyzed and a probability was assigned to the record.

Once the existing customer base was analyzed, then there were many possibilities for use. For example, when a customer calls the company operator, the operator would immediately know if that customer was flagged as one that was likely to leave. Based on this information, the operator shapes the conversation in a manner optimal to keeping the business of the customer.

Another use of the probability assignment is more proactive: mailing campaigns and other promotions. Periodically, the telephone company scans its customer file and selectively sends out promotions that are designed to keep customers loyal. The model that has resulted from the exploration work that was designed to minimize churn is shown in Figure 4.42.

Quality Assurance in Manufacturing

Once there was a steel company that made batches, or "heats," of steel. The steel company was able to measure the quality of a heat by measuring the percentage of usable steel at the end of a pouring. The higher the percentage, the higher the quality. The greater the usable steel ratio, the more productive the company.

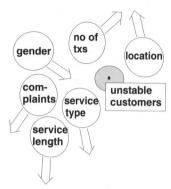

Figure 4.42 The model built by the telephone company.

The engineers at the steel company wish to improve the quality of the manufacturing process, but with 35,000 different variables per heat, they do not know where to start. It is suggested that the heats be arranged in order of quality. The heats with the lowest quality are ranked first, going up to the heats with the highest quality. Then, one variable after another is measured with the heats to see if there is a correlation between quality and the different measurements of the variable. Figure 4.43 shows the arrangement of heat quality versus the individual variables. Once the engineer starts to detect a pattern, the likely variables are then graphed together, as seen in Figure 4.44.

After analyzing many variables, the steel company can finally say which variables in which settings correlate to higher quality. Once this becomes estab-

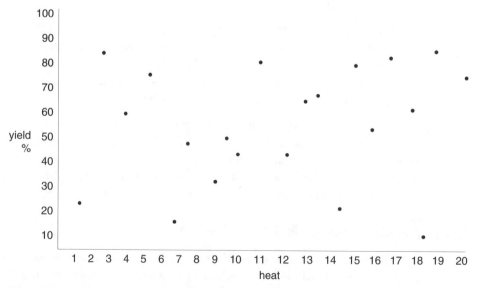

Figure 4.43 The yield of a heat is measured.

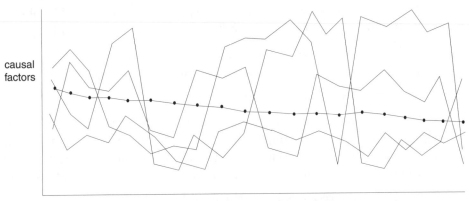

heat quality in order of highest to lowest

Figure 4.44 The top yields of the heats are correlated against other manufacturing variables to see what patterns there are.

lished, the steel company can improve its quality simply by knowing to which variables the heat process is sensitive. The model of quality that results from this analysis is seen in Figure 4.45.

In Summary

The chain of beneficence represents exploration processing at the highest level. At a lower level, exploration processing consists of:

- Gathering data and finding patterns of behavior
- Identifying external forces to address causality and correlation
- Interpreting patterns and translating them into business practices

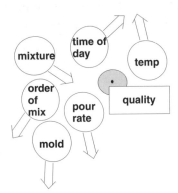

Figure 4.45 The model created by the steel company.

A simple methodology for exploration processing has been described that correlates to the steps previously outlined. The origins of insight lie:

- Between detail and summarization
- Between variables that are reasonably homogeneous
- Beyond a single observation

Heterogeneous variables may be compared when it is suspected that there is a hidden pattern connecting the heterogeneous variables. The explorer must constantly be aware of the fact that when there are many patterns, false positives will occur. When comparisons of variables don't focus, the analyst can:

- Reduce the scope of homogeneity
- Increase the scope of homogeneity
- Alter the X-axis measurement
- Alter the Y-axis measurement
- Alter the time span being analyzed

Analysis results lead to the creation of a business model. There are two approaches to the creation of the business model. One is the pattern-to-business-model approach, in which known patterns are used to create the business model. The second is the business-model-to-pattern approach, in which the business model is first created, then the search for patterns commences. The business model consists of:

- Point of interest
- Variables surrounding the point of interest that can be used to measure change
- External forces

The movement of the point of interest is a function of all of the factors at work. Some effects of the external forces are causal; other effects of the external forces are merely correlative. One of the challenges facing the explorer is the identification of unknown or unrecognized external forces. Companies with well-constructed business models are in a position to be proactive in understanding where the business is heading.

CHAPTER 5

Analytical Exploration Processing

There are lies, damn lies, and statistics.

—MARK TWAIN

The previous chapter was primarily concerned with a process that is sometimes referred to as "mucking in the data." There is no preexisting supposition as to patterns in the data. A good mining analogy is that of the casual geologist who walks across an expanse of land picking up rocks that look interesting. Upon arrival back at the laboratory, he splits them apart and out of 100 samples he might, by intuition and luck, find 5 of interest. The 5 of interest lead him to a hypothesis worthy of testing in detail. He then proceeds to perform, in a systematic and scientific way, a series of analytical tests, each one used in sequence to determine whether the hypothesis is true.

Most scientists have the unique advantage of being both knowledge domain and process experts. This is not true in other areas of endeavor. Thus, even in medicine today, the doctor does not perform the analytical tests for a particular disease; rather, a medical laboratory with predefined procedures runs the tests and returns the results to the physician for interpretation. The exploration process is an iterative interaction between the businessperson and the analyst for both process and meaning.

For the balance of the chapter, a single business problem will be used as a hypothetical case study to define the analytical exploration process. Remember that the analytical exploration process can best be equated to strip mining. In strip mining, ore is removed from the earth near the surface, at relatively low cost, without precision. Many low-cost techniques are available to analyze data. The majority of business analysts use the technique of cross-tabular analysis, which produces simple tables in a standard format. The analysis can be taught and performed by relatively junior staff because it does not require extensive training in statistics. (Note however that one must never confuse the process of performing the analysis with interpreting the results. Interpretation of results requires substantial business acumen and experience.)

The objective of this chapter is not to be a definitive work on statistical analysis. The goal is to define some easily understood concepts in business using business English so that the reader can get value immediately.

A Defined Business Problem

The company in question is a large toy retailer who has begun to look at issues related to profitability by store. When doing the initial exploration, the busi-

A Word about Tools

Today, we are in the middle of a tool explosion. The reason is an exponential increase in demand for analytical services with an arithmetic increase in the number of trained analysts. Figure 5.1 illustrates the gap between the availability of skilled analysts and the demand for high-level analytical services. The absence of adequately trained professionals to fill the demand has forced industry to look for alternatives. This has led to the substitution of a tool for experience and understanding. The unfortunate side effect is that increasingly, large amounts of analytical output are generated automatically, without insight as to the meaning of the information. A technician is not an analyst. The analyst has the ability to translate the output of the tool into meaningful bullets. The analyst then has the ability to interact with the businessperson in a meaningful and consultative way to assist in the interpretation of results. A great tool will make a good analyst more productive. The result of better analytical production is usually more iterations of the analytical process in the same time period or a faster turnaround on any single iteration. This should lead to quicker positioning, exploitation, and business return. A great tool will not make a poor analyst or a poor businessperson successful. At best, poor results will be generated faster. Tools are only as good as the workers who use them. The right strategy is to structure the work in such a manner that the highest level of analytical resource supervises the analytical process but only interprets the high-level work product. Tools, in and of themselves, are not the solution to business problems. If the analytical process is structured correctly, the participants will show preference for certain tools but will be flexible enough to use any tool in a given category.

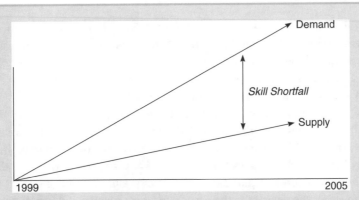

Figure 5.1 Supply and demand for analytical services.

A Word about Sampling

Many businesspeople ask the question, "Why run all the data, why not a sample?" The answer lies in the dimensions of time and complexity. Most of the statistics with which we are all acquainted deal with how well the sample we have picked reflects the population from which it was drawn. In general, on a single variable, a small sample will reflect trends in the general population. Exit polling in elections, within a few percentage points, will accurately reflect the outcome for a much larger population. As dimensions are added to an analysis, the quality of the sample becomes a concern. One should remember that in an exit poll, time is of the essence. If an exit poll cannot return a result in a timely fashion, then the event being predicted will be over before the data is of any use. If the analysis requires a large number of predictor (independent) variables, then the concern becomes skewing in the sample.

Skew occurs when the values in a sample do not reflect the distribution on the particular variable in the total population being sampled. Thus, if the gender distribution in a sample is 75 percent female, 25 percent male, but the population is 50 percent of each, the attributes on any dependent variable will be overly weighted toward what the female sample reports. In cases where prediction is a matter of a few percentage points, this skew can result in an absolutely wrong prediction. As more predictor variables with skew enter into the analysis, the skewing interacts to a level at which dramatic errors on percentage can occur. In general, however, a statistical principle called the *law of large numbers* prevails. Most often the skewing on multiple levels actually has a self-canceling effect. Again, time becomes the issue; in many cases, ascertaining the quality of the sample, in a complex analysis, can take as much or more time than running the entire population.

Much of the disposition toward sampling came from a time when computer power was expensive and tools were difficult to use. When the analysis is not under a real-time constraint, why not run all the data? It is important in the analytical process to remember the real objective. In the retail example we are using, sampling the point-of-sale (POS) data gives us information about the people who have bought. However, is that the real analytical objective? If the intent is to increase market basket size (number of items in a single shopping session), then perhaps the objective can be met. If, however, the objective is to understand the behavioral differences between those who have come into the store and those who are in the sphere of influence of the store and have not come to shop, then the sampling of the POS data leaves the usability of any findings of questionable value. In reality, what is then required is a sample of people who have not shopped in the store; the process is then to compare and contrast these people on a number of predictor dimensions. This process is typically what happens in market research when the population is too large or complex to collect massive data. Running the full POS data allows for inferential application of the analysis upward to the general population. In reality, running the full population of buyer data and comparing it with parametric data about the general population shows clear patterns of differential buying behavior by socioeconomic group.

There is another case when sampling is more desirable than running the full population. This is when capturing the full data can operationally interfere with the functioning of a primary system. This is a common phenomenon associated with operational analysis of computer platforms. If the time sampling is too frequent, substantial cycles are stolen from the application using the platform. Usually, this problem is not associated with commercial applications; however, demands of e-business may show this problem. We will discuss the special challenges of e-business at the end of this chapter.

nessperson notices that several stores in the chain show markedly higher revenue than the other stores in the chain. In Figure 5.2, the revenue per store is represented in a bar chart in ascending order.

Stores 4 and 7 are located alongside a major highway. The first hypothesis is that *the type of road where the store is located determines revenue.* What facts are needed to ascertain the truth of the hypothesis? The revenue of each store over the same time period and information about the access road are important. In reality, the size of the access road is a determinant factor in choosing store location. Often, however, the businessperson may not have access to the factors used to choose store location; therefore, this hypothesis is both reasonable and proper.

This hypothesis is now subject to testing. This is a key step in the chain of beneficence and is the prime focus of the analytical exploration process. "Mucking in

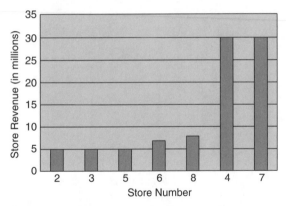

Figure 5.2 Store revenue by store number.

the data" is an intuitive process, and there are no rules. The analytical process is the antithesis of mucking: It is nonintuitive, process-driven activity that is focused on proving or disproving a single idea. Before we can derive business value from mucking in the data, an analytical process needs to be performed.

Inductive versus Deductive Processes

If a businessperson looks at data and creates a hypothesis for testing, he or she has performed an *inductive* act. For example, if he or she looks at data and hypothesizes that whenever a store is located on a high-traffic-volume road, it will have a higher revenue than if the same store was located on a low-traffic-volume road, an inductive process has been performed. Determining that a hypothesis is true is a *deductive* process. As a class in an ideal world, each and every occurrence of the class has to exhibit a causal relationship.

It is important to understand that the interaction between the businessperson and the technical analyst is based upon different roles in the analytical process. Figure 5.3 illustrates the cyclical relationship between the businessperson and the analyst. The businessperson creates the hypothesis, and the analyst executes the verification process. If the exploration process is properly executed, the interaction goes on in a spiral, not a circle.

An ideal team follows a variation of the Hegelian dialectic. Figure 5.4 illustrates the application of the Hegelian dialectic to the analytical process and the iterative nature of the process. Each cycle of hypothesis testing leads to a new cycle of testing with a more defined hypothesis. Each hypothesis generates its own antithesis or opposite hypothesis. In the example, the hypothesis is that road location may show a covariance with store revenue. The antithesis is that there is no relation-

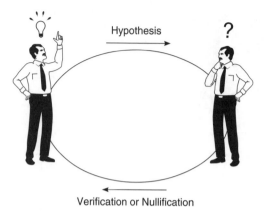

Hypothesis →

?

← Verification or Nullification

Figure 5.3 Businessperson-to-analyst relationship.

ship between store location and store revenue. Relationships are never perfect. Thus, when the results are returned, the businessperson now forms a new hypothesis that population density of the area may well also help to determine store revenue. This formation of a modified problem statement is known as *synthesis*. With a new hypothesis, the analysis begins the iteration again. The introduction of another factor creates a complication in causality, which we will explore later in this chapter. There are two key concepts that should be explored before proceeding: *validity* and *reliability*.

Validity and Reliability

Validity is the truth that we discover from the exploration process. The philosophical problem is that there is no absolute way of knowing whether the findings of testing are absolutely true. This is the old problem of, if a tree falls in the

Hypothesis (Thesis)

Test (Antithesis)

New Hypothesis (Synthesis)

Iteration

Figure 5.4 The testing of each hypothesis leads to a new cycle of testing with a more defined hypothesis.

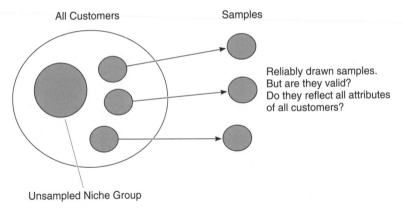

Figure 5.5   Validity and reliability.

forest and nobody is there to hear it, does it make a sound? Intuitively, it is commonly believed to be true because it is common sense. However, often in exploration, what is being examined is in an area where there is no knowledge base or the knowledge base is proven wrong. It is known that a tree makes a sound when it falls because every tree that ever was observed falling has made a sound. This ability to observe repeated occurrences with the same result is the basis of the concept of reliability. Figure 5.5 demonstrates the sampling process as it applies to the reliability of the sample reflecting the general population it was drawn from. High reliability imputes validity, but this is not a guarantee; it is simply the best tool we have.

Reliability in business is the province of the farmer. In exploration, if you can obtain incremental value, the breakthrough will rarely result in a vertical leap for the business. It is the explorer who finds the counterintuitive finding and converts it to value. An example from retailing was an exploration in market basket analysis of items most frequently found with chocolate chip cookies. The intuitive answer was milk. However, in an explorative case, using tools that are covered in the next chapter, the answer turned out to be cola. This is a perfect example of the thesis, antithesis, and synthesis cycle.

Defining Analytical Relationships in Exploration

Going back to the original problem, the businessperson believes that store location as defined by access road type causes revenue variation by store. There is a relationship between the two variables, but is it causal? Figure 5.6 illustrates a plot between store location along a highway and store revenue, represented as a linear graph. This type of variation is referred to as *covariance*. The finding of covariance may be helpful to the business but, once again, the impact is usually minimal. In the retail chain example, it is well known that there are toys

Figure 5.6 Noncausal covariance.

(i.e., swim goggles and fins) whose sales vary with season. However, the season change is not necessarily the causal factor. It is the change of temperature, which is caused by seasonal change, that leads to increased sales. In the case of an early-season heat wave, the savvy store manager already has the merchandise in the store ready to be staged on the selling floor to leverage this unexpected opportunity. This type of activity can yield minimal value. It is derived from intuitive knowledge and not from the analytical explorative process. It becomes explorative when the analyst returns a statistical interpretation to the businessperson as part of the process and the cycle iterates based upon a formal methodology.

Causal Relationships

Causal relationships occur between a predictor variable and a dependent variable where no intermediary factor (variable) can "explain away" the covariance. A single independent variable causes a single dependent variable to change in a consistent manner. Causal relationships are the nirvana of business. A classic business assumption is that price alone is a determinant factor for volume in any given item. The assumption (hypothesis) is that if the price of a particular item is lowered, sales will go up. There are numerous cases in which this hypothesis has been proven false. In the cases of many trend-driven items, increasing price will actually increase sales because the consumer perceives scarcity of supply to be more important than price. Causality is the objective of all analysis.

Many different factors can mask a causal relationship in exploration. Assuming good data and dispersion, another factor includes masking intervening variables in the causal chain. The nature of how variables enter the analysis is also critical. Often, in the analytical process, the consumers' education levels and

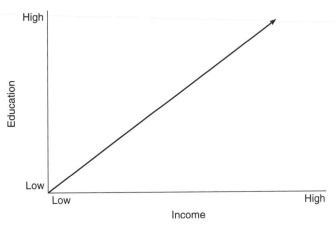

Figure 5.7 An example of a known causal relationship.

incomes are entered into an analytical model at the same level for predicting buying behavior. Both historical studies and experience tell us that education is a strong predictor of income. It is important when performing the analysis to understand how education plays into the prediction directly and indirectly through income and or occupation. Figure 5.7 shows the relationship between education and income displayed as a line graph. This type of display is useful for visualization purposes. Figure 5.8 shows the causal relationship in node notation. Node notation allows the analyst to illustrate a complex causal chain in two dimensions.

Spurious Relationships

By definition, spurious relations are ones that superficially appear to be causal but when examined further, are not. In the analytical exploration process, failing to detect a spurious relationship can lead to incorrect testing, positioning, and a failure to exploit a business opportunity. Worse than failing to exploit an opportunity can be a total waste of capital and effort based on an incorrect business objective. In the retail chain example, a count of the numbers indicates that the number of units sold is directly proportional to the size of the store.

Figure 5.9 shows an apparent causal relationship between store size and units sold. The hypothesis appears to be reasonable based upon these variables only. When the analytical tool introduces inventory on hand for the reporting period as

Figure 5.8 Causal relationship represented in set notation.

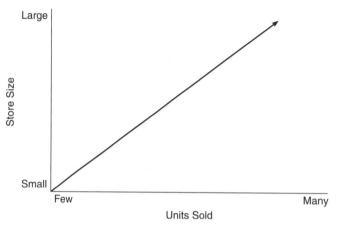

Figure 5.9 Hypothesis: Store size affects units sold.

a "control" variable, it becomes apparent that every store sold the same percentage of inventory on hand. Figure 5.10 shows the effect on the analysis of introducing inventory as a control or intervening variable. In this figure, the analyst has chosen a bar graph for visualization. The way that the analyst has introduced the control variable is to present sales as a percentage of inventory rather than as an absolute number of units sold. Another way to introduce a control variable is to run tables for each category on one dimension. Thus, the analyst could have presented this data as inventory versus units sold for small, medium, and large stores. The same conclusion would have been drawn.

Concomitant Variation

Concomitant variation occurs when two variables vary together in a noncausal manner. Frequently, the source of the concomitant is a dependent variable that has been entered into the analysis as if it were causal. In the case of concomitant variation, the objective becomes finding a common causal variable.

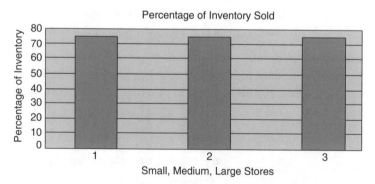

Figure 5.10 Units sold and store size controlling for inventory.

An example of this phenomenon can be seen when examining occupation and income. Most scales of occupational prestige have poorly compensated occupations at the bottom and highly compensated occupations near the top. There are always exceptions. Teachers and businesspeople often are placed on the scale in ranges that are determined by other factors. (Teachers are most notably ranked relatively high on prestige but show relatively low compensation. Businesspeople tend to rank very high on compensation but notably lower on prestige.) When education is added to the equation, it becomes clear that both occupation and income have a high causal relationship with education. Another affirmation of causal order is time sequence. Education almost always precedes occupation and career; therefore, by definition, it is in a causal position in terms of life events.

Specification

Specification is the process of accounting for more change in the dependent variable by adding additional independent variables into the analysis at the same level of analysis. Figure 5.11 shows many independent variables that describe the buyer in node notation format. The figure also shows a multisequence linkage model. When a series of variables are shown as illustrated at Level 2, it implies that they are being entered into the analysis at a peer level and at the same point in time. When exploring (and predicting) income, education is often used as a predictor variable, as shown in the Level 1–Level 2 relationship. Years of education alone, however, do not account for the majority of the variance in buying behavior (Level 3). Adding parents' incomes, occupation, and other socioeconomic variables improves the prediction dramatically.

Although it is important to understand the specification process, predictive modeling is more closely associated with the data mining techniques described in the next chapter. In this type of analytical processing, additional variables follow the

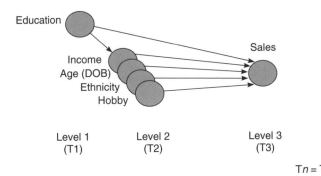

Figure 5.11 Specification: the addition of additional variables at the same level for increased predictability.

law of diminishing returns. It is unusual to glean much additional value beyond the third or fourth analytical dimension (independent variable) in the analysis. Human beings are rather complex creatures and many random factors can mitigate behavior. It is important to go back to the critical measures of success and impact in the retail arena. In a world where cost is allocated in the delivery chain down to the session level, an alteration of a single item per session (market basket) can dramatically alter the profitability picture. For precisely that reason, retail has been at the forefront of this type of analysis for over 10 years.

Drill-Down

Drill-down is the natural progression of activity in the exploration process. Figure 5.12 diagrams the drill-down process in a geographical dimension. Drill-down occurs usually after preliminary value is found but before business action is taken. Drill-down is the businessperson's risk assessment process to avoid overstating the potential gains from the exploration process. Drill-down occurs most often along well-known dimensions. In the retail case study, it is usual to drill down along both the geographical and product category dimensions.

Drill-down performs two functions:

1. It provides a target population to confirm the validity of any hypothesis for testing purposes.
2. It limits the amount of resource necessary to exploit an opportunity.

Target marketing projects often use drill-down to minimize capital while maximizing result. Another use of drill-down is to determine which outlets represent the most potential, not necessarily the most current revenue or profit genera-

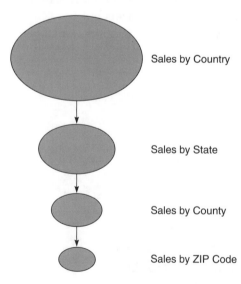

Sales by Country

Sales by State

Sales by County

Sales by ZIP Code

Figure 5.12 Drill-down: as used in a geographical dimension.

tion. This type of modeling is critical in brick-and-mortar companies that are undergoing image rejuvenation. There is extensive literature as well as tools to execute the drill-down analysis. It is important to remember that drill-down can only occur in the analytical process if the next lower unit of analysis is available. Furthermore, linkages between dimensions can occur only at the detailed level; therefore, any linkages above that level and between dimensions are inferential, and causality cannot be traced, it can only be inferred.

This is essentially why detailed data is almost mandatory in the explorative warehouse. That is not to say that value cannot be derived at a summary level, it simply cannot be "hard linked" into other dimensions. It is the concept of interdimension linkage that is a critical distinction between the market and the warehouse in exploration. Defining the lowest unit of analysis is critical to successful construction of the exploration warehouse.

Units of Analysis

The most frequently asked question by those who are new to the analytical exploration process is, Why is detailed data needed? The answer is that aggregation is a one-directional process in which information is always lost. In Figure 5.13, the linkage at one point in time is shown for market basket analysis. Can we answer the question, How much cola did we sell? without going to this level? This can be answered by information that is usually reported in a product category data mart. Can we answer the question, Who bought the cola? Absolutely not. It is the interdimensional linkage at the session level that links a live person to a product. In an examination of an individual's market basket, the linkage is "hard" (i.e., for that individual, actual buying information is had, not "inferred"). Can an analyst ascribe buying behavior at a higher level? It is done all the time.

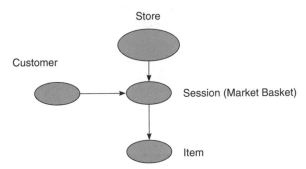

Figure 5.13 Units of analysis: You can aggregate data up, but you can never aggregate data down.

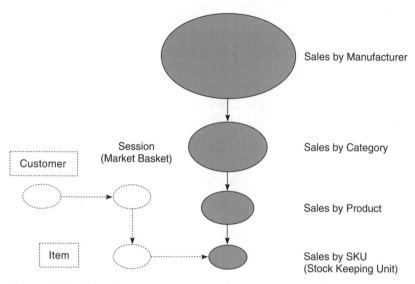

Figure 5.14 Drill-down: as used in a product dimension.

Several leading companies score zip code and census tract into a socioeconomic scale for purposes of getting dispersion patterns in buying behavior. These scores are frequently used for target marketing in mass distribution mechanisms, such as door-to-door flyer delivery and newspaper coverage. When one begins to specify drill-down within the units of analysis, and when one associates additional factors like car ownership with advertising for aftermarket stereo equipment, it becomes impossible to explore. Figure 5.14 shows drill-down in the product category dimension.

Ownership data of cars at the zip code level cannot be driven down to the individual level. In retail, banking, and telephony, the competitive nature of the marketplace has driven every major company back to the individual level for analytical exploration and marketing execution. The business model of the enterprise tempers the need for very detailed analysis and the focus of the analysis. Understanding the proper focus of analysis requires effort to align with the business strategy as well.

Business Models and Exploration

Each explorative process must be set in the context of a business model. Analysis of the same information set in two different business models has very different meaning. In an analysis, the business model will often determine where the most value can be derived using the exploratory process. Figure 5.15 illustrates how a product is placed into the product pipeline in a retail *push model*. In a retail

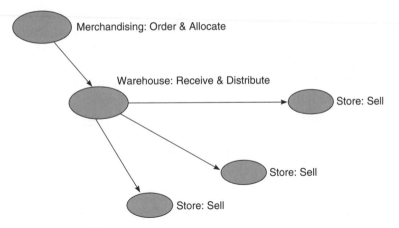

Figure 5.15 Retail push model.

push model, with no ability to categorize the store by the socioeconomic status of the customer base, market segmentation analysis will be of little business value because the distribution mechanism is not geared to support differential distribution at the store level.

In this case, the value of the analytical exploration process takes the form of strategic recommendations to management. The danger is that the recommendations gained in the explorative process may never be operationalized. Very often, the line between the analytical exploration process and true data mining is the line between tactical executable results and discoveries that require strategic actions by the business.

In the retail *pull model*, explorative findings are often easier to implement due to a distribution mechanism that can tolerate small incremental changes. However, dramatic change in a retail pull model is usually uncharacteristic. The dependency on a highly complicated information technology (IT) infrastructure tends to limit change. There is some merit in looking a little more deeply into each of these models.

Push Models and Exploration

In the case study of the particular retailer that we used for the illustrative example, its business model is a push model (i.e., merchandise is pushed to all of their stores). The business implication of this model is that all buying decisions are centralized and allow the business to leverage its acquisition power.

The downside of the business model is that short-term or localized anomalies in activity cannot be exploited for profit. Successful explorers often apply the analytical process to tune the model. This usually takes the form of testing hypotheses and then implementing the results in the distribution model. The impact is immediate and substantial. At the mart level, much of the analysis is performed in the category management mart. The push model is at the heart of the category-killer-type retail chains. Each of these chains is focused on a single segment of retailing (items like toys, sporting goods, and office supplies). Each of the chains provides a facility with large quantities of the specialized goods. Each location is actually a warehouse that is open to the public. The model uses the image of the lowest price to provide the draw that is necessary to enlarge the location sphere of influence.

Very often, the actual causal factor is time, not price. In the highly specialized chains (e.g., golf stores), the probability of finding exactly what is desired in the shortest possible time is what motivates a focused customer (high income) to come to the store. It is not unusual for a highly specialized chain to make the transition from a push model to a pull model as the chain exits the rapid-growth stage and becomes an established market segment retailer.

Pull Models and Exploration

Pull model retailers use the exploration process in a very different way than push model retailers. The pull model retailer utilizes a business process called *replenishment* to keep certain staple bread-and-butter items in the store. Figure 5.16 illustrates the demand process, sometimes known as *fulfillment*, in a pull model retailer. Whereas the push model retailer explores distribution optimization, the pull model retailer optimizes the pipeline supply part of the problem. The ideal result of the analytical exploration process is the optimization of

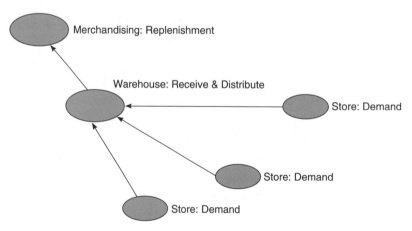

Figure 5.16 Retail pull model.

the demand, order, and supply process to assure minimal waste and maximum retention of profit with minimal inventory.

The analytical exploration process works best for predicting sales with goods that are either seasonal or perennial in nature. To create new demand, the pull model retailer will frequently implement special "events" to drive additional business. *Event-driven exploration* is a special category of analysis.

Event-Driven Exploration

In the retail business arena, event-driven exploration is often called *campaign management*. The exploration warehouse is the ideal vehicle to use for the analytical processes involved. The typical scenario involves staging a causal event to improve sales. Figure 5.17 illustrates how time is critical to event analysis. The event could be a media event such as an advertising campaign, or it could be a special solicitation. The event itself does not matter. What is important is that the event transpires for a finite period of time and that, before and after, data is available for analysis.

The approach of these events is closer to a scientific experiment than classic exploration. It is assumed that during the relatively short duration of the event, all other factors remain the same and, therefore, will "wash out" or, in essence, are statistically controlled. Thus, all change in buying behavior is then attributed to the event. This activity is often viewed as transitory and the data is not retained. It is actually a form of experimentation. The before and after conditions are classical conditions in a scientific experiment. Furthermore, the control group is often simply another set of products or retail outlets, which are not within the scope of the event. The short duration usually implies a quick return. The downside is that the value that is found is often artificially created by short-term expenditures. Although this has value, the object of analytical exploration

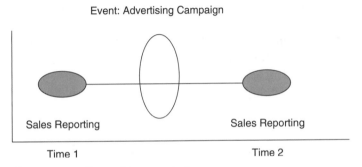

Figure 5.17 Event-driven analysis.

is to find naturally occurring phenomena of long-term value with, hopefully, minimal additional investment.

In terms of the chain of beneficence, sometimes an event is staged as the final confirmation in the analytical process between the discovery stage and the widespread application of the information that was uncovered as a risk mitigation strategy. This is very different from the campaign management strategy that was outlined earlier. In the case of the retailer to whom we previously referred, proving out the findings has created a pilot store phenomenon. Phenomena that are uncovered by exploration are implemented at a small subset of stores before chainwide rollout occurs. This particular chain is extremely successful in implementing operational changes. Unfortunately, the same chain does not apply this principle to implementing change in other aspects of the business. Sometimes, the exploration process's value is lost because of the business management's failure to recognize time as the real challenge of business.

Time and the Exploration Process

Time is the most problematic aspect in the analytical exploration process. The time problem is not covered in the original relational theory. The standard presentation format original was a series of tables with data in rows and columns. Multidimensionality was managed by presenting multiple two-dimensional tables. Time is the only phenomenon in the analytical process that may be managed as an entity, as an attribute of a domain. There is deep and varied theory on how to manage the time problem. For the average businessperson and analyst who are locked in the exploration process, time becomes the enemy of the process.

The first concern with time in the analytical process is the freshness of the data. In an earlier chapter, the option of creating the exploration warehouse on demand was introduced. Although initial costs may be reduced, the time delay that is involved in creating an as-needed exploration warehouse can dramatically reduce the value of the data. The more volatile the marketplace, the less likely the exploration warehouse will be created on demand. Virtually every market researcher in the brokerage retail space would like to have data added to their exploration warehouses in real time. The ability to analyze and to react expeditiously to change in the marketplace can result in millions of dollars of profit in minutes. Thus, the differentiation between the top-line firms and the second-tier firms is the ability to leverage information rapidly, because the exploration warehouse is permanently in place. This same issue is also driving business in the .com space. This will be dealt with in a later chapter.

The second concern is the duration of time that the analysis takes. Again, in rapidly changing business scenarios, time determines the viability of the analysis. In financial market scenarios, time is such a critical factor that the analysis gets broken into two components. The first component is a series of indexes that are sensitive to small changes in both direction and value. These indexes are the result of the larger analytical process. They are then operationalized to cause business actions that have an immediate impact. Programmed trading follows this closed-loop process. The dangers of programmed trading do not come from the link between the explorative process and operational result. This linkage is the beginning of what we know as artificial intelligence. When multiple systems of this nature engage each other in a free-market scenario without any stopgap measures and with a very limited rule base, chaos can result.

The larger analytical process in trading can afford the luxury of time. The unique relationship between the derived operationalized indexes and the detailed analytical research warehouse exemplifies the warehouse-to-mart relationship. The same factors also typify the relationship between the detailed level of data and the summarized level. Perhaps the financial services industry, more than any other segment of business, has derived the benefits of the analytical explorative process. Most of the complex analytical tools that traders use in the day-to-day environment are derived from an exploration warehouse and are constantly refined to account for new evolving factors. In the brokerage industry, the analytical exploration process is precisely what the research departments use. It is in these same research departments that new hypotheses are constantly created. In retail, it is the market research department that owns the responsibility to test new demand hypotheses.

Hypothesis Formation

A businessperson in charge of sales, in the large-item category, examines bicycle sales across a series of stores nationally. He notes that some stores are selling a lot of bikes, whereas others are selling very few. He is particularly puzzled because this is a push model retailer; therefore, all stores receive identical merchandise. He hypothesizes that *factors other than the actual merchandise* are affecting sales.

Before proceeding, the businessperson must document that his observations or intuitions are verified with data. To accomplish this verification, he enters into the stage of the analytical exploration process. Today, most businesspeople get operational reports that provide this level of analysis. Surprisingly, in small businesses, this level of analysis has only become available in the last few years with the advent of inexpensive store-based server systems with integrated applications.

It is surprising how many small businesses can benefit from simple analysis, which traditionally was beyond their financial means. These businesses do not need the full analytical exploration process. Simple hypothesis formation, based on experience and coupled with single-variable analysis, can lead to business improvement and success.

Beginning the Analytical Process: Simple Single-Variable Analysis

The easiest analysis is a simple frequency distribution (i.e., How many bikes did we sell by store). The problem is that this only tells you which stores sold the most; it tells nothing about causality. The businessperson now asks the next follow-on question, What percentage of the bikes in inventory, as of the first of the period, were sold? The analysis still is considered a single-variable analysis, but the businessperson has now controlled for the differences in inventory by using a percentage sold as opposed to a raw count.

The measurement of the successful sales hypothesis has changed to success based upon a percentage of available inventories. *The hypothesis has changed!* The store which is most successful is the store that, by definition, sold the highest proportion of goods on hand. Beyond this point, the analytical process needs more complex techniques to determine causality.

Interpreting Results

Using the simplest analytical tool, *relative percentages*, the introduction of a control variable will cause one of several results. If the control variable causes no increase or decrease in the percentage of bikes sold in inventory by store controlled for store size (i.e., the relative percentage of bikes that were sold was the same, regardless of how big the store was), one can reasonably conclude that store size was not a causal factor. In general, if washout of a predictive variable occurs at this level in the analytical process, the variable should be removed.

That does not mean that the very same variable will not reenter the analysis further up or down the value chain. Once again, in the hypothetical retail case study cited, if on-hand inventory is dramatically increased across all stores, then store size could very well reemerge as a determinant factor. We know that initial store location choice is often determined based upon the socioeconomic profile of the area, the size of the transportation arteries, and other factors. It is also a well-known factor that in suburban settings, parking lot size can affect store sales dramatically. Does parking lot size directly enter the chain at the bike sales level, or does it affect the previous link in the value chain of store traffic? What should the businessperson do with the findings?

To Iterate or to Act?

At each stage of the chain of beneficence, there is an opportunity to wait for more data or to act. The right action is based upon market forces, risk, the culture of the company, and time. Risk-averse company cultures will almost always farm the data to death. That is, until every known permutation of the causal factors is run, the businessperson will make no recommendation to management to act. Risk-oriented companies, on the other hand, will often leap without going through the hypothesis testing process fully.

Continuous-improvement-oriented companies who derive business value from process and are committed to exploration analysis, will engage in a closed-loop process that creates a continuous series of actions based upon rationality and results of the process. Today, in general, there are two categories of business that will cluster to either the risk or the reticence end of the scale. It is worthwhile to differentiate the market imperatives of the Web-based businesses (true .coms) and brick-and-mortar companies.

Exploration in Web Businesses versus Brick-and-Mortar Businesses

Web-based businesses represent a new challenge to the analytical process. This new challenge is broken into two pieces:

1. How did the customer arrive at the site in his or her flight through virtual space?

2. What does traditional channel distribution mean in Web-based commerce?

The nature of Web-based commerce has changed the fundamental way we think about retail commerce. Historically, we advertised based upon a sphere of influence that surrounded a distribution point. The model was essentially a circular model. Again, time was a primary determinant in the equation. The size of the sphere was determined by a number of factors, such as competing distribution points from the same organization, competing points from a different organization, and travel time.

Even the much-admired catalog organizations of the late nineteenth and early twentieth centuries followed a circular model. Although the circle was very wide (national), the distribution was typically done from a single point. The business driver was based on whether the consumer could wait for delivery of goods long enough to offset local availability. The financial advantages of the supply side of the catalog industry allowed the distribution side to use low cost to drive the model. Although advertising was used to help drive sales in certain locations, the model was not all that different than marketing in the traditional distribution model.

In the Web environment, the model is very different. The consumer enters virtual space through a portal, a point in virtual space. Then, the consumer navigates through a series of points to his or her destination. Sometimes, he or she will use an index—a search engine—to find topical information when the end point of the journey is not a finite site, but a subject area.

When this type of journey is undertaken, the position in the engine and the specificity of the information in the index can be extremely important. The circular model of early marketing generations breaks down. The model of the demand-side problem is now a linear point-to-point model. This model has precedent in the data base and in the analytical world. The model for this analysis is called a *transportation schema*.

What is unique about a transportation schema is that it consists of two points and a leg of measurable length in between. In reality, the start point and the destination point are linked as a single leg or as a series of small legs with intermediate destinations or hops. The major portal companies have huge real-time warehouses to explore the patterns. These "click" warehouses are considered mission critical to the portal. One of the largest portals has a disaster recovery mechanism for the entire warehouse. The matrix of navigation continually changes in virtual space. The true Web-based company must, in real time, constantly readjust the company's positioning. Web space exploration analysis is not a decision support system or a nice-to-have system in this arena; it is a mandatory operational system. Sometimes, the exploration is outsourced to companies that are set up to do nothing but Web impact analysis. The key, always, is time.

Time also plays into the distribution side of Web business. The speeding up of information to the consumers causes a change in delivery expectations by the Web-based consumer. It is unrealistic to expect an individual who finds a desired product in minutes to wait weeks for delivery. The most successful .com retailers have learned that delivery must take place in a day or two, or they must ask the consumer's consent to back order goods. How do you stock and distribute goods for worldwide delivery? Can a .com company risk the traditional drop shipment business process? What do brick-and-mortar and .com companies have in common, and why do they need to perform analytical exploration?

In Summary

Whether the business is Web based or traditional brick and mortar, the need for analytical exploration touches every portion of the business chain. To successfully manage continuous rapid change, a fully linked analytical model is required.

Figure 5.18 illustrates some major components of a fully defined exploration model. This model provides the business with an opportunity to farm for more value on both the supply and the demand sides of the business. The exploration

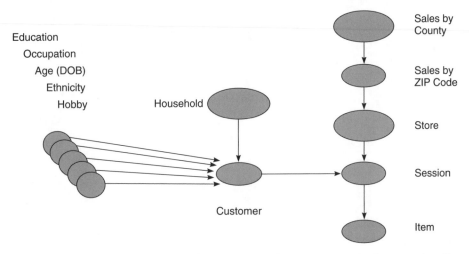

Figure 5.18 A fully linked analytical model along the customer and sales reporting dimensions.

warehouse also requires large numbers of predictor variables to mitigate risk from false hypothesis and imprudent actions. The real-world metaphor for a business without an analytical exploration capacity is an airplane pilot who plans a flight without weather reports and radar. The risk will exceed the return and sometimes the results can be fatal. The explorative warehouse and the analytical exploration process are the radar and flight instruments of business.

CHAPTER 6

Analytical Data Mining

Where no man has gone before!

—GENE RODDENBERRY

There are no easy answers in data mining—the analogy to hard-rock mining is very accurate. With lots of hard work and appropriate preparation, diamonds can be had. Without proper methodology and work, you can get a financial sinkhole and frustration.

Data mining is useful for finding unexpected patterns in data. It requires an organizational structure that values research and that understands the derivative value of information. In the physical sciences, this has become an accepted technique as part of the analytical process.

Data mining is not a panacea. If the product or service provided is substandard or if the fundamental business processes are flawed, the data mining process will add little or no value. Often, businesses look to mining as a mystical solution to save a lost niche in the marketplace. This is not the purpose of the analytical mining process; rather, it is to find additional value in a viable business. When fundamental business processes break down, it is doubtful that the data quality and freshness required to get meaningful results will endure. Mining old data will reflect patterns that will not be meaningful in a highly fluid environment.

Data mining is not a new phenomenon. Its roots go back at least 35 years to the early application of computers to data analysis. Two early packages, Biomed and Statistical Package for the Social Services (SPSS), contained the statistical routines that are at the core of today's higher-level tools. The real change in tools is in terms of ease of use. Historically, it often took days to set up the programs, which included the notorious Job Control Language.

The first widely distributed program, Biomed, had its roots in the physical sciences. The routines included many simple statistics that were focused on sampling. The analysis therefore often assumed a limited amount of data with some degree of control integrity. By the time the SPSS package became commonly available, the focus of most analyses had shifted to the social sciences. Like business, the social sciences are more concerned with human behavioral patterns than physical phenomena. Because much social data is derived or interpreted, it was necessary to provide tools that were capable of dynamic recategorization on the fly. Furthermore, the massaged data could be directed to a series of different analytical routines without necessitating a separate setup. For the first time, the average social scientist could vary analysis without a statistician at his or her side.

As business worked the value chain in buying back from brick and mortar to human motivation, social science sampling and analysis techniques merged with marketing techniques into the field of market analysis, which centered on panel studies. Although they were effective in determining simple opinion such as new product acceptance, these panel studies were not effective for driving out opportunities that involved segmenting the marketplace. Segmentation requires critical mass in the data along with tools that could be run by analysts who were not necessarily trained in the more abstract statistical arts.

This democratization of data gave rise to the demand for a set of tools that anyone could run. This demand was accelerated by the availability of lower-cost computing platforms and the spread of computer literacy. These data mining tools mask the internals of statistical routines and plow through the data, removing many assumptions and automatically alternating algorithms to find a best-fit solution.

These tools moved data mining from an obscure, backroom activity into a standard business practice. Even the best tool, however, has requirements. Among these requirements is the preparation of data.

This chapter is intended for the businessperson who needs a basic conceptual understanding of data mining. For an in-depth study, see *Mastering Data Mining and Data Mining Techniques* by Michael Berry and Gordon Linoff, John Wiley & Sons, Inc., 2000.

Data Preparation for Data Mining

Cleaning data is often the most cumbersome part of the data mining process. Anomalies are found that can be resolved only by interaction with the business. Improper codes, out-of-domain values, and missing results all impact the qual-

Table 6.1 Relative Cleanliness of Data Missing Values

SESSION	SKU*	PRICE	QUANTITY
123	12765	1.88	10
123	123456	1.23	5
123	321456	0.29	
124	321457		17
124		1.17	10
124	321111	1.15	20

* SKU, Stock Keeping Unit.

ity of the end results. In addition, improperly cleaned data can extend the analytical process and add unnecessary cost.

Even though the cleansing process can assure data quality from the internal data source, it cannot assure the quality of data from external secondary sources. Some data mining techniques require that every row have a full set of values. To fulfill this requirement, imputed values or default values are sometimes used. Imputed values can skew results toward the normal (mean) value, eliminating many of the benefits of cluster analysis and often offering false results. Default values can indicate spurious patterns.

In most cases of missing data, the analyst uses and weights only good rows. It is this possibility of spurious results that sets a requirement that every potential finding be verified through the analytical exploration process. Table 6.1 shows a series of rows with missing values, which would make them unusable in many data mining processes.

Another requirement for data mining is ordinality. Ordinality is described in the previous chapter as the amount of spread in the data with clear directionality between less and more. Figure 6.1 shows two variables with weak dispersion; that is, there are only four possible values, and, therefore, many of the statistical techniques will not reflect accurate measures of association. Almost all mul-

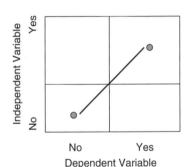

Figure 6.1 Weak dispersion pattern.

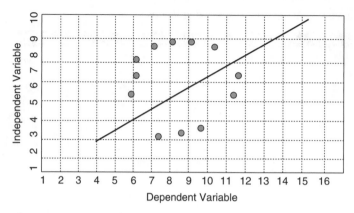

Figure 6.2 Strong dispersion pattern.

tivariate analysis requires a fair amount or spread in value to assess causality. Figure 6.2 shows two variables with high degrees of dispersion. Techniques like multiple-stepwise and multiple-stagewise regression work well with this type of data, if a relationship exists.

It is common practice in low-level discovery to group the data. Age, for example, is often grouped into 10-year ranges to examine basic buying behavior. In data mining, however, the lowest level of detail is necessary to help find subpatterns in the data, which are "washed out" in grouped data. In data mining, actual age is critical to predicting buying behavior. It is well known that there are financial service opportunities with recent college graduates. By their late 20s, different acquisition patterns emerge, most notably home acquisition. If the data is not aggregated, data mining tools miss this bimodal acquisition process and time series analysis becomes impossible. The ideal dispersion is interval-level data in which the distance between points is consistent, such as in the measurement of age.

Having described the quality of data issues, it is worthwhile to examine several data mining processes.

Basic Types of Mining Processes

All forms of data mining have the objective of discovering patterns in the data that are not obvious. To accomplish this objective, mining tools apply one or more statistical techniques. These techniques are constantly evolving and becoming more sophisticated. It is the intent of this chapter to demystify the common techniques, giving analysts insight into available options and approaches. The key to success in data mining is choosing a technique that fits the business problem and with which the businessperson and analyst are both comfortable. Let us examine the various techniques, beginning with one of the oldest and most popular approaches, *regression analysis.*

Regression Analysis

The first requirement of regression analysis is that the data approach interval-level specification. This sometimes occurs naturally in the data, but more often, it has to be created by recategorization, especially with data from market research. Sufficient dispersion is critical to getting meaningful results in regression analysis.

The second criterion for successful regression analysis is knowing causality. Causality implies an existing hypothesis, placing this technique in the data mining process as opposed to exploration processing. In classical regression analysis, there is a single dependent variable and multiple independent (predictor) variables. The predictor factors can enter into the equation in a prespecified order, or they can be allowed to enter the process based upon how much of the variance in the dependent variable they account for. Iteratively entering additional predictor variables is ideal when attempting to define specification.

The most understandable statistic reported in the process is *R squared*. This number roughly equals the amount of change or variance in the dependent variable accounted for by the introduction of the independent or predictor variable in the equation. The order of entry is very important:

- If entry is constrained, the first variable introduced will maximize its prediction value. Each succeeding variable will account only for the predictable variance left after the preceding variable has entered into the analysis.

- In unconstrained entry, the tool will search for the one variable that accounts for the most variance. Once entered, each succeeding pass follows the same process until all are entered. In pure data mining, unconstrained entry is usually the process that is selected.

The key to understanding regression analysis is remembering that the analytical model is based on the concept of *best fit*. The mining tool performs a series of least-squares calculation that would otherwise be time consuming and, quite frankly, boring. Figure 6.3 shows a dispersion plot illustrating how least squares are calculated to a mean. The iterative nature of these calculations made this approach the exclusive province of the statistician prior to the widespread advent of computers. In the 1960s and 1970s, social scientists began using these techniques. Widespread data mining only became possible when business had enough cycles to both supply primary and secondary exploration functions.

An example of regression analysis is a retail market survey analysis of factors leading to store traffic. Predictor variables include circular advertising, television advertising, in the mall (general visit), and routine visit. Table 6.2 illustrates the

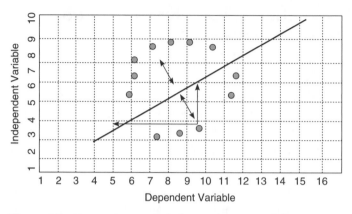

Figure 6.3 Regression analysis: least-squares model.

statistical output from a regression analysis. The four causal variables explain 81 percent of the reasons why people come to the store. The results also indicate that television advertising accounts for a relatively small amount of the traffic.

Regression analysis tools are found at all levels of the computing platform. For analytical work with soft data like market surveys, a Microsoft Windows platform is excellent and inexpensive. Because regression analysis uses a smoothing, or averaging, technique, sampling can be used to quickly bring about meaningful results.

Cluster Analysis

In cluster analysis, the analyst looks at detailed data for paired occurrences and assesses the distance between these pairs. If two pairs share a common member, the analyst can infer that the remaining members in the pair are grouped as well. Figure 6.4 shows data, ready for cluster analysis, that is already tokenized. Data mining software looks for associations with weaker pairs that are not apparent to the casual observer. Analysis becomes geometrically more complex as the number of columns or variables and rows or records increases.

Table 6.2 *R*-Squared Values for Market Study*

Life event	.40
In mall (general visit)	.20
Circular advertising	.12
Television advertising	.09
Total variance	.81

* Dependent variable = visited store.

```
                        01, 03, 03, 03,
04 - 20817, 04, 04, 01, 04, 02, 04, 02, 04, 01, 01,
05 - 19082, 03, 05, 02, 05, 02, 05, 15, 04, 02, 02,
06 - 17620, 05, 03, 01, 06, 01, 01, 10, 01, 01, 01,
07 - 01982, 05, 04, 01, 07, 01, 06, 21, 06, 01, 02,
08 - 20813, 06, 01, 02, 01, 01, 01, 14, 07, 01, 03,
09 - 18726, 02, 05, 01, 07, 01, 02, 13, 08, 01, 02,
10 - 01872, 03, 06, 02, 06, 01, 01, 19, 06, 02, 02,
11 - 00287, 01, 07, 01, 01, 01, 07, 12, 01, 01, 01,
12 - 01876, 06, 04, 02, 07, 01, 02, 15, 09, 02, 03,
13 - 17765, 07, 08, 02, 05, 02, 06, 10, 05, 01, 02,
14 - 29871, 08, 09, 01, 07, 01, 08, 18, 10, 02, 01,
15 - 00189, 09, 04, 01, 03, 02, 09, 19, 06, 01, 02,
16 - 01862, 11, 03, 01, 04, 02, 09, 18, 10, 02, 01,
17 - 08972, 10, 08, 02, 08, 02, 09, 21, 09, 01, 03,
18 - 10662, 11, 07, 01, 07, 01, 06, 21, 11, 02, 01,
19 - 02663, 03, 10, 02, 04, 02, 01, 18, 12, 02, 02,
20 - 01887, 05, 11, 01, 04, 02, 02, 18, 11  02, 01,
```

Figure 6.4   Tuples in cluster analysis.

When categories are predetermined, cluster analysis belongs to the data mining world. When there are no predetermined categories, cluster analysis can be considered either an exploration technique or a mining technique. Because the data is usually narrow and deep, it is most frequently categorized as a data mining technique. It requires linear passes through detailed data. Processing time increases linearly with the size of the data. Cluster analysis is frequently used in market basket studies, where item buying patterns are differentiated by characteristics of consumers. Occasionally, the information that is derived from a pattern alters a basic business model.

In a subsequent section, the impact of a data mining result on the business model is explored. Cluster analysis can be run on all levels of the computing platform; however, in the learning mode, the best results are achieved with large data sets on high-powered platforms. Here, minor elaboration of the taxonomy will be discovered that will be missed in sampling techniques.

In our retail example, cluster analysis would specify groups of buyers by their characteristics. This could include high-income, large-ticket shoppers or low-income impulse buyers. The first group of buyers would be identified by a combination of external zip code data and shopping cart items over a certain price. The second type of buyers would also be typified by the zip code data, but they would show a market basket characteristic of purchasing end-of-aisle (end-cap) and register stand items. The first group would be a target of focused, direct-mail advertising. The second group of buyers might require a different type of advertising.

Neural Networks

Conventional mining techniques rely on fixed algorithms and variable data. Variation in the dependent variable is measured by a single calculation, which is

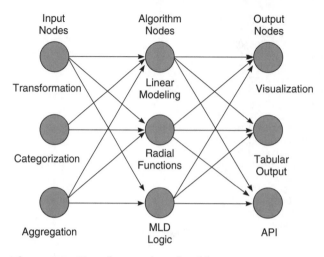

Figure 6.5 Neural network tool architecture.

repeated incrementally. In neural networks, data can be passed node to node at will. The data and algorithm are both variable. Receptor nodes pass data to intermediate nodes containing a variety of algorithms. Finally, a series of output nodes allows the data to be displayed or reused in various formats. Figure 6.5 shows a logical construct of neural network software. It is the ability to choose a variety of logical paths with different decision-making criteria that makes neural networks so appealing to the data miner. Using the same preparation, the miner will pop-out unexpected results from a series of different simultaneous operations. This speeds up the mining process.

There are two fundamental techniques in neural network technology. The first involves training the network based on a prepared set of data. This type of learned behavior sets an expectation in the model for all subsequent passes. This is sometimes referred to as a *back-propagation neural network*. The various inputs in the matrix are differentially weighted from the learning experience. This technique is also referred to as *supervised learning*. This technique is most often found in "black box" applications, in which data passes through the software and a determination is made as to whether the current set of data is a match to the profile based on prior experience.

A real-world example of this technique is fraud detection in retail. By passing detailed point-of-sale (POS) transactions for a particular register through the neural network, prior normal register activity would show a criterion match or mismatch. Figure 6.6 shows a categorization taken from a hypothetical POS retail application. In the example, each register shows a series of transactions that is typical in retail. These transactions include register open, register close, session open, session close, item ring, coupon ring, payment cash, payment credit, refund, and total out. There is a normal pattern and distribution in these transactions.

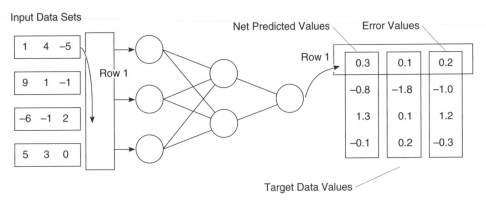

Input Data Sets

Net Predicted Values ╲ Error Values ╲

Row 1

Figure 6.6 Results from back-propagation.

Given this expectation, a variation in the pattern (too many refunds or a register closing) will alert a fraud detection supervisor.

The second technique is unsupervised learning (Figure 6.7). Here, the patterns are detected as data is passed through the software. There is no a priori weighting—patterns are detected as a by-product of the process. This is the most common use of neural network tools. A typology is derived from the process for subsequent use. This technique is also used to set up the fraud detection criteria. Another use is market segmentation analysis for target marketing. This type of analysis is both data and calculation intensive and can be expensive. Although software is available to run an analysis in a Windows environment, it is more commonly found in a mainframe or symmetrical multiprocessing environment of large Unix machines. When the objective is to set a learning criterion in relatively simple data, like POS transactions, a small amount of data can be used in a Windows environment, and then the learned behavior can be replicated on a more powerful platform. When the learned behavior is used for support checking by means of random inspection (sampling), again, a lower-power platform can be used. If the taxonomy is complex or massive, a high-horsepower platform is recommended.

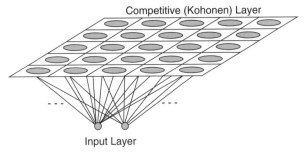

Competitive (Kohonen) Layer

Input Layer

Figure 6.7 Kohonen layer in unstructured learning.

Other primary uses of neural network technology in business include credit risk analysis and scoring, prediction of stock and commodity prices, pipeline supply requirement, and future sales.

Like many other techniques, neural networks are not designed to handle time. Time-based analysis requires a rotation in thinking.

Time Series Analysis

Traditional analysis manages the complexity of time by collapsing it into a point rather than a continuum. Thus, when we do traditional sales analysis, we talk about sales per month, sales per quarter, or sales per year. We essentially take slices of time, make them a point, and then compare these points two at a time. However, what if we want to follow customers through several months or many years? Each point in time becomes a category along one axis of a two-dimensional table. As human beings, we can easily manage two dimensions on paper. Cognitively, we can handle three dimensions in the real world. What we can't conceptualize is time in the two-dimensional space. To do this, data mining software traces the behavior of fixed entities over time periods. Table 6.3 shows data that is prepared for time series analysis.

Of what real-world use is time series analysis? The financial services industry uses it to determine what mix of products to offer customers at various stages of their lives. The retail industry uses time series analysis to help in the retention of frequent buyers, because it is has been found that the cost of retaining customers is lower than the cost of acquiring new customers. It is also easier to run a revenue improvement program with customers of known characteristics. These programs touch the customers immediately before critical life cycle events, so they are dependent on time series analysis.

Data Mining in Brick-and-Mortar Companies

The traditional retail company tends to focus data mining operations in two principal areas. The first area is market basket analysis. In the case of the reference company, a critical determinant of profitability is the number of items in the market basket. A shift of an average number of items per session in the tenths of a percentage point range will alter profitability dramatically. Data mining techniques show associations that are not intuitive. The famous diapers and beer illustration from the convenience store business illustrates this type of association.

This type of finding allows for drag-through on both ends of the tied pair. In the case of the diapers, kiosking with baby ointments, baby toys, and clothing, coupled with the display of the beer with chips, salsa, and pretzels, allows for significant increases in the market basket size.

Table 6.3 Time Series Analysis—Number of Active Products

	QUARTER														
CUSTOMER	1/96	2/96	3/96	4/96	1/97	2/97	3/97	4/97	1/98	2/98	3/98	4/98	1/99	2/99	3/99	4/99
1	1	2	1	3	3	5	4	4	2	2	1	3	4	5	5	4
2	2	2	1	1	2	3	1	2	3	3	2	2	2	2	2	3
3	1	2	1	1	1	1	2	2	2	2	1	2	2	2	2	2
4	1	2	1	3	3	5	4	4	2	2	1	3	4	5	5	4
5	1	2	1	1	1	1	2	2	2	2	1	2	2	2	2	2
6	1	1	1	2	1	1	2	2	2	2	1	1	1	1	1	1
7	2	2	1	1	2	3	1	2	3	3	2	2	2	2	2	3
8	1	2	1	3	3	5	4	4	2	2	1	3	4	5	5	4

Sometimes, the findings are intuitively obvious but are masked by the standard operational procedures. For instance, it is a known profitable business practice to follow the release of a major motion picture with appropriate theme toys. Operationally, the toys are distributed by category throughout the store. Intuitively, the different toys are displayed in one section, because children will most likely want more than one.

The second area of data mining interest is market segmentation, in which buyers are categorized by a series of socioeconomic variables. It is well known that different segments of the population have different buying behaviors. However, is this differential behavior true for a warehouse-style retailer whose principal strategy is goods on hand at everyday low prices? The complex relationships between what is in the shopping session and the attributes of the buyer are virtually impossible to understand without data mining tools. Why? The sheer number of analytical combinations possible, based on the number of independent variables and the number of categories for each of these variables, must be taken into consideration. Thus if you have two variables with 10 possible choices you have 10×10 or 100 combinations. Add one more variable and the number increases to 1000. It becomes clear that even if patterns were visible in the data, it would not be intuitively obvious.

Data Mining and e-Commerce

The importance of data mining in e-commerce is well known to portal companies. Access to information is a portal company's only asset, so it is critical to understand patterns of navigation through virtual space. To that end, the major players all have built data warehouses to record end-to-end patterns of user sessions. These click warehouses are used for everything from load analysis to banner placement. The portal company centers around the customer, and presentation is constantly being refined to present as much individualized customer information as possible in the initial page. This drive is referred to as the *one-click, one-call, one-mile objective.* In a service-based economy, the customer expects that the information provider will provide all necessary information in the shortest possible path.

What the customer needs can be ascertained by either his or her explicit request or by his or her past pattern of behavior. The latter type of analysis falls under the category of analytical exploration. The difference between the good and the great Web sites is the ability to formulate a solution to the problem of "this is what he or she asked for, but this is what the customer really wants." The customer asked for this information, but what other information should we offer? Data mining tools, particularly cluster analysis and neural network tools, allow us to find small subpopulations whose needs would otherwise be masked by a large population, which is one of e-business's greatest assets.

The other concern in e-commerce and a Web-based economy is the rate of change. Historically, communication and transportation have acted to slow the rate of change in society. The impact model was usually circular around a distribution point, or sometimes elongated along a transportation corridor. This model is almost useless in a Web-based economy. The portal company may own its infrastructure or leverage a partner's infrastructure.

Other than the initial physical connection, which may be local, geography is largely irrelevant. The traditional sphere-of-influence model has no meaning in virtual space. New Web sites create their own demand. Point events skew the behavior of customers. Traditional customer loyalty techniques such as frequent customer programs may have little meaning in a Web-based world. Rapid changes require constant reanalysis of patterns in the Web itself.

To respond in a timely fashion, usually minutes and hours, it is necessary to turn data mining efforts toward external data sources rather than the traditional internal data. There are a number of concerns that collect, stream, and analyze data on a constant basis. These companies collect actual screen-to-screen navigation directly over the Internet.

Platform Selection for Data Mining

Among the most frequently occurring errors in data mining is platform selection. Explorers often pick platforms to match the tools—a classic case of putting the cart before the horse.

The right platform is a function of horsepower, input/output capacity, and time frame. Workstation- or NT-based solutions can handle row quantities in the thousands to tens of thousands. High-power Unix servers can handle hundreds of thousands to millions of records. Traditional mainframes are able to handle millions of records. There are sampling-based techniques in data mining that eliminate the need for larger-capacity platforms, but the vast majority of the tools continue to use techniques that sequentially pass records.

The advantages that massively parallel processing (MPP) platforms bring to data mining are limited. However, because tools can be redesigned to utilize a multiprocessing environment, platforms are usually chosen based on cost concerns and not necessarily utilization.

Tool Selection for Data Mining

There is no single, definitive "right" tool for data mining—a range of tools is capable of adding value. The criteria for tool selection should be set before you begin your search:

- Does the tool fit appropriately into the chain of beneficence? Can the tool be applied in a timely fashion so that any discovery can be cycled back into the hypothesis testing loop for verification and then be implemented? This is the determinantal factor in selection.

- Are you familiar with the tool?

- Is the time that is necessary to transfer data from the warehousing environment to the mining environment available?

- Does the platform have the adequate horsepower?

- What is the cost of setting up the mining environment? The strategic value that is gained by mining diminishes this factor, however.

Most of the tools that are available are predicated on very clean data and exotic algorithms. Several tools include the ability to alter their patterns dynamically as they navigate data.

The Value of Mined Information

The value of the exploration process, as outlined in the previous chapter, is to incrementally improve supply side availability or to refine demand side market specification. In either case, the expected value is incremental to the standard business activity. Often, the result of an analytical exploration is a single-digit change in revenue generation or profitability. The average businessperson is usually happy with such results. However, especially in small companies, the businessperson will question whether his or her capital could be better spent in other aspects of the business to gain the same result.

The business perspective on the data mining process tends to be different. The results found by data mining are almost always nonintuitive. To the businessperson this represents an unexpected opportunity, sometimes referred to in sales as a *bluebird*. If properly operationalized, findings often have double-digit revenue implications. In other cases, spin-off businesses are created from the findings. Once again, the ability to act on the information in a rapid manner is crucial to exploiting the value.

Impact of Mined Data on the Business Model

Sometimes, the information that is obtained from a data mining operation presents a dilemma to the business. What if a pattern is missing where one is expected? In the retail case study, an entire high socioeconomic group is missing in the analysis. What is happening? Is the data faulty?

In this particular case, a fundamental business assumption was faulty. The theory of many warehouse-type retailers is "everyday low prices (EDLP)." This model was developed in opposition to the traditional high-low model, whose key business driver was price. The assumption was that price, coupled with availability, overrode all other buying factors. Historically, and in tight economic times, this is a reliable assumption.

Business, however, is not a static world. New market forces constantly arise and this assumption is not appropriate in a rich economy with high-speed guaranteed delivery of goods. In an economy in which many members have significant disposable income, factors like scarcity of goods, quality of goods, and time all become important factors. Time cannot be replenished, making it more important than money in this environment. We conclude that a new business proposition must be created to exploit this segment.

In Summary

Data mining is an integral part of the analytical process and is necessary to run a successful competitive business today. Firms that have integrated the data mining warehouse and the analytical data mining process enjoy competitive advantage. Each data mining technique has its own niche and advantages, and not all techniques are appropriate for a particular hypothesis. In the next chapter, we will explore how best to exploit mined knowledge.

CHAPTER 7

From Pattern to Competitive Advantage

To be a success in business, be daring, be first, be different.

—STEWART MARCHANT

There is no predetermined formula for turning information into competitive advantage, but there is a process that tends to produce desired results. This chapter will look at this process step by step and apply it to various real-world examples to demonstrate how the explorer turns information and ideas into a plan of action.

A Basic Formula for Gaining Competitive Advantage

Converting corporate information into competitive advantage requires the following:

- That factors that describe the general health of the company—called *environmental factors*—are well defined
- That a strategic plan is formulated that reflects the company's market share and profitability goals as well as the environmental factors that will affect its ability to achieve these goals
- That specific objectives are determined based on the assessment of environmental factors and the company's goals

Identifying Environmental Factors

Environmental factors describe the general state of the company. They include the following:

- The products/services that a corporation sells, including their:
  - Type and number
  - Pricing
  - Length of time sold
- The market share of specific products and services, including such functions as:
  - Competitive products and services
  - Integration of the products and services
  - Barriers to entry of the products and services
- The market positioning of the corporation:
  - Its leadership in the industry
  - Its current market share
  - Its target market share
- The financial management of the corporation:
  - Its overall profitability
  - Its percentage of retained profits
  - Its current financial picture
  - Its distribution channels
  - Its overall size
  - Its number and types of partnerships
  - Its current management
  - Its ability to respond to change
  - Its multinational capabilities

These environmental factors are different for each company. The explorer who wishes to use quantified analysis to its greatest effect must be fully aware of all of them. The factors can be discussed informally if the explorer has a long history with the company, or they may be spelled out in a formal assessment. (Note that it does a company no good to look at environmental factors through rose-colored glasses. The purpose of an environmental assessment is to gain an honest portrayal of the corporation as it really is, not as it would like to be.)

Formulating a Strategic Plan

Once the environmental factors are assessed, they are matched up against the company's strategic plan. Some corporations have a formal strategic plan, others have one or two senior managers who keep the plan in their heads. The strategic plan includes such information as:

- Identification of opportunity
- Statement of strengths and weaknesses
- Current positioning versus desired positioning
- Financial goals
- Measurements of objectives
- Timing of objectives
- External influences
- Schedule for evaluation and reevaluation
- Current, midterm, and long-term strategic plans

If management has already undertaken an analysis of the opportunities that are available to the corporation, this, too, serves as input. From this plan, a simple list of corporate directions is created. It can be useful to prioritize the list, but remember that the point is to get a general sense of the intent of management— Don't make this exercise more complex than it needs to be!

The strategic plan can be as formal or as informal as the business dictates. Lifting strategic plans from the heads of executives is often the best approach because:

- Information received is very current. If a formal written strategic plan is used, the plan is sure to be out of date, sometimes by a wide margin.
- Management tends to be concise, because their time is valuable. They don't waste time on subjects of little importance.
- Management is more likely to support projects that result from its direct input.

However it is done, the explorer needs to match the strategic plan to the environmental factors to gain a context for proceeding. For example, if the strategic objective is to gain market share, then exploration to reduce cost is not going to have the right business context. If the explorer does not go through these exercises, it is quite possible that he or she will look for the wrong opportunity or bypass important opportunities.

Determining Specific Objectives

At this point, the explorer can take one of several approaches:

- Take the corporate objectives and proactively look for patterns in the exploration warehouse. This is effective only if there are patterns waiting to be found.
- Compare the corporate objectives with patterns that have already been discovered. The problem here is that the patterns may not bear any resemblance to the corporate objectives.

- Wait until new patterns and associations turn up, then compare them with the corporate objectives. This passive approach requires the least energy and can be effective over the long haul.

- Do all of these approaches. This approach requires the most resources but is the most effective.

However it is done, the explorer arrives at a point at which the corporate objectives match up—either wholly or in part—with the patterns and associations that are observed by participants in the exploration process. The explorer then attempts to fill the following template:

> Based on the information—that _____—if we _____, then we can optimize _____.

In this template, *information* is the pattern or association that is discovered by the process of exploration; *if we* refers to the action that the corporation will take as a result of connecting the pattern to the corporate objective; *we can optimize* refers to the corporate objective(s) that will be satisfied by the proposed action.

There are some important trade-offs. For example, when a company is optimized for market share, it is not optimized for profitability, and vice versa. The explorer needs to be keenly aware of managers' stance, and it helps if they make a clear statement about their priorities:

- Based on environmental factors and the corporate strategic plan, the corporate stance to gaining market share and protecting existing market share is to _____.

- Based on environmental factors and the corporate strategic plan, the corporate stance for increasing profitability, enhancing revenue, and reducing expenses is to _____.

The reason this trade-off needs to be considered carefully is that as the explorer starts to sort through different patterns and relationships that come out of exploration processing, there will be many opportunities: to enhance market share, to enhance profitability, or possibly both. The explorer needs to know which path is the most important to management. Otherwise, he or she may waste much time developing a case for something that management has no taste for.

Examples of Finding Competitive Advantage

The following sections look at some examples of how companies find and exploit advantages.

A Financial Institution

A financial and securities corporation has the objective of widening its marketplace and, if possible, of increasing profits at the same time. The explorer begins with a survey of the products offered by the firm. Then, he or she reviews the corporate strategic plan with management. The explorer learns that the management's objective is to widen the customer base as much as possible; short-term profitability is not an immediate objective. The strategic plan is to attract as many customers as possible, then to entice the customer to use as many services as possible once a bond has been established.

Next, the explorer begins analyzing both the existing customer base and the available industrywide data bases. The explorer segments the customer bases by:

- Gender
- Age
- Net worth
- Occupation
- Financial services used

A profile is created for each market segment. Next, he or she finds historical data for customers and subjects it to the same market segmentation that the current data was subjected to. The explorer combines the marketplace profiles to create a market segmentation over time, revealing the following patterns:

- As people age, the ownership of money passes from men to women.
- People start to take savings and investments seriously at about age 45.
- People start their retirement savings with simple accounts, then graduate to mutual funds when they are about 54.
- Average people think that social security will be their retirement; only about a quarter of people actually invest and save beyond any company savings plan. For diverse reasons—mergers, financial insolvency, misrepresentation, poor management, and so forth—company savings and retirement plans do not meet the expectations of participants. Unfortunately, participants usually do not discover this until they are close to retirement.
- There are certain people with considerable disposable income who are not diverting that income to savings. This group includes teachers, government workers, craftspeople, and office professionals. The amount of disposable income in this group is proportionally higher as percentage of total income than for other groups.

Once the explorer has thoroughly analyzed these patterns and relationships, he uses the template to draw the following conclusion:

Based on the information—that women over 59 control most investments and that investments made are likely to be in mutual funds—if we create programs that cater to older female investors, then we can optimize the number of new investors who will enter our portals.

A second strategy that is gleaned from the analysis of the behavior and from patterns of investors' activity is as follows:

Based on the information—that school teachers, office professionals, government workers, and paraprofessionals make up a group of currently inactive but potentially active investors—if we create promotions that entice these categories to start investing, then we can optimize the number of new investors who will enter our portals.

Golfers

An entrepreneurial company in the business of making golf equipment finds itself being squeezed very hard by its competitors. The company offers brand recognition and a quality line of products. However, what once was a very comfortable business is no longer easy. Margins are low and are getting lower all the time. Market share is holding steady, but marketing costs are increasing. New competitors with new ideas are entering the market place daily. Management wishes to come up with new approaches to marketing existing equipment and possibly opening up new opportunities for revenue.

Because traditionally there has been little need for information technology inside the walls of a golf equipment manufacturer, an outside explorer must be hired. She or he begins the process by making a quick assessment of the environmental factors, then has several in-depth conversations with management about strategic direction. The explorer learns that these managers had few ideas about strategic direction until competition began and profit margins were affected. Management is now interested primarily in profitability, but it is open to ideas about increasing market share.

The explorer then sets out to find relevant information. The first place to look is in the information systems of the golf equipment manufacturer itself. These systems show very little information about the golfers themselves; rather, they show a remarkable shift in golf equipment sales from country clubs and public golf courses to distributors. Over the years, more golf equipment was sold to large retailers, such as Kmart, Sears, and Wal-Mart. Then, another shift occurred when golf equipment was sold to specialty retail outlets that specialized in golf equipment. The explorer noted that some of the retailers were moving to magazine and Internet sales, although this segment of the marketplace was not yet developed to the extent of the other outlets.

The explorer then sets out to examine who the golfers are by using several indirect sources. One source is the registration of new equipment. The manufacturer sporadically offers special programs to golfers who buy a set of clubs. The second source of information is the golf magazine subscription list. The lists contain a fair number of individual subscribers who can easily be segmented by gender or zip code. A third source of information is handicap organizations, found in most states. Handicap organizations record all scores made by individual golfers at all courses at which they have ever played. These sources provide enough information to begin creating a representative data base about golfers.

The explorer then identifies market segments from the data and looks at the segments from many different perspectives, including:

- Gender
- Number of rounds played
- Handicap
- Demographics of where golfers live
- Time of year golf is played
- Age
- Affluence
- Day of the week when golf is played
- Season of the year when golf is played
- Time of day when golf is played
- Rate at which new equipment is sold
- Total quantity of golf balls sold
- Amount of rainy golf equipment sold
- Amount of golf played at resorts
- Amount of golf played at country clubs and private clubs

When looking at historical information, the explorer finds that:

- More rounds of golf are being played in comparison to the total population.
- The average handicap is 19.6 and rising. More new golfers enter the system with high handicaps than current golfers improve.
- Women are entering the golf system at a faster rate than men. However, men still make up 78 percent of active golfers.
- The average golfer plays 7.9 rounds per year.
- Country clubs make up 15 percent of golf sales.
- Public courses make up 21 percent of sales, large retailers make up 38 percent of sales, specialty retailers make up 17 percent of sales, and other sources make up the rest.
- The rate of sales via magazines and the Internet is growing slowly. The feeling is that people like to touch and feel the golf equipment that they are buying. Only commodity items such as golf balls are selling well across the Internet.
- International golf equipment sales are blossoming.

Once the explorer has the basic information in hand, the template is applied:

> Based on the information—that there is a movement for people to play more than one course, even when the person is a member at a home course—if we create a series of "local multiclub" championships that is to open to people who must play at several courses and if we give away sets of clubs and other equipment as prizes, then we can optimize a new channel for sales and the opportunity for additional promotion of our product line. In addition, if handled properly, additional revenue may be generated by creating the program.

It is noticed that people play golf frequently on courses other than their home course. This cross-course play could have several origins—boredom, social and business occasions at other courses, and so forth. The golf company sees this as a revenue-building opportunity.

The company also sees an opportunity to capitalize on the international popularity of golf:

> Based on the information—that international golf is becoming very popular—if we create a program in which we put a set of our golf clubs at selected overseas courses and then coordinate travel packages in which the traveler does not have to carry a set of clubs overseas, then we can optimize the number of sales of our clubs and the loyalty to our line of golf products.

Another trend that is noticed by the explorer is that golf clubs are often lost or stolen. This leads to another suggestion:

> Based on the information—that people lose clubs quite frequently—if we create a program in which we replace old clubs along with several dozen of our golf balls, then we can optimize sales and profitability.

To implement this program, the golf company must go to other manufacturers and buy several sets of clubs. Fortunately, the manufacturer can buy at wholesale rates, and the clubs bought are being discontinued and are, therefore, relatively inexpensive. These clubs will be sold at a break-even rate. Selling individual clubs will more than pay for the set of clubs purchased by the golf company. The real profit, however, comes with the inclusion of golf balls that are sold at normal prices.

Supermarket Sales

A supermarket executive is struggling with how to optimize profitability. Margins are being squeezed by competition, and vendors are becoming increasingly aware of their profitability.

The explorer begins by assessing environmental factors: Who is the competition? How do sales operate? How is the supermarket chain structured? What is the history of the organization? Next, the explorer chats with the management about its strategic plans. The management's concern is not about market share for the existing stores in the chain; rather, it is about maximizing profits.

The explorer then gathers all available information about:

- Point of sale (checkout ticket)
- Customer loyalty program
- Coupon discount
- Promotion response
- Vendor stocking
- Sales trends over time by store and by product type
- Spoilage and breakage
- Returns
- Competitors
- Sales and in-store promotion
- Pricing over time
- Product placement
- Stocking
- Weather
- Extraordinary factors such as disasters (fires, hurricanes, riots)

The explorer sets, organizes, and analyzes the information, finding so many patterns that the issue becomes sorting through them. Some of these patterns are probably false; other patterns are real but irrelevant. Some of the patterns found include the following:

- Products have different price elasticities.
- Product price elasticity correlates in part to the day of the week and to the month of the year.
- Different items of data are sold in conjunction with other items.
- Some external events, such as the Super Bowl or the World Series, correlate to one-time demands for certain items.
- Weather contributes to the price elasticity of certain products.
- Total store revenue does not seem to be affected by promotions.
- Competition has a big impact on store revenue.
- Pricing is very sensitive to the selection of brands inside the store.
- Positioning of items on the shelves correlates to the units sold.

There are many opportunities for capitalizing on this knowledge, including:

> Based on the information—that there are some products that sell well together in the same market basket—if we create an understanding that market basket profitability is as important as item profitability, then we can optimize profitability.

Suppose two beer manufacturers are competing for space on the supermarket shelf. One is a large national manufacturer and offers high margins of profitability; the other is a local manufacturer with lower profit margins. Based strictly on item profitability, the store chooses to stock the national beer. Customers, however, purchase the local beer along with other items—cheese, spreads, crackers, colas—which makes it more profitable for the store to stock the local beer manufacturer than the national beer. Although the national beer manufacturer has a higher profit margin, it does not offer market basket profitability.

Another perspective is frequency of purchase. The national beer manufacturer may attract a few quantity purchasers, whereas the local beer manufacturer attracts many purchasers. A real case can be made for the local beer manufacturer who is achieving equal footing even though the item margin is less than the national brand beer.

The second important analysis dealing with profitability of the supermarket chain is determining the price elasticity of products:

> Based on the information—that some products sell more if their price is reduced, but other products sell the same regardless of pricing—if we create a pricing strategy that sets items with price elasticity on sale but that does not set price-inelastic items on sale, then we can optimize profitability.

Analyzing sales during normal pricing and during sale pricing can tell the supermarket what items are price-elastic or -inelastic. Once the store is armed with this information, it can begin to maximize profitability. Price elasticity, though, is not a static subject. The explorer discovers that it correlates with both the weather and the time of year. In some cases, the explorer finds that the elasticity of a product varies with the day of the week. Yet another opportunity for the maximization of profit arises:

> Based on the information—that some products sell more if their price is reduced, but other products sell the same regardless of pricing, and that pricing elasticity varies by the weather, the time of year, and the day of the week—if we create a pricing strategy that sets price-elastic items on sale but that does not set price-inelastic items (based on weather, time of year, and day of the week) on sale, then we can optimize profitability.

To be successful, the explorer must constantly monitor sales to see if the elasticity factors have changed.

Travelers

A travel agency wants to expand its client base to diversify its revenue. The explorer first investigates the basic environmental factors: the types of people who make trips, the types of trips that are taken, the profitability of booking and managing trips, the number of trips booked, international and domestic trips, the interactions of the agents required, and business trips and pleasure trips.

Next, the explorer interviews management to determine its priorities and objectives. He finds that management hopes to create a broader base of customers so that the agency will be less sensitive to business downturns. Profitability is not an issue, or at least, it is not the most important issue. The explorer finds a surprisingly large amount of data from different sources:

Bookings made by the agency

- Destinations
- Customers
- Form of payment
- Length of the trip
- Nature of the trip
- Number of people going on the trip
- Frequency of travel

Travel arrangements

- Airlines
- Hotels
- Other forms of transportation

Industry statistics

- Total number of people/trips
- Marketwide destinations
- Demographics of travelers

The explorer makes several interesting discoveries:

- The total number of pleasure trips is increasing at a rate far beyond any other form of travel.
- The average age of the traveler is 42 years old, an increase from 10 years ago.
- Seventy-three percent of travelers are male.
- The average pleasure trip is 10 days.
- The most traveled-to pleasure destination is Orlando.
- Conference travel accounts for 18 percent of all trips.
- Travel peaks at two times of the year—early September and at Christmas.
- Air travel is the favored form of travel for trips of over 250 miles.
- Seventy-eight percent of all air travelers rent cars.
- Fifty-one percent of all travel is to destinations that are oceanside.

Based on the information that is gathered as a result of the analysis, the explorer comes to the following conclusion:

> Based on the information—that nontraditional destinations (Cambodia/Angkor Wat; Nepal/the Himalayas; the Yucatán, Mexico/Chichén Itzá; Peru/Machu Picchu) are increasingly being selected by customers—if we create exotic travel packages that offer unusual activities and locations, then we can optimize the niche market of "rugged" travelers.

The explorer also notices that the business marketplace can be extended:

> Based on the information—that there are a lot of business travelers, that they usually travel on corporate budgets, and that the accommodations offered are somewhat limited—if we create a program that tells the business traveler about nighttime activities available in that city (concerts, sports activities, comedy acts), then we can optimize new opportunities for cash flow.

Steel Manufacturing

A steel manufacturer has a problem. World steel prices are dropping, and with this drop comes a reduction in profit margins. Although there is a relatively constant demand for steel, the steel company feels squeezed. Management brings in an explorer to help find ways to optimize profits.

The explorer sets out first to understand the environmental factors facing the company, including products made, who the customers are, the way that sales are made, and the past history of the steel company. Interviews with management reveal that the steel company is interested in maximizing profit, although it is concerned about shrinking market share because of competitive prices. Management also makes it clear to the explorer that it would not look favorably on any option that involves new capital expenditures, especially for new plants or for renovation to existing plants.

The explorer then starts to examine available data, including:

- Products—past and present
- Sales—past and present
- Who the customers are and were
- Length of time required to fulfill an order
- Rejection rate of the customer
- Customer complaints
- Products made from the steel
- Worldwide cost of steel
- Shipping costs of steel
- Manufacturing process
- Rejection rate within manufacturing
- Quality control process for manufacturing
- Speed of manufacturing
- Engineering of the final product
- Backlog rate
- Percentage of idle time at a plant
- Number of times that a new product has been introduced

Over the years, the steel company did a good job of archiving its internal data, so the explorer can also factor time into the analysis. The problem that the explorer faces is choosing on which variables to focus to satisfy the parameters of management. The explorer decides to look at:

The quality of steel production. Each batch of steel has a percentage of usable product. The quality rate varies significantly, from 50 to 99 percent.

The variables of manufacture include:

- When the batch is run
- Which plants made the batch
- The heat of the mixture
- The rate at which the mixture was poured
- The gauge of the mixture throughout the pouring process
- The length of time in which the batch is heated
- The chemical composition of the batch
- The percentage of undesirable product that is eliminated
- The engineers of the manufacturing process

The explorer then takes the variables and comes up with the following conclusion:

> Based on the information—that the quality of manufacture varies wildly—if we create a data base of the different variables that are most relevant to manufacture and track how those variables relate to the quality of steel created, then we can optimize profitability by making our plants more productive with no extra capital cost.

One of the challenges that the explorer faces is that each batch of steel operates under many variables. It is not unheard-of for a batch to have as many as 35,000 variables attached to it. The explorer creates a small table of 100 variables that the engineers say are most relevant to the manufacturing process. This table is easy to create, and it is even easier to implement. The remaining variables are placed in an archival store from which they can be accessed if needed. By separating the data in this manner, the explorer creates a more manageable environment for further exploration.

Once a manufacturing data base is created, the explorer does a correlative study. Over time, we can see which variables correlate with both those batches of steel with the high productivity ratios and those with the poor production ratios. Understanding how different variables correlate with the success or failure of the production process helps the explorer raise the quality of production. This has had several benefits:

- Customer satisfaction has risen.
- The costs of manufacturing have gone down, in some cases significantly.
- As the costs of manufacturing have gone down, profitability has gone up.

Furthermore, changes in the manufacturing process have been achieved with minimal capital investment.

In Summary

Going from patterns to competitive advantage begins with a description of the business environment—including germane aspects of the competitive environment, the technological environment, and the business climate. Next, the corporate strategic plan is incorporated. From these two inputs, we derive the strategy for capturing and maintaining market share and enhancing profitability. After these factors are identified and synthesized, the explorer assimilates the patterns and turns the business model into the following template:

Based on the information—that ____—if we ____, then we can optimize ____.

CHAPTER 8

Designing the Exploration Warehouse

A problem well stated is a problem half solved.

—CHARLES KETTERING

Strictly speaking, it is not necessary to build an exploration warehouse to perform exploration processing. An enterprise data warehouse will suffice for limited amounts and types of exploration processing. For specialized projects with limited data and processing requirements, data can even be extracted directly from the legacy application environment. Once a company needs to perform a significant amount of exploration processing, though, exploration warehouses become important.

In a way, there is no such thing as a data base design for an exploration warehouse. Data and analysis requirements are constantly changing, and each iteration of analysis leads to a change in the design of the exploration warehouse. The magnitude and the rate of change of design in an exploration warehouse is a function of the analysis being done and is a result of an ever-changing understanding of the requirements being analyzed. Therefore, it is properly said that the initial configuration of the exploration warehouse is designed, but all further modifications to the design are a result of the iterative analysis.

The initial exploration warehouse design is based on a cursory understanding of where the business opportunity lies. If the business-model-to-pattern approach is used, exploration warehouses are likely to be initiated:

- Where the external forces intersect, such as the recent acquisition of Time Warner by America OnLine (AOL), changing the business definition of *distribution channel* and *content*.

- Where there are many occurrences of data, especially transaction-based *data*. Typically, call detail records (CDRs) in telephony, point-of-sale (POS) data in retail, and transactional data in banking fall into this category.

- Where there is a correlation of data. Market penetration analysis is often based on POS data, census data, and market survey research data.

If the pattern-to-business-model approach has been used, patterns that have already been discovered are used as the basis for the initial exploration warehouse design.

At the end of the first iteration of analysis, the exploration warehouse is refined, and the design is altered to reflect new insights. At this point, data may be added to tables, tables may be added, and foreign key/key relationships may be changed. The second iteration of analysis uses the new exploration warehouse, and the processes of design, reconstruction, and analysis continue.

Data Flow into the Exploration Warehouse

As noted in Chapter 1, data flows, traditionally, into the exploration warehouse from any or all of the following sources:

- External sources
- Enterprise data warehouse
- Near-line storage

Flows may feed continuously or on a one-time basis. The number of feeds and how they interrelate are strictly up to the explorer.

Each flow into the exploration warehouse has a separate set of considerations:

From external sources:

- Data must be integrated into a structure that is compatible with other data that is residing in or flowing into the exploration warehouse.
- Data may require special cleansing and integration routines.
- The explorer must consider the frequency of updates.
- Data must be fresh.
- The external source is usually a one-time flow or a very infrequent flow.

From the enterprise data warehouse:

- Data needs to be reshaped as it moves to the exploration warehouse.
- Performance of the enterprise data warehouse can be affected by periodically moving the data into the exploration warehouse.
- Proper subsets of data must be selected.

■ The explorer needs to choose to feed either a static or a dynamic exploration warehouse.

From near-line storage:

■ Data must be chosen and moved into the exploration warehouse.

■ Data must be condensed as it moves from near-line storage to the exploration warehouse.

The designer does not merely load all available data into the exploration warehouse. Instead, the designer must make an educated guess as to which data will most likely yield the best results. Let's examine that process now.

Using the Data Model

Suppose the designer knows that analysis and exploration will focus on manufacturing productivity. He or she knows that it is unlikely that sales promotions will have much to do with the exploration analysis in this case, so it's safe to cut out such areas from the analysis.

The designer can go even further, though. Suppose that in another case, he or she knows that the exploration centers around sales. For the first iteration of the population of the exploration warehouse, the designer may choose to place sales from the year 2000 in the exploration warehouse, knowing that subsequent iterations will need data from years 1999, 1998, and so forth. The designer deliberately does not put all the historical data that will be needed into the exploration warehouse because he or she knows that the initial design will change. It will be easier to change the sales data for 2000 than it will be for 1997, 1998, 1999, and 2000. Therefore, for the first iteration of design and population of the exploration warehouse, the designer puts only a useful representation of historical data into the exploration warehouse. This approach of not completely fulfilling requirements for the first two or three iterations of development is typical and normal for the design of the exploration warehouse.

The Partial Design Approach

The *partial design approach* is especially applicable for data coming from near-line storage and external sources. There is usually so much volume that resides in near-line storage that great care must be taken when accessing and selecting it. The same is true of data coming from external sources. Data coming from external sources is said to be "brittle," meaning that there is very little manipulation that the company can do to further condition the external data. It therefore makes sense that external data be used sparingly until the explorer starts to get a good feel for its characteristics.

The data model that describes the contents of the exploration warehouse is usually created in an informal manner. It seldom makes sense to go through a formal data modeling exercise to create the exploration warehouse data model. Usually, the data model in the enterprise data warehouse will suffice as the data model for the initial design of the exploration warehouse. Of course, as successive iterations of the exploration process are executed, the data model will change.

Data Model Constraints

The initial design of the exploration warehouse is shaped by the data model. However, there is considerable freedom to design and redesign the exploration warehouse based on the results of iterative analysis and exploration. Figure 8.1 shows that, at least initially, the exploration warehouse is shaped by the explorer's choice of data model. However, the designer has only a loose interpretation of what the contents and structures the exploration warehouse should be.

The exploration warehouse environment is fundamentally different from almost any other computing environment in that the explorer is free to change the structure and content of the data residing inside the exploration warehouse at any time. The very essence of the exploration warehouse is agility and flexibility. The only real constraint that the explorer has is finding data sources and making them compatible enough to reside and be used in the same data base.

Data Mining Design versus Data Exploration Design

There is little or no difference in the data base design for data mining and data exploration when a company first begins these activities. As an organization becomes more sophisticated, however, differences between exploration warehouse data base design and data mining data base design start to unfold. Those differences are expressed in Figure 8.2.

Figure 8.2 shows that the exploration warehouse's data base design is aimed at breadth of information. For example, there will be many subject areas, many foreign keys in support of joins, and a representative supply of historical data. The intent of the exploration warehouse data base design is to provide a foundation for spontaneous thinking and browsing; the design of this data base is made with very few presuppositions about the data, because its purpose is to allow the analyst to discover or flesh out his or her assumptions about the analysis. Furthermore, the internal structure of data for the exploration warehouse needs to be as flexible as possible. Therefore, normalization of data is a design norm for the exploration warehouse.

The data base design for the data mining data warehouse is quite different. A whole set of hypotheses and assumptions are made at the outset about the data

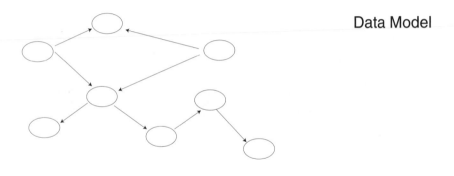

Data Model

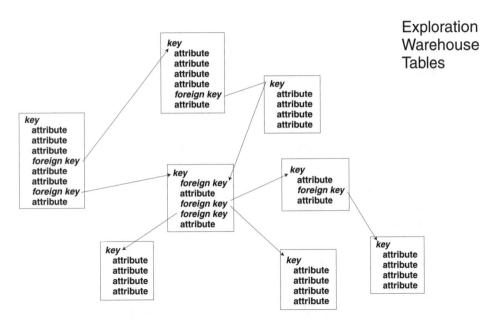

Exploration
Warehouse
Tables

Figure 8.1 The data model shapes the tables of the exploration warehouse.

mining data warehouse. The intent of data mining is to prove or disprove a set of hypotheses, or to examine the strength of the hypotheses within the confines of the assumptions. Therefore, the design for the data mining warehouse need only address the hypotheses and assumptions that have been identified from the outset, which greatly limits the scope of the design.

There is no need for the flexible, normalized structure of data found in the exploration warehouse. The structures of data inside the data mining data warehouse can be flat. The focus of design is on the efficiency of processing rather than the flexibility of processing.

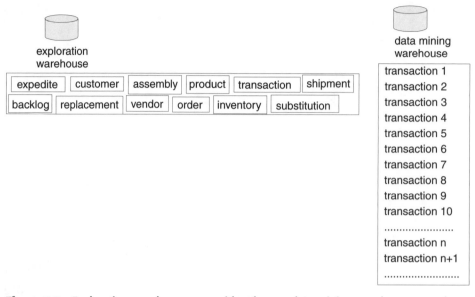

Figure 8.2 Exploration warehouses are wide whereas data mining warehouses are deep.

The data mining data warehouse also contains more occurrences of data than the exploration warehouse. The data mining data warehouse needs to contain as many detailed occurrences and historical references as possible, so that the data miner can be as thorough as possible. The essence of the data mining data warehouse is depth, in contrast to the breadth of the exploration warehouse.

The design of both warehouses should allow their structure and contents to be quickly and easily changed, as shown in Figure 8.3.

Creating Exploration Marts

Figure 8.3 also shows that exploration marts are first created at the advanced stages of exploration. An exploration mart is a structure that is dedicated to the analysis of only one aspect of exploration analysis. Just as data marts are separate structures that are optimized for departmental processing of a data warehouse, exploration marts are specialized exploration warehouses dedicated to focused aspects that are of interest to the explorer.

For example, in building a sales exploration warehouse, an explorer may find out that it is necessary to study sales in South America on their own, separate and apart from all other sales. Also, the explorer may find that, for an exploration warehouse that is dedicated to manufacturing, a separate exploration mart may be required just to study the manufacture of part XYZ. Although the data that is found in the exploration warehouse reflects the entire company, the exploration mart focuses on only one aspect of the corporation. With this focus, data can be optimized for processing based on the limitations set by the explorer.

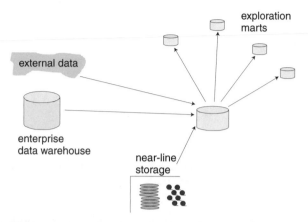

Figure 8.3 Exploration marts can be created from an exploration warehouse.

Temporary or Permanent Exploration Warehouses

The exploration warehouse is often created with the attitude that it will be gone as soon as the project is completed. This should not imply that there is a great deal of waste in the exploration warehouse. Machine and storage resources are reusable. It behooves the exploration analyst to carefully consider which parts of an exploration warehouse should be permanent and which should be temporary. As a general rule, an exploration warehouse should be temporary unless there are extenuating circumstances that would dictate otherwise. An example of an extenuating circumstance would be the discovery of an unexpected secondary effect requiring additional exploration.

Of course, when a temporary exploration warehouse is discarded, the explorer should determine whether the project should be placed in mothballs or if it should be permanently discarded.

Manipulation of Data in Flight

Data is often manipulated and filtered before being placed in the exploration warehouse, as shown in Figure 8.4.

There are a variety of reasons why data is altered as it passes from the source to the exploration warehouse:

- Some types of data are simply not needed. For example, when analyzing human resource data, it may not be necessary to carry social security numbers and personal names with the records to be analyzed.

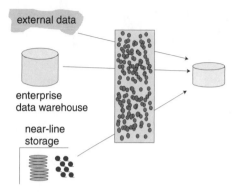

Figure 8.4 Data can be filtered as it passes into the exploration warehouse.

- Some types of data are best represented in another form. In the previous example, the source data may have date of birth. It may be easier to convert date of birth into actual age for the purpose of exploratory analysis.

- Some types of data need to be represented in a compact form. Suppose a source has sales amount, sales tax, sales commission, and sales shipment cost. The explorer may wish to create a single column in the exploration warehouse called "net sale," where net sale = sales amount − (sales tax + sales commission + sales shipment cost). The explorer may simply find that it is easier to create one element of data rather than to have to manipulate the data each time that it needs to be used.

- Some types of data need to be converted. To achieve integration, the explorer may have to take the source data and convert it into a format that is common to other sources.

There are then a whole host of reasons why data may be altered as it passes from the exploration warehouse sources into the exploration warehouse itself.

Maintenance of Granularity

The explorer should be aware that there may be an undesirable loss of granularity. In some cases, when data passes into the exploration warehouse, it is summarized and, consequently, there is a loss of granularity. The explorer needs to be aware that the design will have to be fundamentally recast to recapture this loss of granularity. This can certainly be done, but the recasting may require considerable effort and may have an impact on the analytical work that has already been done. The explorer needs to consider carefully what happens if the granularity of data in the exploration warehouse is not at the lowest level necessary.

Design Approaches

The basic data structure of the exploration warehouse is normalized. Figure 8.5 shows a simple example of the normalized structure that one would expect for

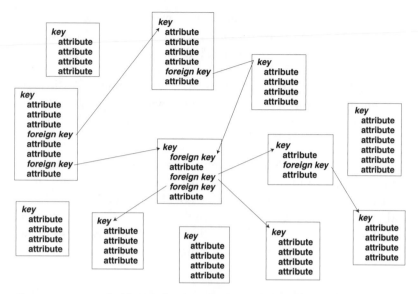

Figure 8.5 A typical internal structure of an exploration warehouse.

an exploration warehouse. In Figure 8.5, data is organized into little tables in which each table logically contains data that relates directly to the key of the table. The tables are related to each other by means of a key/foreign key set of relationships. A key exists in one table. A foreign key exists in one or more other tables. The two tables can be related by matching logic for the keys. For example, there might be a table for human resources describing an employee:

Employee social security number (key)

Employee name

Employee address

Employee date of hire

Employee gender

The key to the table is Employee ID. Now, suppose that there is a payroll table that looks like:

Employee ID (key)

Month

Year

Pay amount

Taxes paid

FICA paid

Other deductions

Social security number (foreign key)

The foreign key is social security number. Now, suppose the explorer wished to find the address of the person being paid. The explorer would join the two tables on social security number. That is, the system would search the employee file. It would find a record for Kevin Gould. Next, the system would find the social security number for Kevin. It would then look through the payroll table and find all the occurrences when Kevin had been paid. It would know that a payroll record belonged to Kevin when it discovered a record with his social security number in it.

Such a process is called a join. By joining data, the structure of data is very flexible. In addition, should the explorer wish to add another table—for instance, an employee education table—the table could be added independently with no disruption to the existing tables. Figure 8.6 shows that many different combinations of joins can be created. The diagram in Figure 8.6 also illustrates the profound flexibility of data when it is stored in a normalized form.

Integrated Exploration Warehouse Data

Data in the exploration warehouse must be integrated. Expressed most simply, this means that the key structure for any given entity must be unique. Figure 8.7 shows this characteristic of data residing inside the exploration warehouse.

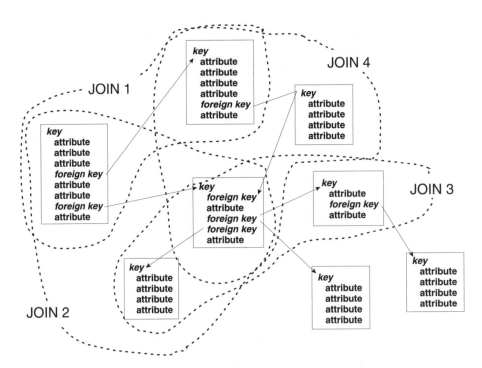

Figure 8.6 The same data can be joined in many ways.

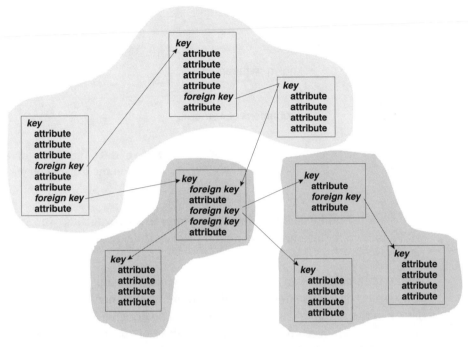

Figure 8.7 The data inside the exploration warehouse is integrated.

Suppose an exploration warehouse contains data from an external source and from the enterprise data warehouse. The key of the external record is sale of a part. The key for part is 16 bytes and is determined by a standards industrial committee. The key for data coming from the enterprise data warehouse for parts is 10 bytes and is determined by the business practices of the corporation over the past 20 years. In one part of the exploration warehouse, a broom is -BR100-980. In another part of the exploration warehouse a broom is -549-ppi-str4. In other words, the system has no way of knowing that the same item goes by two different names. The result is poor integration and an inability to do effective exploration processing.

Attributes of the Exploration Warehouse

Figure 8.8 shows that there are three types of attributes that can be placed inside the tables inside the exploration warehouse:

1. Attributes for which there are known requirements.

2. Attributes for which there are probable requirements.

3. Attributes for which there are possible requirements.

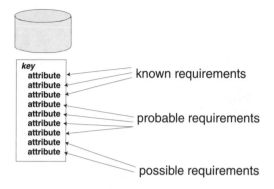

Figure 8.8 The types of attributes placed in the exploration warehouse.

The explorer addresses the three attributes in the order shown. An attribute with a known requirement gets higher priority than an attribute with a probable requirement.

Unlike data base design done elsewhere, when creating the exploration warehouse, there is a loose definition of attribute requirements. This stems from the nature of the iterative development that will be done with the exploration warehouse. The explorer knows that if he or she fails to include the proper attributes, they can be included at a later time. Indeed, spending too much time on a rigorous definition of attributes delays the real work of the exploration warehouse—iterative analysis.

Volumes of Data

One of the very real issues of design that the designer faces is managing massive volumes of data. Detail and history are normal for the exploration warehouse environment. Exploration warehouses regularly contain very large volumes of data, which designers manage by:

- Sampling techniques.
- Subdividing the data into separate tables in which each table can be handled individually.
- Operating at less than the lowest level of granularity. This usually is a very poor option and is done when there is no other way to accomplish the task.
- Breaking the analytical process up into a series of small sequential steps and executing each of the steps one at a time and independently of each other.

Each record in the exploration warehouse has a time stamp. The time stamp is used to identify the moment in time to which the record is relevant. To create a summary record, the explorer selects all exploration warehouse records that lie within the time frame. Once the records are selected, they can be aggregated, summarized, and counted. Given that the enterprise data warehouse or near-line storage is the source of much of the data in the exploration warehouse, having a time stamp on individual records is natural.

Purging an Exploration Project

When a project and results have been attained, enthusiasm for further expenditure tends to wane. Indeed, a project can simply be abandoned; however, if there is ever a need to resurrect the project, formal closure is in order (Figure 8.9).

Some of the activities that result from formal closure of a project include:

- Documenting what has transpired
- Saving any relevant data
- Saving relevant reports
- Describing who conducted the analysis
- Saving any queries or algorithms that have been developed
- Describing assumptions
- Identifying sources of data used
- Describing the cleansing and integration algorithms that were used

In short, anything that can be useful in re-creating the project, should it be necessary for such a re-creation, should be saved and documented.

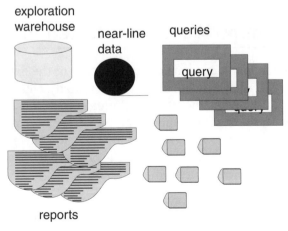

Figure 8.9 A variety of objects needs to be saved at the end of a project.

Meta Data and the Exploration Warehouse

One of the most elusive yet potentially useful aspects of the exploration warehouse is the meta data component.

During the analysis and exploration process, the analyst needs a road map to tell him or her as much as possible about the exploration warehouse. Meta data in the exploration warehouse environment acts as a road map to tell the analyst what data is where, how it got there, what its source is, and what meaning the data has. In short, meta data in the exploration warehouse can greatly enhance the exploration experience.

There are, however, some problems with a formal infrastructure for meta data in the exploration warehouse. First, meta data requires a fair amount of resources to create and keep current. Given that many exploration warehouses are temporary, it is difficult to create the infrastructure required for meta data.

The second problem is that the exploration warehouse changes very rapidly. Theoretically, each time the exploration warehouse changes, the meta data should also be changed. Soon, the maintenance of the meta data becomes a drag on the development and exploration process.

The third problem is that the technological infrastructure for the creation and maintenance of exploration meta data does not exist. The world of meta data in general is undeveloped. The world of exploration meta data is even more undeveloped.

There is, then, a challenge for the explorer to build an infrastructure for meta data that is informal, easy to build, easy to change, and cheap.

Dynamic/Static Exploration Warehouse Differences

A final design consideration is the dynamic or static nature of the exploration warehouse. The static exploration warehouse is created initially, changed a few times, then frozen for analysis. When the static exploration warehouse reaches the state of being frozen, little ongoing support infrastructure is required. No more data will be loaded, no updates will be done, there is no concern for the freshness of the data, and so forth. There is, then, little concern for the technological infrastructure of the static exploration warehouse.

The dynamic exploration warehouse is, however, another matter altogether. The dynamic exploration warehouse requires capacity planning, monitoring, management of periodic loads, management of periodic updates, and purging. A very different technological infrastructure is required for the dynamic exploration warehouse, one that is much more rigorous and disciplined than the infrastructure required for the static exploration warehouse.

In Summary

The exploration warehouse environment is built in a spiral manner. The data model is at the foundation for the design of the first iteration of development for the exploration warehouse, but successive iterations of development are a result of exploration processing.

The scope of the exploration warehouse is broad, whereas the scope of the data mining data warehouse is deep. The output of exploration processing is assumptions and hypotheses. The output of the data mining process is the examination for truth and strength of those outputs that are discovered in exploration processing.

CHAPTER 9

The Politics of Exploration

*There are some politicians who, if their constituents were cannibals,
would promise them missionaries for dinner.*

—H. L. MENCKEN

E
xplorers are driven by the need to hit "home runs" and find new, strategically useful information. Companies can benefit mightily from these efforts, in terms of both market share and profitability. The benefit of exploration and data mining can often run upward of tens of millions of dollars.

Explorers and data miners are not singles hitters, but the problem with swinging for the fence on every pitch is that you strike out a lot. Even Babe Ruth struck out more times than he managed to hit a "tater." Therein lies one of the fundamental problems of the politics of data mining and exploration processing. Organizations do not like to invest in ventures that strike out a lot. Management is used to predictability when it comes to making investments in projects, and it favors the singles hitter, who has a high batting average and seldom strikes out. With singles hitters, there is a reasonably predictable expectation of success.

The explorer, however, cannot predict whether exploration and data mining will be successful prior to exploration. Periodic checkpoints, setting goals and objectives, and analysis review are about the best that we can do to manage the exploration process.

Even with these mechanisms in place, management sponsorship of exploration is much like betting at the racetrack. If you win, the payoff can be very great. If you lose, you end up with nothing. The explorer needs to perform exploration and data mining without risking the ire of management if he or she fails. Of course, once the explorer hits a home run, everyone lines up for congratulations.

The Exploration Crucible

Three things drive explorers:

1. *Explorers are curious.* They notice things that no one else notices— changes in business, customers, rate of sales, and demographics of sales. Explorers look for the data behind the data, which explains what they observe.

2. *Explorers are motivated.* Explorers do not rest until a phenomenon is explained. This bulldog mentality is, in some respects, the root of their problem. Explorers' investigations will inevitably take many wrong turns, for which the organization receives no payback; however, when they ultimately take the right turns, payback is spectacular.

3. *Explorers understand opportunity when it is presented to them.* Explorers are not satisfied until observations are turned into business opportunity. Explorers are the original capitalists, except that their venue is information rather than capital goods.

All three of these factors are necessary to become a successful explorer. Successful exploration and data mining depend on insight and inspiration. Organizations can create an environment in which insight and inspiration are fostered and rewarded, but actually scheduling them is impossible. This drives management crazy, because it is used to projects in which results can be measured.

How Does Exploration Start?

At the initial stages, explorers usually start with very crude tools, such as a simple spreadsheet. The spreadsheet is a good entry point for exploration because it is easy to use and is ubiquitous. However, spreadsheets have their limitations, which the explorer quickly discovers. They don't work with large amounts of data, data that needs integration and scrubbing, or data that needs more than simple calculation.

After a short while, the explorer graduates to a data base, often a relational data base. The data base can handle much more data than the spreadsheet; data can be integrated before entering the data base; data loaded into the data base is much more versatile than data found in a spreadsheet.

Most data bases, though, serve lots of masters—the explorer is just one of many. Because data bases are so popular, the explorer finds that he or she quickly becomes an outcast, relegated to operating the time-consuming analyses in the wee hours of the morning or over the Christmas holidays.

The explorer decides that if he or she cannot get to the data in the data base, then he or she will extract it into an environment that can be controlled by the explorer. However, even here we find problems:

- *Keeping the extracted data current.* The minute at which the explorer extracts the data, it starts to age.

- *Adding more data to extractions.* The explorer never gets all the data that is needed the first time. Or the second time. He or she is constantly going back to the data base for more data, frustrating the data base administrator.

About this time, the organization discovers data warehousing. The explorer immediately falls in love with a data warehouse. A data warehouse contains detailed data, integrated data, and historical data. As soon as the data warehouse administrator takes one look at the explorer's large queries, he or she is removed from the list of warehouse users. At this point, the explorer feels like a kid looking in on a candy store without a penny in his or her pocket.

However, all is not lost. The explorer now discovers (or invents!) the exploration warehouse, which belongs exclusively to the explorer. There is a catch, though: The explorer has to pay for the exploration warehouse. Up until this point, he or she has been using common corporate facilities that were paid for by someone else. The data warehouse belonged to corporate services. The data base belonged to applications. The extracted set of data belonged to the explorer, but it was so small that paying for it was not usually a problem. However, the exploration warehouse, which can be quite large, needs to be paid for.

Very soon, the explorer finds him- or herself in strange territory—that of corporate budgets, corporate politics, and the world of a priori cost justification.

Budgets for the Exploration Warehouse

The exploration warehouse budget is usually much smaller than the budget for the enterprise data warehouse or for other parts of the information technology (IT) environment. The final user (for example, marketing, finance, or sales) usually foots the bill for the exploration warehouse.

Occasionally, the budget lands in the lap of the IT organization. Ironically, the benefits of the exploration warehouse may not go to the organization that sponsors it. Often, the benefits of exploration processing are scattered around the company, regardless of who originally sponsored the exploration effort.

Positioning of the exploration function usually follows the funding. If the marketing department sponsors exploration, then the exploration function will fit the marketing department. One exception occurs when there is a centralized exploration function that many departments plan to take advantage of. In this case, all departments pay for the centralized processing facility. However, most corporations evolve to this position only after a long time.

After the Home Run

Once the infrastructure for exploration processing has been formalized and the exploration warehouse has been placed in an organization chart, management expects to see results on a regular basis. This is usually not the case.

In a way, formalizing the infrastructure of exploration processing is poisonous to exploration processing. Exploration processing has always been for out-of-the-box thinkers. Creating an infrastructure gives explorers a sandbox to play in. Given the right incentive (see the upcoming section, entitled "Explorer Motivation"), it is likely that explorers will prosper. Be aware, though, that some free-thinkers will feel frustrated by a more formal infrastructure, which can result in stagnation.

One high-level by-product of exploration warehousing is the shaping of corporate policy. Once it becomes aware of the factors critical to its success, the company can change its corporate strategy accordingly. Results of exploration processing can also be used at the lowest, most detailed level. For example, when exploration processing is used to determine the elasticity of the pricing of a product, the results can help the product or department manager to determine what goes on sale and at what price.

Critical Success Factors

The following sections look at other critical factors in successful exploration warehousing.

Explorer Motivation

One of the key ingredients for successful exploration is proper motivation of the explorer. The first motivation is satisfaction of curiosity. Universally, explorers are curious people. Exploration carries its own reward system: There is a powerful sense of satisfaction in discovering the underlying reasons for a particular phenomenon.

Intellectual satisfaction is usually not enough, however, to create a highly effective exploration environment. Other rewards are necessary to create an optimal environment, including:

- Recognition from the organization
- Promotion

- Bonus based on performance
- Sharing benefits

At this point, we should discuss a delicate subject—Should an explorer share a percentage of the rewards for making a discovery? One the one hand, if an explorer makes a discovery that is worth $10 million to the business, should the explorer be paid a percentage or a flat fee? One percent of the revenue is a lot of money, but $1000 might not be enough of a reward to keep the explorer with the company. Explorers tend to be entrepreneurial people, and entrepreneurial people like to be paid what they are worth. The best way to avoid this sticky situation is to discuss compensation up front.

Management Communications

The exploration infrastructure needs to provide constant feedback to management; otherwise, they will look upon it as a cost center. Costs need to be quantified and regularly presented to management. This communication is also valuable in determining who is responsible for successful exploration. Communications with management can be formal or informal. It can be:

- A regular meeting
- An e-mail
- A memo
- A companywide function
- A magazine article
- An interview

The explorer should be innovative, give management regular updates, and offer an honest picture of ongoing exploration. By *innovative*, what is meant is that the process of exploration should be constantly run as a proactive function. In this way opportunity is presented to management as an ongoing change facilitator rather than an analytical, after-the-fact assessment of business breakage. Management needs to be apprised of both success and failure.

Putting Discovery into Action

The first step in turning discovery into real business advantage is making management aware of the exploration-processing results to determine a course of action. This action is broken down into a series of finite steps. Because it is often difficult to determine how to apply a broad concept to the business, the explorer designs a series of specific instructions for the implementor.

Once the steps are implemented, it behooves the explorer to measure the results of implementation over time. This way, the cost/benefit ratio can be calculated.

In Summary

Because exploration processing is an all-or-nothing affair and results for exploration cannot be scheduled, management is often loath to fund exploration efforts. Only after exploration processing has proved successful will management acknowledge sponsorship. The likely place to look for support for the corporate budget for exploration warehousing is the marketing, sales, or finance department. Management communications throughout the exploration process are essential.

CHAPTER 10

Data Mining:

From Analysis to Business

Do not put your faith in what statistics say until you have carefully considered what they do not say.

—WILLIAM W. WATT

D ata mining can be used sometimes to prove or disprove an assertion from exploration processing. Examples of assertions include:

- Children, from the ages of 2½ to 4, love Barney.
- Baseball is the national pastime.
- Republicans run Congress.
- People save more money as they grow older because their children demand fewer resources.
- Flight attendants are less fertile than the average individual, because the time spent at a high altitude affects their bodies.

Hypotheses that come from the exploration process have been deemed:

- Useful to the corporation
- Likely to be true

It is the data miner's job to determine the truth of the assertions made by the explorer.

A Symbiotic Relationship

There is a symbiotic relationship between exploration processing and data mining, as demonstrated in Figure 10.1. Figure 10.1 shows that there is an ongoing

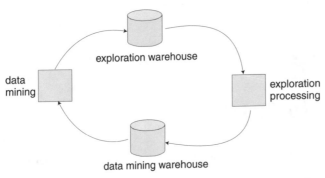

Figure 10.1 The symbiotic nature of exploration processing and data mining.

loop between exploration processing and data mining. Exploration processing feeds hypotheses to the data miner and is, in turn, fed an analysis of the hypotheses as well as suggestions for future investigations. It is very normal for the data miner to make discoveries and observations along the way to data mining. The data miner feeds these discoveries and observations to the explorer for future reference and refinement.

The data miner operates within boundaries set by the businessperson. The data miner is concerned both with the scope of the assumption and the source of data needed to populate the data mining data warehouse.

As a rule, the explorer will supply the data miner with data that is useful for analysis, a sort of "starter kit." Upon receiving the starter kit, the data miner will want to supplement with more data for in-depth analysis. The data miner is looking to create as large a data mining data warehouse as possible with as many occurrences of data as possible. The data miner needs the large volume of data to thoroughly prove or disprove assertions made by the explorer. As a general rule, the explorer provides only a fraction of the data that is needed by the data miner.

The data miner is free to go to as many sources as possible to obtain more occurrences of data: external sources, internal sources, and archival sources. Of course, the miner must take care that the data being sought is of the proper quality. To this end, he or she is often faced with the task of scrubbing the data as it comes into the system.

Another issue facing the miner is the structure of the data that is inside the data mining data warehouse. The flexibility of the data allows the explorer to shape and reshape data as desired; however, the data miner has a different set of needs. He or she does not need flexibility nearly as much as he or she needs performance. The data miner has already identified assumptions and the hypotheses at the outset of the mining process. The most efficient form of data for the data miner is a flat file: Data relationships are already created inside the record, and the flat file addresses nothing but the hypotheses and assumptions that are of interest to the data miner. The flat-file structure is ideal for selecting, counting, and summarizing data efficiently. Because of its efficiency in processing, the flat-file structure is able to accommodate very large amounts of data.

The flat-file structure amalgamates data of different varieties into the record, for example:

- Part ID
    - Part description
    - Part unit of measure
    - Vendor ID for part
    - Vendor description of part
    - Engineering bom ID
    - Engineering cost of production
    - Engineering length of production
    - Sales amount
    - Sales list price
    - Sales-expediting code
    - Sales order lead time
    - Sales forecast amount

- Production control manufacturing resource planning (MRP) code
    - Production control inventory-to-assembly time – production control item code
    - Marketing time-to-market code – marketing marginal cost ratio
    - Marketing source supplier code

Once the data miner has selected and cleansed the data, the miner merges it into a single record that can be processed efficiently and simply by using tools of calculation.

Degrees of Truth

The data miner looks at data in two ways:

1. Is the assertion true at all?
2. If the assertion is true, then to what degree is it true?

The first proposition is deceptively simple, because there are many ways that an assertion can be true:

- An assertion can be true because A caused B.

- An assertion can be true because A is directly correlated to B, but A does not cause B.

- An assertion can be true because A is indirectly correlated to B.

Even if an assertion is untrue, it can take different forms:

- An assertion appears to be true because A appears to correlate to B, but in fact A is not related to B at all.

- An assertion is simply not true. Any relationship between A and B is purely random.

The data miner is faced with a series of choices. If there is some element of truth in the assertion that is handed to the data miner, then a second level of analysis applies. The second level of analysis is not so much concerned with proving or disproving truth, but with examining the degree of truth. In other words, if something is true, is it true all the time? Part of the time? Some of the time? Only on certain occasions? Under some conditions?

Examples of Degree of Truth

Suppose the explorer has passed the assertion to the data miner that people who drive red cars have more accidents than people who drive cars of other colors. The data miner finds that people with red cars have:

- About 0.07 percent more accidents than people who drive black cars
- About 0.12 percent fewer accidents than people who drive white cars
- About 0.01 percent more accidents than people who drive tan cars
- About 0.04 percent fewer accidents than people who drive green cars

Although there are small differences in the rate of accidents, the difference is not meaningful. There is, then, no statistical significance to the rate of accidents that a car owner has and the color of his or her car. The assertion can be stated to be not true.

Now let's examine another assertion: Female voters like Bill Clinton. On the surface, the assertion is true because there certainly are women voters who like Clinton. However, not all women voters like Clinton. In this case, the strength of the assertion needs to be investigated. A good measure of the strength of the proposition is how many women voters cast their ballot for Clinton. In the 1996 Presidential election, 65 percent of women voted for Clinton. Therefore, the strength of the assertion is that it is true (or at least was true at the time of the election) about 65 percent of the time.

Now, let's consider looking at another assertion: College graduates by the age of 40 make more money than non–college graduates. A simple way to examine this assertion is to find the average salary of college graduates at age 40 and compare that number with the average salary of non–college graduates at age 40. The data miner finds that the average salary of the college graduate at age 40 is $52,000, whereas the average salary of the non–college graduate at age 40 is $39,000. Therefore, the assertion is true.

The economic analysis that is presented by the data miner is a bit misleading because some non–college graduates make much more money than college graduates. The data miner digs deeper and comes up with a different, more sophisticated representation of the differences between the salary levels of the college and non–college graduate.

Figure 10.2 shows two bell-shaped curves placed on top of each other. One bell curve represents the salaries of college graduates at age 40. The other bell curve represents the salaries of non–college graduates at age 40. The juxtaposition of the two bell curves on top of each other shows a much more accurate picture of the strength of this assertion.

There are other ways to portray the strength of an assertion. Consider the assertion: As men age, they tend to become more overweight. The calculation of overweight is determined by taking the average weight of a population and comparing it with the medically accepted ideal body weight. The data miner creates the following analysis that shows the strength of the assertion:

AGE	POUNDS OVERWEIGHT
20	2.6
25	3.1
30	3.4
35	6.2
40	5.6
45	7.8
50	10.1
55	11.6
60	9.3

Not only is this assertion true, but the data miner has also quantified exactly how true it is.

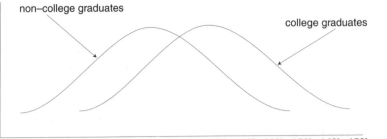

Figure 10.2 Comparing the salaries of college graduates with non–college graduates.

Exploration, Mining, and the Value Development Process

Data miners are not born, nor do they function only as data miners. At times they function as explorers, businesspeople, consumers, and in a host of other roles. Roles are functions performed at a point in time when particular tasks need to be executed. Thus "real-world" exploring and mining have to be distinguished from the ideal type categorizations presented here. On the road to business value, an effective team does not rigidly define roles. The most effective data miners, in trying to return value for effort, migrate through roles during various stages in the process.

The first role usually assumed by this individual is that of the business consultant. The most effective participants come to the value chain with a base knowledge of the business. While this knowledge is not absolutely necessary, having business knowledge accelerates the discovery process and allows for more effective communication. Having expertise in the business also opens the door to full partnership between the business individual and the individual performing the mining or exploration. These types of partnership lead to rapid acceleration of activity from the brainstorming process. The acceptance by the business individual of the support individual as a partner in the process blurs the line between steps in the value process. This is akin to the concept of *fuzzy logic*. That is, in the most effective teams, role inversion occurs. Role inversion leads to a better perspective for both parties. For example, it is the business individual who winds up arguing the implications of the data while the analyst focuses on marketing implications and profitability concerns. Another effect of this teaming is the generation of multiple parallel points of interest in the value chain all being examined together.

As the analyst slides into the exploration phase, he or she begins to construct the exploration warehouse. This does not imply that at times this individual does not go back to business partner role or consider data mining implications. The only characterization of this phase is that the majority of the time is spent in the process of setting up and using an exploration environment. Nor is the analyst necessarily the technician who sets up the exploration environment. More often, the individual communicates the requirement to a host of players including system administrators, database administrators, infrastructure support personnel, and of course the all-important businessperson who provides the funding for the process. Often during this phase, in addition to being explorer, the individual is playing project manager. As with any individual who brings new functionality to an organization, in order to obtain the business value, it is necessary to train and educate a host of peripheral players based upon the key players' prior experience.

Out of the exploration phase rises a set of ideas that require more confirmation. The change in focus determines a change in tools and a change in data. The change in tools and data signals the transition to the mining phase. While the idea type states that this is a confirmation process, discovery does occur during the mining process in the real world. Further, there are individuals who begin the value process using mining techniques and return to exploration for additional value. This too is perfectly acceptable. Most often there is an iterative relationship between exploration and mining requiring the acquisition of data from the data warehouse several times and the reloading of both environments.

The only absolute is that the objective of both exploration and mining is new net business value. This value most frequently is incremental. To obtain the value of the process, the circle closes with business action and follow-up. Too often, the value of exploration and mining is lost because of the failure of the business to seize opportunity. Why does this happen?

There are many reasons why a business does not or cannot seize opportunity from the results of the exploration and mining processes. Some are valid resource-based reasons such as lack of capital or staff. Others are procedural or cultural and can be watched for as obstacles to opportunity.

One pitfall involves understanding the real decision-making process in companies. In many companies information is only utilized to support a position that is intuitively held by the key decision maker. These decision makers will usually return to the analyst with a request to explore a slightly altered hypothesis. The hope is that the narrowed or altered scope will support the already firmly held opinion-based decision. While this type of organization provides work for the analyst, that work is often less than gratifying. This type of behavior is most frequently found in family-owned businesses or in young, rapidly expanding organizations where the original entrepreneur is still operationally involved.

A second pitfall is referred to as the "NIH" or "not invented here" syndrome. Unfortunately, this seems to be collateral to the famous first-mover effect. In the first-mover effect, a company is often successful because it moves decisively into a new, evolving business area with adequate resources. This effect has been seen in retail warehousing (i.e., toys, sporting goods, home maintenance materials) and the Internet. While the business is rising to the market saturation point, the initial paradigm works. Unfortunately, as market success begins to crown, the very approach that caused the initial success becomes the limiting factor. Thus, not one of the key first-mover companies in the retail warehousing marketplace was capable of also being the first mover into the same specialty in the Internet space. It was inconceivable that an alternate marketing approach could invade the same content space; after all, it was "not invented here."

A third pitfall is the classic "analysis paralysis." This is characteristic of firms that have large, slow-moving bureaucracies. The exploration and mining processes are supported and sanctioned in these firms, but that does not imply that the work product is used in a timely fashion. Frequently when results are presented a request is made to go back and "confirm" the work product. This occurs when the results indicate a need for change or potential organizational exposure. The response is to then to send the analyst back to the information factory to reconfirm the results. In a highly volatile business environment, the time needed to reanalyze is often just enough to miss a key opportunity.

If these are the attributes of organizational behavior that can subvert the work product of exploration and mining, what are the attributes of an organization that can leverage the work product for business advantage?

The first characteristic is that the organization values information. It assumes that the work product is meaningful and therefore has value. Often this attitude is conveyed by the way in which data miners and explorers are interacted with. When the business decision makers call for exploration, listen and ask for clarification, and are willing to take risks, the conditions are right to seize opportunity.

A second characteristic required for success is the means to execute. Many firms see opportunity but do not have the financial resources to execute the idea. Successful firms exploit the knowledge themselves, seek partners in funding, or sell the information. All three approaches result in revenue and profit to different degrees. All three use the work product produced to gain benefit for the firm's stakeholders.

A final characteristic of a firm that seizes opportunity is a propensity to act. This requires recognition that change is perpetual. In a firm that accepts perpetual change as the norm, data mining can reach the highest form. Rather than reactive description, much of the effort goes in into proactive prediction. This predictive modeling function is well known in the high-stakes financial services industry. Predictive modeling is also extremely well established in operations research. With the democratization of exploration and data mining due to tools at all platform levels, small and medium-size firms can seize opportunity.

In Summary

Data mining not only proves or disproves an assertion, it also assesses the strength of the assertion. It is necessary to link data mining to the business so that the company can use data mining to examine avenues of interest and possible exploitation. Data mining and exploration are mutually complimentary processes in the chain of beneficence. Data miners can be explorers, farmers, business consultants, and technologists at different stages of the value generation process. To some extent, data mining is defined in the real world by what data miners do. There are obstacles to success in data mining and exploration beyond the technical realm. These obstacles are primarily cultural. Successful firms often have altered their cultures to accept information as valuable and to deal with perpetual change. The secret to success in the data mining process is to act upon the information.

CHAPTER 11

Exploration and Data Mining Technologies

Production is not the application of tools to materials, but logic to work.

—PETER DRUCKER

E xploration processing entails loading data into a data base, selecting and analyzing rows of data, comparing and calculating against those rows, and displaying the results. Data mining technology differs from exploration processing in a few minor respects. Among these differences data mining has these characteristics:

- Linear processing
- Lack of joins
- Analysis of relatively clean data
- Use of algorithms
- Unanticipated groupings of observations

Exploration processing and data mining technology do not cover online transaction processing (OLTP), complicated backup and recovery processing, or update integrity, making them much simpler than their OLTP database management system (DBMS) brethren.

However, exploration processing and data mining technology are not without complications. The DBMS that accommodates exploration processing and data mining technology must deal with large amounts of data, due to the history and the detail encompassed. Also, data often gets tangled into unrecognizable shapes. This occurs because of the diversity of sources of data and the fact that in the real world there are less-than-perfect definitions of the data, some that overlap while others are actually in conflict. The explorer and data miner need to shape, and reshape data into forms never imagined by a traditional data base designer. Finally, the explorer and the data miner are constantly looking for relationships and associations in the data that are hidden across different kinds of data types. The only way to make those associations come alive is through Boolean processing. This additional consideration slows the technical processing and often requires intellectual pauses in the analytical process to reevaluate the true meaning of a definition after several AND, OR, or NOR conditions are put together. What started out as a simple meta data definition ends up far from simple.

It is true that any standard DBMS can be used for exploration processing and data mining. It is also true that almost any language—COBOL, PL-I, Fortran, C—can be used to do exploration processing and data mining processing. However, using a general-purpose DBMS and language technology for exploration processing and data mining is like using a Model T car in the Indianapolis 500. To be effective, specialized tools are required.

This chapter will outline two approaches to exploration processing and one approach to data mining:

1. The token-based approach of the Sand/HDS Nucleus product for exploration processing.

2. The in-memory hardware and software approach of the White Cross Systems Data Exploration Server product for exploration processing.

3. The analytical approach of SAS Institute for data mining.

The Token-Based Approach

Despite the similarity of names, the *token-based approach* to exploration processing has nothing to do with token ring technology. The token-based approach to exploration processing compresses data in a specialized manner and is optimized for Boolean expression processing. The token-based approach provides an infrastructure that is optimal for exploration.

The token-based exploration warehouse is fed from external data, from the enterprise data warehouse, or from near-line storage (Figure 11.1). All three are legitimate sources for data going into a tokenized exploration warehouse.

To understand tokenization, consider a simple relational table, as seen in Figure 11.2. It shows relational data that might exist for a human resources table. The data shown is in third normal form, but there are still redundancies: The same first name occurs in many places, the same last name occurs in many places, the value for city and state appear in many places. The more data there is, the greater the amount of redundancy.

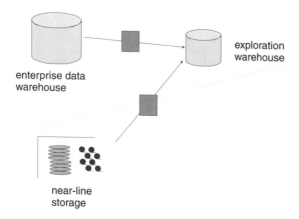

enterprise data
warehouse

exploration
warehouse

near-line
storage

Figure 11.1　The exploration warehouse is fed from
external data, the enterprise data warehouse, or the
near-line storage component.

Redundancy can be minimized by putting the relational table in a tokenized
form. The first step to creating a tokenized table is to create token tables. Figure 11.3 shows the token tables that are created from the data found in the relational tables.

In Figure 11.4, the token tables that are created are really domain tables. In
other words, the domain of values found in the relational table is used to create
separate token tables.

rows in a relational table -

1 - 20398	Bill Inmon	male	San Diego	CA	Jul	18	1997	programmer	Mills Annex
2 - 10982	Joe Lautze	male	Los Angeles	CA	Aug	13	1982	analyst	Fort Mason
3 - 10827	Mary Jones	female	El Paso	TX	Sep	01	1987	end user	Johnson Terrace
4 - 20817	Jim Wilson	male	Ft Worth	TX	Jan	02	1962	programmer	Mills Annex
5 - 19082	Mary Johnson	female	Dallas	TX	Feb	15	1996	analyst	Fort Mason
6 - 17620	Don Jones	male	San Francisco	CA	Jul	10	1997	programmer	Mills Annex
7 - 01982	Don Wilson	male	San Jose	CA	Jun	21	1995	analyst	Fort Mason
8 - 20813	Jean Inmon	female	San Diego	CA	Jul	14	1992	programmer	Johnson Terrace
9 - 18726	Joe Johnson	male	San Jose	CA	Aug	13	1991	programmer	Fort Mason
10 - 01872	Mary Donzetti	female	San Francisco	CA	Jul	19	1995	analyst	Fort Mason
11 - 00287	Bill Thomas	male	San Diego	CA	Nov	12	1997	programmer	Mill Annex
12 - 01876	Jean Wilson	female	San Jose	CA	Aug	15	1998	analyst	Johnson Terrace
13 - 17765	Martha Kirk	female	Dallas	TX	Jun	10	1996	programmer	Fort Mason
14 - 29871	Pat Thompson	male	San Jose	CA	Apr	18	1994	analyst	Mills Annex
15 - 00189	Rick Wilson	male	El Paso	TX	Mar	19	1995	programmer	Fort Mason
16 - 01862	John Jones	male	Ft Worth	TX	Mar	18	1994	analyst	Mills Annex
17 - 08972	Joan Kirk	female	Austin	TX	May	21	1998	programmer	Johnson Terrace
18 - 10662	John Thomas	male	San Jose	CA	Jun	21	1993	analyst	Mills Annex
19 - 02663	Mary Trepte	female	Dallas	TX	Jul	19	1999	programmer	Fort Mason
20 - 01887	Don Smith	male	Ft Worth	TX	Aug	18	1997	analyst	Mills Annex

Figure 11.2　A simple relational table.

the token tables

first name	last name		city	month	
01 - Bill	01 - Inmon	gender	01 - San Diego	01 - Jul	year
02 - Joe	02 - Lautze	01 - male	02 - Los Angeles	02 - Aug	01 - 1997
03 - Mary	03 - Jones	02 - female	03 - El Paso	03 - Sep	02 - 1982
04 - Jim	04 - Wilson		04 - Ft Worth	04 - Jan	03 - 1987
05 - Don	05 - Johnson	state	05 - Dallas	05 - Feb	04 - 1962
06 - Jean	06 - Donzetti	01 - CA	06 - San Francisco	06 - Jun	05 - 1996
07 - Martha	07 - Thomas	02 - TX	07 - San Jose	07 - Nov	06 - 1995
08 - Pat	08 - Kirk		08 - Austin	08 - Apr	07 - 1992
09 - Rick	09 - Thompson	position			08 - 1991
10 - Joan	10 - Trepte	01 - programmer	location		09 - 1998
11 - John	11 - Smith	02 - analyst	01 - Mills Annex		10 - 1994
		03 - end user	02 - Fort Mason		11 - 1993
			03 - Johnson Terrace		12 - 1999
					13 - 1997

Figure 11.3 Token tables created from the relational tables.

After the token tables are created, the tokenized data base can be created by taking each row in the relational table and replacing the values of data that are found in the row with the bitmap representation of the data. In doing so, the row is greatly shrunk. Figure 11.4 shows the creation of the tokenized table.

As the data is tokenized, it is also compressed. Depending on the type and amount of data, it is not unusual to see an order-of-magnitude compression. If the relational table were 100 gigabytes, then the tokenized table would be 10 gigabytes. The larger the exploration warehouse grows, the more compressed the tokenized data becomes. Therefore, the more data there is, the greater the compression ratio.

There are several implications of tokenization and compression of data in the exploration warehouse. As data is compressed, the cost of hardware goes down. As data is compressed into sets that are optimal for Boolean processing, the data

the tokenized data

```
01 - 20398,01,01,01,01,01,01,18,01,01,01
02 - 10982,02,02,01,02,01,02,13,02,02,02
03 - 10827,03,03,02,03,02,03,01,03,03,03
04 - 20817,04,04,01,04,02,04,02,04,01,01
05 - 19082,03,05,02,05,02,05,15,04,02,02
06 - 17620,05,03,01,06,01,01,10,01,01,01
07 - 01982,05,04,01,07,01,06,21,06,01,02
08 - 20813,06,01,02,01,01,01,14,07,01,03
09 - 18726,02,05,01,07,01,02,13,08,01,02
10 - 01872,03,06,02,06,01,01,19,06,02,02
11 - 00287,01,07,01,01,01,07,12,01,01,01
12 - 01876,06,04,02,07,01,02,15,09,02,03
13 - 17765,07,08,02,05,02,06,10,05,01,02
14 - 29871,08,09,01,07,01,08,18,10,02,01
15 - 00189,09,04,01,03,02,09,19,06,01,02
16 - 01862,11,03,01,04,02,09,18,10,02,01
17 - 08972,10,08,02,08,02,09,21,09,01,03
18 - 10662,11,07,01,07,01,06,21,11,02,01
19 - 02663,03,10,02,04,02,01,18,12,02,02
20 - 01887,05,11,01,04,02,02,18,11,02,01
```

Figure 11.4 The tokenized table.

can be processed very efficiently. In cases in which most or all of the tokenized data can be placed into main memory, processing speeds are very fast.

One of the interesting features of tokenization is how queries are processed. Figure 11.5 shows the important steps in the life of a query. As a query enters a tokenized system, the parameters of the query are tokenized. Once the query parameters are tokenized, the query can be issued against the tokenized data. The result set is created and is then detokenized. To the end user, it appears that regular Structured Query Language (SQL) or other query processing has occurred. In fact, the query has been executed against very different data than that found in the regular SQL relational environment.

One feature of token-based processing is executing in main memory. Main memory execution can occur because of the shrinkage of data that occurs during the tokenization process. Figure 11.6 shows that as much processing as possible occurs in main memory.

As long as most or all tokenized query processing occurs in main memory, performance is very good. However, in the case of very large amounts of data or very small amounts of main memory (or both!), performance of tokenized data will suffer. The more query processing that has to occur in the hard disk, the worse performance becomes.

One of the important considerations of the tokenized approach is the tokenization algorithm used to create the token tables.

As data is entered into the tokenized tables, it must be tokenized. Some data is very easy to tokenize and other data is not. Tokenized vendors offer prefabricated token tables for such data as names, cities, streets, and states. By offering prefabricated token tables, the vendor short-circuits many complex problems.

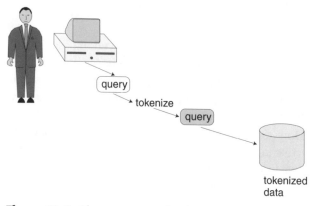

Figure 11.5 The parameters in the query are tokenized before the query is sent into execution.

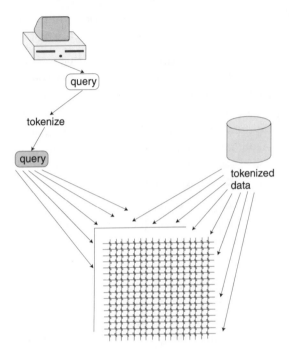

Figure 11.6 As much data as possible is placed in main memory before the execution of the query.

In-Memory Exploration Processing

The second approach to exploration processing is *in-memory processing*. An example of in-memory processing is White Cross Systems Data Exploration Server. This sophisticated exploration DBMS engine for large databases actually uses several technologies, of which in-memory processing is one. See the upcoming section on White Cross for more information.

The White Cross Data Exploration Server was conceived and designed from the ground up to interrogate all of the detail in large data bases. It produces answers at a speed that allows knowledge workers to perform in-depth investigations and ask ad hoc questions. High-speed exploration of all the detail in massively sized data bases is impossible for technologies that have grown from yesterday's information architecture. However, White Cross started with a clean sheet, allowing it to leverage their expertise in massively parallel processor (MPP) database design and merge that with a vision that random access memory (RAM) would become a cost-effective approach for data base processing.

Figure 11.7 shows that an in-memory exploration warehouse can be created from an enterprise data warehouse, external data, or from near-line storage. The

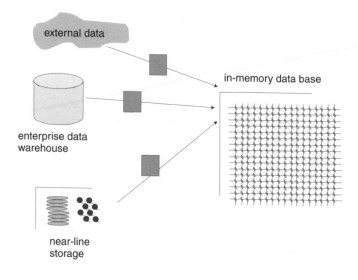

Figure 11.7 In-memory data can be loaded from external data, the enterprise warehouse, and near-line storage.

process of creating an in-memory exploration warehouse is straightforward. Data is simply loaded directly from its source into the exploration warehouse into a server that is memory based. Once the data is loaded, there is no input/output (I/O) that is required to search and access the data in the in-memory exploration warehouse. As such, many standard data base constraints do not apply. Figure 11.8 shows that no indexes are needed, for example.

When a query is made against the in-memory data base, it is faster to search the entire data base than it is to create and maintain an index. Most data base designers and technicians have never before worked in an environment in which this was the case.

Full table scans are also not a problem. In a conventional DBMS, the DBA avoids full table scans like the plague, because they eat up system resources. However, with an in-memory DBMS for exploration processing, a full table scan

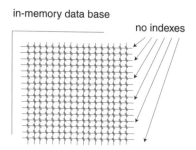

Figure 11.8 No indexes are needed for an in-memory exploration warehouse.

is natural and easy. Because full table scans are not a problem with an in-memory DBMS, doing complex joins and merges is also not a problem. There is a very comfortable fit between exploration processing and in-memory DBMS.

White Cross

White Cross is an exploration platform for large databases used for data exploration that processes very large volumes of data. However, in-memory processing is only one element of White Cross's architecture that is used to satisfy the explorer's needs.

The challenge is that the explorer's paths to data during exploration cannot be predetermined. The classic methods for minimizing response times in OLTP are dependent on minimizing I/O by using key indexes to key data items and by clustering data that tends to be accessed together.

In OLTP or simple fixed-reporting applications, the optimization of a predetermined path is a good strategy, because in the database design, the designer can predict how the data will be accessed and thereby decide upon which indexing strategy will be employed and/or how data should be colocated. Even in online analytical processing (OLAP) systems, the designer has some foreknowledge of how the data will be accessed to determine the optimal content and structure of the multidimensional cubes.

This is not the case at all for exploration processing. By definition, no one knows which data will be accessed or how the data will be accessed until the very moment the query arrives. Furthermore, queries are likely to be different from each other.

The problem of not having foreknowledge or predictability of access becomes even worse for large bodies of data. Approaches that rely on multiple indexing strategies, predetermined summaries, or multiple different organizations and orderings of the data become exponentially more complex, difficult, and costly as the volume of data rises.

As processing power and RAM decrease in cost, it has become practicable to conceive of systems that can bring brute force to bear on the problem. Even more recently, standard communications technologies have become economical and fast to the point that large numbers of processors can be linked together. This has made it possible to place large amounts of data in memory and to apply large amounts of processing power to search and analyze data extremely fast in a random manner.

The big advantage of an in-memory DBMS is that of speed. An in-memory DBMS is the fastest in the world. If raw speed is needed, an in-memory DBMS is what is required.

For example, suppose a company is monitoring market conditions that are changing by the minute. With an in-memory DBMS, the user can keep track of different conditions dynamically. At one second, one set of conditions can be checked, then at the next instant another set of conditions can be checked, and so forth. The results can be recalculated across many different sets of variables instantaneously.

This is a vital capability for Web-based enterprises in which patterns of behavior are changing and developing at point-and-click speed. For example, many organizations now seek to combine analysis of Web site activity with other data to better understand preferences, tendencies, and needs, and thereby offer more relevant information to Web site visitors. This is not a trivial activity—Web sites record millions of page views every day.

One of the major misconceptions of an in-memory DBMS for exploration processing is that an in-memory data base cannot handle as much data as desired. There is no technological limit on data placed inside an in-memory DBMS. If there is a limit, it is an economical one, not a technological one. You can load as much data into an in-memory DBMS as you can afford.

One of the peculiar attributes of an in-memory DBMS is that it is capable of detecting massive and instantaneous "sea changes." Figure 11.9 illustrates this capability. A sea change occurs where massive amounts of detail data change simultaneously and instantaneously. (The term *sea change* refers to the phenomenon of when whole schools of small fish that are swimming together simultaneously change direction. A marine drill sergeant would look at such coordination in awe!) With an in-memory DBMS, such a phenomenon can be detected and observed with ease.

In-Memory versus Token-Based

An interesting thing happens when exploration technology is applied to the 72-hour query. With standard relational technology running a standard DBMS technology, an explorer query is likely to take 72 hours or more. The reasons why an explorer's query takes so long in a standard environment are that:

- A lot of detail is required.
- A lot of history is required.
- The data needs to be reshaped.

By going to either token-based or in-memory technology, performance improves dramatically. Why does performance improve so much? Because:

- The software that is used for exploration processing is specially designed for set processing and has special "smarts" for analytic operations.

9:10 A.M.		9:35 A.M.	
Oracle—	+.75	Oracle—	−.25
Coca Cola—	+.25	Coca Cola—	−.16
IBM—	+.1.00	IBM—	−2.25
ATT—	+1.25	ATT—	−.25
Microsoft—	+1.16	Microsoft—	−.16
GM—	+.50	GM—	−2.50
EMC—	+.1.16	EMC—	−.75
Merck—	+.75	Merck—	−1.75
Disney—	+1.00	Disney—	−2.25

Figure 11.9 A sea change that has occurred as the stock market goes from 9:10 A.M. to 9:35 A.M.

- The majority or all of the processing occurs in memory where I/O is not a consideration.
- The most advanced DBMS combines in-memory processing with architectural constructs that are suitable for large-scale DBMS processing such as MPP.
- The processing is exclusively exploration, so that there is no interference from other transactional processing.

What, then, are the considerations for choosing between an in-memory approach or a token-based approach? The two key criteria are volumes of data and how static or dynamic the data is.

Large Data Bases

A parallel in-memory approach is capable of handling much more data than a token-based approach. The token-based approach works fine until the point is reached at which it can no longer handle all the query processing in memory. At that point, performance begins to degrade. In addition, the reload or refreshment of large volumes of data cannot be done frequently in a graceful manner.

Conversely, an in-memory system that employs parallel load and update methods can be scaled to readily achieve fast data update or load times as well as fast query response times.

Static or Dynamic

When comparing the in-memory approach with the token-based approach, it is instructive to ask which approach fits into which environment the best. Figure 11.10 shows that if the environment is static, then the token-based approach probably works best. However, if the need is for a dynamic exploration warehouse, then the in-memory approach is probably optimal.

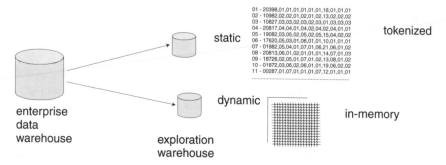

Figure 11.10 There is an affinity for tokenized technology in static warehouses and in-memory technology in dynamic warehouses.

Another difference between the capabilities is in terms of the amount of data that is handled by each approach. The token-based approach works fine until the point is reached at which it can no longer handle all the query processing in memory. At that point performance degrades. However, an in-memory DBMS is capable of handling as much data as the explorer can afford.

In any case, an interesting thing happens to the explorer's 72-hour query. With standard relational technology running a standard enterprise data warehouse, it was a given that when an explorer ran a query, it would run in 72 hours. In actuality, although explorer queries ran a long time, very few actually ran in 72 hours. The reason why the queries ran for so long is because the explorer was looking at:

- Detail
- History
- Contorted data

By going to either token-based processing or in-memory processing, performance improves dramatically. Why does performance improve so much? Because:

- Data is optimized for Boolean set processing.
- Most or all processing occurs in memory where I/O is no consideration.
- Processing is exclusively exploration. There is no interference from transaction-based processing.

SAS Institute's Enterprise Miner

For many years, SAS Institute has been the world leader in data mining. Long before data warehousing became popular, SAS was supporting data mining. The advent of data warehousing merely provided a framework for SAS's data mining products to become institutionalized.

SAS provides a holistic approach to data mining under the name Enterprise Miner. Enterprise Miner is part of a larger infrastructure that provides support for OLAP processing, data warehousing, and visualization of results.

To begin data mining, data can be loaded from virtually any platform into SAS Institute's Enterprise Miner. Once the data is captured and cleansed, analysis done by SAS Institute's Enterprise Miner can execute on a wide variety of platforms—mainframe, Unix, NT, desk top.

One of the features of SAS Institute's Enterprise Miner is the integration of process with product. SAS Institute's Enterprise Miner provides a methodology for data mining called Sample, Explore, Modify Model, Assess (SEMMA). SEMMA is the result of SAS and their customer base doing data mining for many years. SEMMA provides guidance for executing data mining along with the SAS product line.

One of the features of SAS Institute's Enterprise Miner is the ability to operate on samples. The importance and effectiveness of using sampling techniques is an integral part of the SEMMA process. By using sampling techniques, SAS is able to accommodate analysis against very large amounts of data.

Another feature of SAS Institute's Enterprise Miner is the support of standard data mining models, in particular:

- Linear and logistic regression analysis
- Decision tree analysis
- Neural networks

SAS also features sophisticated displays of data and user interfaces of almost every variety:

- Three-dimensional Pareto charts
- Simple point-to-point displays
- Colored pie charts

One of the really nice features of SAS Institute's Enterprise Miner is the ability to integrate the software into an exploration and data mining environment. SAS Institute's Enterprise Miner can be used strictly for data mining, or it can be used as a general-purpose tool for both data mining and exploration. Of course, SAS Institute's Enterprise Miner can be used also for exploration by itself, should that be something that is desired. The SAS analytical environment is versatile and robust, well beyond the capabilities of other products. In addition, the SAS Institute's Enterprise Miner fits inside a DSS environment in which the other components of the corporate information factory are also supported.

Why Focus on SAS?

There are many fine analytical tools in the marketplace. On any given day, a new tool or technique may evolve for a finite time into a niche position of leadership. However, over the long haul, certain organizations set the "gold" standard of the industry. SAS Institute is one of these organizations.

Under the leadership of Dr. James Goodnight, the SAS Institute nurtured the art and science of information discovery from a fledgling set of statistical routines run on a mainframe and primarily targeted at physical and social scientists into a robust set of commercially viable tools applicable to all known platforms and all approaches to knowledge discovery. In essence, the reason such attention is paid to SAS in this chapter is that it has moved from being simply a product to being regarded as an architectural standard. It is this standard against which other vendors and tools are often compared.

Additionally, by making the tool set available for use in academic institutions, the SAS Institute has provided industry with a base of trained analysts. The value to industry of this contribution should not be underestimated. It is estimated that there are over 3 million SAS users today.

In Summary

There are a host of exploration and data mining techniques. While three that are of interest have been discussed here, there are literally dozens. The choice of tool and technique is based upon the business need and available resources to meet that need. There is no one right technique. The explorer or miner should pick the technique that is appropriate for the problem at hand. Sometimes, when time is of the essence, a tool that is well known is preferable to a tool that may be technically superior and requires extensive technical setup. The object of the analysis is *to return business value!* The single biggest pitfall is called tool fixation! This occurs when the selection of the right tool becomes the focus, as opposed to obtaining business value. In conclusion, any technique that causes value to be obtained is the right technique.

CHAPTER 12

Business Communities of the Corporate Information Factory

A society of people having . . . common interests.

—WEBSTER'S UNABRIDGED DICTIONARY, 1979

The corporate information factory (CIF) is an ideal decision support environment for both tactical and strategic analyses. However, it is important to realize that different types of analyses and different types of users need their own milieus. We label users as farmers, tourists, explorers, miners, and operators. By grouping users with similar characteristics, we can gain a valuable head start in understanding, anticipating, and satisfying their needs.

This chapter will look at each of the five communities, broken down into the following topics:

- Description and examples
- Business characteristics
- Architectural requirements

Farmers

What comes to mind when you think of farmers? Old McDonald? Straw hats and tractors? They cultivate soil, sow seeds, pray for good weather, harvest their crops, go to market, and repeat the cycle the following season. Although this is a bit of an oversimplification, it's remarkable how well the farmer description fits certain CIF users, who also have:

- Well-defined requirements—crops.
- Consistent requirements—limited crop rotation.
- Data to create the answers—fields.
- Clear, concise queries—seeds.
- Access tool expertise—they know how to drive the combine.
- Sound business understanding—they know what their crops are worth.

Farmers usually come from the management or business-planning groups within the organization. Typical farmers in your corporation include:

- Financial analysts who are responsible for reporting on revenues and costs
- Sales and product analysts who determine how well a product is selling in some part of the world
- People who track campaigns or promotions from week to week
- Analysts who monitor the budget versus actual reports

Wherever they are in your organization, you can bet that they have a very good handle on the types of reports and analyses that they need to perform. Examples of farmers in businesses include:

- Product category managers
- Financial analysts
- Sales analysts

Farmer Business Characteristics

When you are building an environment for farmers, you will find they have the following:

Well-defined requirements.   Corporate information factory farmers know what they want and can generally express it clearly and concisely. For example, people who analyze product profitability or sales reports each month know exactly what data they want, how they want it displayed, when they want it, and what media they want it in.

Consistent requirements.   Farmers' requirements change very slowly, if at all, giving us a solid basis to begin growing our strategic decision support environment. This allows us to stabilize the environment, understand the iterative process, set up appropriate technologies, establish proper processes, and develop infrastructure for the less stable requirements of explorers, miners, and tourists.

Because their queries are predictable and routine, farmers also expect good response times. It is not unusual or unreasonable for the farmer to expect a subsecond's to a few seconds' response time on a report that he or she runs every Monday morning at 8:05 A.M. Because we have been fore-warned, we can set up the data base to facilitate these queries.

Data to create the answers. Most farmers struggled for a long time to capture strategic information without the CIF, so they understand the value of integrated, cleansed data. They tend to be some of the most satisfied users of the CIF because their requirements are so easily met and managed. The farmers are often the primary users of standard query data within the CIF.

They look to the CIF to supply automation (of reports), consistency (of data), reliability (of the technology), standardization (of calculations and algorithms), and reproducibility (of information).

Clear, concise queries. Farmers in the Decision Support System (DSS) world ordinarily submit repeating queries. What are the total sales for product A in market segment B over C time frame? How many customers bought product A through sales channel B during campaign C in the last month? They can also tell you the parameters that they will need to run these types of questions. They submit these queries with precise regularity (e.g., every Monday morning, every month end, every end of quarter). These queries are generally short and require only a small number of rows from the data base. Often, the farmer is only interested in current data—sales from this month, for example. They may do simple comparisons as well—this month to last month, this quarter to the same quarter last year.

Farmers almost always get an answer to their queries. Whereas the miner or explorer may or may not get an answer to their question, the farmer knows that he or she will get a response, even though it may not be what he or she expected or wanted to see.

Access tool expertise. For years, farmers were left to build their own reporting data bases to gather information. Therefore, they readily adopt new data access tools and easily begin using them.

Sound business understanding. Farmers run basic business intelligence reports routinely, glean information from them, study their trends for the future, and then report their findings back to the corporation. They are also, without doubt, the largest population of users of the CIF.

The farmers in our business enterprise track key performance metrics that report on the health of the business. Standard reports show the return on investment (ROI) of major decisions (e.g., opening a new store, running a new campaign, offering a specific mix of products), the costs and revenues associated with doing business, and balanced scorecard reports.

Many times, the farmer provides feedback on an explorer's predictions, which are based on patterns discovered in the exploration warehouse. The explorer may predict that the sale of a particular product may show a 50 percent increase in a certain segment of the country. It then falls on the farmer to track that prediction and to determine whether it is indeed increasing as predicted.

Architectural Requirements

The farmer sees the world in terms of both dimensions (product, market segment, campaign, sales channel) and metrics (revenue, cost, counts, transactions). Therefore, the farmer's DSS environment consists of multidimensional data marts found within the CIF. Each data mart is created from the known requirements for a particular function or capability (such as product profitability or sales channel analysis). Typically, these marts use either relational or multidimensional technologies. The slice-and-dice world of these technologies fits the usage patterns of farmers quite nicely.

If relational technology is used, data base design uses a star or a snowflake schema. If a multidimensional OLAP tool is chosen, a hierarchy of the dimensions along with the aggregated facts is determined for the predefined and pre-made cubes. Again, the ease of access and the response times that are associated with these technologies fit the farmer's world quite nicely. If a new report, cube, or query is needed, they often turn to a central information technology (IT) person for help.

Farmers' data is usually aggregated or summarized to a fairly high degree. Because the farmers know what they are looking for, they rarely need to see massive amounts of data. Nicely aggregated and summarized data gives them all the information they need to understand whether a product is doing well or as expected, whether a sales region is performing according to plan, whether a channel should be eliminated, and so forth. They will rarely need to drill down to the lowest level of detail found in the warehouse, so the farmer's access to the data warehouse itself may be restricted.

Farmers use the following technology and functionality:

- OLAP
- DSS
- Reporting
- Data Visualization

Tourists

Tourists generally come from the executives of companies or from very technical, Internet-savvy resources. Executives are among the most critical users of the CIF because their satisfaction—or dissatisfaction—can significantly impact the future viability of the factory.

Executives can be compared with tourists who are planning to visit Europe in seven days. They know that it's impossible to see everything in a week, and they typically focus in on a few cities, and within those cities, on a few sites. Experienced tourists leave some free time in case they want to spend additional time at one of the sites. Executives look at data the same way. They typically have key indicators of interest, and when one of these has an unexpected value, they want the ability to get more information.

Most tourists come from:

- Upper management (chief officers, vice presidents)
- Middle management (directors, group managers)

Tourist Business Characteristics

It is very important for the CIF architect to recognize the characteristics of tourists. Tourists, just like in the world of travel, often lack patience and knowledge; therefore, some immediate gratification is necessary to keep them happy.

Broad business perspective.   Tourists have a broad perspective of business in general, the industry within which the company operates, and the company itself. They often have detailed knowledge of at least one major aspect of the business, but not of many areas.

Tourists need to have basic information to assess the overall health of the company. They receive information about the profitability or sales volume of the company as a whole first. If they are satisfied, they move on to the next metric of interest. If something seemed out of line (for example, sales volume significantly exceeded expectations), then tourists would look further into the sales volume measures, possibly requesting a breakdown by product line or division.

Many tourists have an intuitive feel for the direction and health of the company. Tourists' need to validate their intuitions makes them hard to please and difficult to predict and plan for.

Internet awareness.   The advent of the Internet has been helpful in drawing tourists to the computer. It has also been responsible for high expectations with respect to data access. As a user of the Internet, the tourist becomes accustomed to a fairly consistent graphical user interface. This interface does not require a lot of typing, giving him or her the ability to search large banks of data and to use information from one search to trigger another search by finding a place on the screen that is highlighted. When the pointer is over that place, it changes shape and the executive knows that by selecting it, another screen will appear.

Tourists in the CIF expect the same ease of use from corporate information. They want the environment to produce only the data that they need at that moment and to not flood them with extraneous data. A proactive interface indicating when information of importance or interest is available would be ideal for this community.

Selection criteria. Because of the plethora of information that is available to tourists, they need to be selective in what they read. For example, the tourist who is planning a trip has access to a myriad of books, tapes, and Internet sites. He or she cannot possibly read everything available. Using some set of criteria, he or she focuses on a few resources, perhaps based on previous experience with a particular series of tour books, other books referenced in the series chosen, or friends' recommendations.

Corporate information factory tourists operate in a similar manner. They do not have the time to look at everything; therefore, they need a way to help them quickly identify the items of interest. Through experience, they have identified key performance indicators, and they look at these regularly. Other information needs are not as predictable. If they read an article about a competitor in a business magazine, they may want to find corresponding information from their company for comparative purposes. In addition, they may need to find facts to substantiate information from a fellow executive. This characteristic, more than any other, makes life difficult for the IT professional who is responsible for the tourists in the CIF environment. An interface must be created so that the CIF tourist can select topics and areas of interest, and then a mechanism must be created to monitor these and to indicate to the tourist that an event requiring his or her attention has happened.

Tourists use the following technologies:

- Query
- Reporting
- EIS
- OLAP
- Intranet/Internet

Architectural Requirements

The tourist's usage characteristics dictate aspects of the architecture. The most significant areas that are impacted are the meta data and the meta data interface, the end-user interface, and the support. When tourists request information, they expect a very small return set, as well as an architecture that is resilient enough to meet the needs of the farmers and explorers and that also satisfies their volume-related needs.

Meta Data

Tourists have two types of queries that they usually execute. The first type is research that is related to key performance indicators. For these queries, once the tourist knows how to get to the information, he or she is unlikely to look at the meta data. When the tourist receives the requested information, he or she will assume that it is complete and accurate. Should there be a problem during the loading process (e.g., data from one of the regions was not processed), or perhaps a quality problem that impacted the completeness or accuracy of any requested data, the architecture should be structured to automatically alert the tourist of the problem.

The tourist may also want to get information to satisfy a special request, and the architecture should provide a means to find it. One approach is to provide keywords for searching the meta data. If an automotive executive reads in an industry periodical report that sales of sports utility vehicles to women aged 35 to 44 are on the rise, he or she should be able to locate the company's data without needing to start with the sales key performance indicator and drilling down. The appropriate information can be obtained by providing a keyword search to the meta data, and by providing the ability to seamlessly execute the required query. In addition to finding the query, meta data about the query must also be provided. The meta data also provides information about the quality of the data, the subset of the company included (for example, is the information provided for worldwide sales or just for U.S. sales?), and so on.

End-User Interface

Many tourists are comfortable with the Internet; therefore, they expect predictable responses using icons, to receive information both textually and pictorially, the ability to search for additional information, and the ability to drill down for more information based on the answer to their initial questions. For these people, minimum expectations are set. The CIF must provide similar capabilities, and it needs to provide them in a comparable way.

Some tourists don't use the Internet and rely on their assistants to retrieve information. These users will require some training on obtaining information. Once they understand the concepts, an interface must also be provided. For some, it may be advisable to introduce them to the concepts incrementally. Initially, they may be provided with a set of icons, one for each key performance indicator, and they receive the indicator metrics simply by pressing the icon. Once they are familiar with that concept, drill-down capabilities can be provided so that they can navigate through the information. After they become comfortable with this, they can be provided with the full search capabilities of both the data and the meta data.

Support

As we have noted before, executives are important CIF users because they influence future funding for the CIF. The CIF program manager must recognize their perspective. Their commitment to the program is dependent on both their satisfaction with the retrieval mechanisms and with the support provided. Although the Help desk may provide acceptable service for the majority of users, tourists may not be willing to wade through several people (or sets of audio-response questions) to get to the person who can help. They need a direct line to someone who can provide quick, professional service to address their needs.

Tourists who use the CIF typically expect very little data in response to queries, and the interface needs to be intuitive. Some requests that are related to the key performance indicator queries (e.g., the constraints or dimensions that will be used to drill down through sales figures) are predictable. These requests should be satisfied using data marts that are based on dimensional models. In some cases, it may be useful to create a multidimensional cube and load it on the tourist's workstation.

Unpredictable requests are more difficult to satisfy. For these, the meta data and its search engine hold the key. The tourist needs the ability to locate and execute a query that satisfies the information need without loading the query tool itself, and the meta data architecture needs to provide this capability. The data itself is likely to reside in a multidimensional data mart, and the pertinent data mart needs to be accessible to the tourist based on the search selection criteria.

Finally, the Internet/Intranet interface must be available and should mimic the browsers that the tourist is used to. An interactive and proactive mechanism is needed to inform the tourist when an item of interest has been discovered.

Explorers

Perhaps the most misunderstood member of the CIF community is the person that is known as the explorer. The explorer is the original corporate out-of-the-box thinker, an individual who does not look at the life and commerce of the company in the standard ways. Instead, the explorer looks at corporate business differently than anyone else. In some cases, these insights are very valuable; in other cases, they are merely a mirage.

Most corporations have only a few true explorers, but their value to the company is immeasurable. Examples of these out-of-the-box thinkers include:

- Marketing analysts
- Actuaries
- Strategic analysts

Explorer Business Characteristics

Due to the unusual nature of explorers, their business requirements are quite different and, therefore, are often difficult to understand and satisfy.

Random Queries

The queries and analyses that are submitted by the explorer are very random. He or she operates on intuition and observation, trying to find relationships between obscure pieces of data and events. The explorer is often wrong in the conclusions that he or she draws. On occasion, however, the explorer is correct, and on those occasions, the rewards can have tremendous payback for the company, easily paying for the many misses that were made.

Uninstitutionalized Procedures

The explorer operates in an unstructured, heruistic world. He will go six days or weeks with no queries, then will submit six queries in a day. These queries tend to be oversized. There is a variety of reasons why he or she submits large queries:

- *The explorer operates on detail.* Finding subtle patterns often requires looking at minute pieces of data.
- *The explorer requires significant history.* The patterns sought occur infrequently. Therefore, the explorer needs robust amounts of historical information.
- *The explorer needs to look at the data in a manner unknown to other users.* The data will be twisted around to suit his or her mood.

In short, the queries submitted by the explorer are huge because the characteristics of the query are.

Pattern and Relationship Determination

Explorers look for patterns and relationships. They care about the conditions that cause a notable event. Once the conditions surrounding a notable event are established, the explorer can seek predictability. Once predictability is determined, it is relatively easy to create an environment with business advantage.

Explorers create hypotheses out of their analysis. Then, they pass these hypotheses to the data miner for proof or disproof and an analysis of the strength of the hypothesis. Often, the explorer will create a repeating query of his or her findings and then pass that query on to the farmer for routine creation.

The explorer uses the following technologies:

- Specialized exploration data bases
- Online analytical processing (OLAP)
- Query
- Business intelligence with embedded data mining
- Data visualization
- DSS

Architectural Requirements

Today, there are several technologies that are available to support explorers. We can now create an exploration warehouse just for their usage. The exploration warehouse takes advantage of specialized data bases, such as token or memory-resident technologies, to create an environment that permits any and all queries. The response time is reasonable for such large queries. Explorers can change their minds as often as needed and not be penalized.

The exploration warehouse is a component of the CIF. It consists of data that is drawn from the data warehouse and reformatted into either a token-based data base or into a memory-resident data base. Then, the explorer uses a variety of tools that access these technologies to launch their queries, receive their results, study their results, and then launch yet another query.

The explorer has other needs, though, that may only be satisfied by using the full data warehouse and data marts, and possibly near-line stored data. In this case, access to the data warehouse and archived data becomes an important consideration.

The data base design that explorers find most useful is a normalized one rather than a multidimensional (star schema) one. Because their queries are ad hoc in nature and very unpredictable, this type of data base design seems to work best. Rarely will they use a predefined data base design.

Miners

The implementation of the CIF has unleashed a gold rush of sorts. A new group of CIF users—data miners—are equipping themselves frantically with tools to find rare and valuable nuggets of information from mountains and mountains of data that is found in data warehouses and data mining data marts. They analyze data to find meaningful correlations. If the data looks odd, they check it out, because data outliers might be just what they're looking for (finding an instance of fraud, for example). There are pitfalls—false starts, dead-end paths, and erroneous or meaningless findings—in determining what activities, tools, and techniques are necessary. Data miners need to have great resilience and patience.

Miners usually have mathematical or statistical backgrounds, such as:

- Statisticians
- Logistics specialists
- Marketers
- Actuaries

Miner Business Characteristics

Data miners have fairly straightforward requirements, and they are usually quite capable of expressing their needs:

Large amounts of detailed, historical data. Data miners scan large amounts of detailed data looking for the confirmation of a hypothesis or for suspected patterns of activities (e.g., buying habits of valued customers, fraudulent claims). These mountains of data must be of high quality and/or consistent.

Generally, the data is preconditioned to aid in a particular study. For example, they may select a statistical subset of data to study, a particular population of customers, or a particular market segment. The data will most likely be presented in a flat-file format rather than a multidimensional or relational format.

Specialized data mining tools. The advent of tools with "intelligent agents" has been a great boon to the data miners. These tools greatly increased miners' productivity and ability to sift through the tons of data available. They offer the miner a variety of analytical devices, such as decision trees, neural networks, memory-based reasoning, cluster detection, genetic algorithms, and statistical analyses.

Known queries. Data miners often have a good idea of what they expect before they execute a query. They set up queries based on this preconceived notion. For example, they may set up a query to determine the frequency of submission of claims with the likelihood of fraudulent claims. They may set up a query to determine the likelihood of two products being purchased together (market basket analysis) or one to determine the pattern of equipment failures (mean time to failure) and so on.

Predictable pattern of usage. The best news for the CIF architect who develops an environment for data miners is that they generally have predictable usage patterns. Indeed, they may know more about how they use the data than any other member of the CIF community. They may tell the CIF administrator to simply supply them with an extract and they will load it into their specialized data mart for their usage.

Mining activities. Data miners approach decision making with basically six different activities in mind:*

1. *Classification.* Assigns records to one of a predefined set of classes.

2. *Estimation.* Determines values for an unknown continuous variable.

3. *Prediction.* Classifies records according to some predicted future behavior or estimated future value.

4. *Affinity grouping.* Determination of which things go together.

5. *Clustering.* Segmentation of a heterogeneous population of records into a number of more homogeneous subgroups.

6. *Description.* Portrayal of a complex data base to increase understanding of the underlying data.

Data miners use the following four technologies and functionality:

1. Statistical languages.

2. Core data mining.

3. Query.

4. Data visualization.

Architectural Requirements

Data miners are heavy users of the data warehouse or of a specialized data mining data mart. They can also use exploration warehouses, if one exists. The data base design scheme that best serves the needs of miners is a denormalized relational one in the data warehouse or the data mining data mart. Aggregated or summarized data usually does the miner no good, because he or she is searching for detailed data to support trends or patterns. The data mining data mart, usually a fairly flat file structure containing preconditioned data for analysis, is designed specifically for miners' use.

Data miners require massive amounts of historical data. Therefore, the CIF architect would be wise to look toward near-line storage mechanisms to help reduce the costs of maintaining these massive sets of data, yet still making it available when the miner needs it.

Operators

Operators are the most common users of the CIF. Most of the time, they need current detailed information on a scheduled basis, so they rely heavily on stan-

---

* From *Data Mining Techniques* by Michael Berry and Gordon Linoff, John Wiley & Sons, New York, 2000.

dardized queries. In general, they simply hope that critical information is available and immediately accessible. As computers have increased information storage capabilities, more operators have adopted the view that the information that they need is in the system somewhere. If only they could get someone to give them access to it—and now!

Understandably, IT departments have been besieged for years by requests for current information from their ever-increasing customer base of operators. Later, when multiple operators clamored for the exact same information, IT took notice and consolidated duplicate extract programs. Still later, the random, ad hoc evolution of multiple extracts feeding multiple-satellite operational systems frequently turned out to be inefficient, if not unmanageable. As a result, many of today's operators continually struggle to consolidate and evaluate current information from disparate sources.

The good news is that an alternative exists for effectively satisfying operators' needs for current, detailed, enterprisewide, consolidated tactical information— the operational data store. Operators are a unique and large class of business users for the CIF. Typical operators include:

- Product category managers
- Financial analysts
- Sales analysts

Operator Business Requirements

Usually, operators come from the administrative or clerical staff in your organization; therefore, their focus is much more tactical than the previously discussed users. Their requirements are as follows:

A need for current, tactical, integrated data.   Operators are easily identified by their administrative, tactical focus on today's problems. They may be individuals functioning in the role of first- or second-level managers, line or shift supervisors, or even customer service representatives who need current information from the CIF. They also represent the largest portion of the business community.

Fast response times.   Their questions require immediate answers that are based on the best and most current data available. For example, which depot should we use to ship products for a special order? What is the financial impact of an impending hurricane on our insurance company's policies? Has the production line made enough of a certain product to satisfy current orders? How many telemarketing calls must still be made to complete the current campaign? Operators require data that is as comprehensive or enterprise focused as possible, because a decision must be made *now*.

Current performance metrics. Operators are generally responsible for monitoring the day-to-day performance metrics of the business. Although they may interact with multiple operational systems, they need consolidated, integrated information to track the current state of the performance metrics.

Predictable usage pattern. Often, operators perform routine processes and queries. They have a predictable usage pattern and are veterans of online transaction processing (OLTP) environments. Therefore, they expect transaction-like performance and response times (subsecond to a few seconds) to their requests.

Minimal historical data requirements. Rarely do operators require significant amounts of historical data because they address the current state of the business. The time aspect of their analyses is usually limited to today, yesterday, this week, or perhaps this month. Although they may not need a large amount of historical data, they do need a broad range or scope of data. Frequently, operators must look at all angles of a problem before making decisions. Because of this, they present the data architect with a significant challenge in maintaining the integrated, detailed, broad-scoped, third normal form-style table structures.

Structured, simple interface. Tools that facilitate unstructured access, such as those in the OLAP family, are generally not necessary for operators. Although the operators strain IT infrastructure to provide current, detailed, accessible data, their interface or presentation requirements are often relatively simple. Many simply need online access to the few lines on the green bar reports that are of interest to them each day. Given the predictable pattern of usage that is demonstrated by most operators, their interface should be intuitive, simple, and menu-driven. Interfaces that facilitate structured access and invoke a series of standard queries using only a few keystrokes are very effective.

Web-based query and reporting tools also may be extremely useful. Browser access to standard and performance-metric information utilizing Web-based tools is very close to online access to the green bar reports.

Rather than querying the information themselves, managers may want key performance indicator information to be broadcast automatically as changes occur, or at a set frequency, such as every half hour. Today's information-broadcasting tools can send information directly and efficiently via e-mail, voice mail, pages, or fax.

Architectural Requirements

The architectural constructs that are used most by operators are an ODS and/or operational applications, although they may use a multidimensional data mart some of the time. Like a data warehouse, an ODS is subject oriented and integrated. In contrast, though, it also contains frequently updated, current data that operators need to make their tactical decisions.

Economy and simplicity are the strengths of an ODS structure in the CIF. An ODS embodies one-stop shopping by providing operators with a single source of integrated, enterprisewide data, and by providing a single destination for disparate source system extracts. Simplicity is a natural by-product of integration and consolidation. It's simpler to load and access one system, as opposed to many.

On the other hand, centralization can be a double-edged sword. The biggest challenge that an ODS poses is frequently updating timing. Assuming an iterative approach to construction, the average ODS starts out small, satisfying a limited number of needs. A small ODS means that updating the data fast enough is not a problem at first. Several iterations later, after its success is proven, an ODS may become so large that it takes significant effort to coordinate the updates to its content. A separate batch process may be needed to handle the integration and transformation process alone.

Even with such potential problems, it's obvious that operators and IT resources can both benefit from an ODS. The ability to make sound tactical decisions from a reliable, up-to-date source of data is becoming a mandatory requirement in many organizations.

The operators' need for normalized structures in the ODS is another unique design aspect. Current, detailed, updatable data is dynamic in nature. Of course, the true meaning of *dynamic* depends on how often you update or refresh the ODS database and on how much of it gets updated. In terms of content, the potential exists for change to every attribute in every row. In terms of frequency, many operators need "zero latency" or instantaneous updates. Whatever the combination, the most stable data structure for updating dynamic data is a normalized data base (generally in third normal form).

Operational Data Stores (ODSs) represent specific and challenging business and technical requirements. These include:

- The business need for subject-oriented and integrated operational data to perform business management functions
- The business need for data as current as it is technologically feasible to get (updated as frequently as possible from the operational applications)
- The access to very detailed information with performance response times of seconds or subseconds
- The ability to analyze detailed information rapidly to act immediately
- The interface that is relatively simple and easy to use
- The ability to have key performance metrics published or "pushed"

In Summary

By recognizing the various communities that use the CIF, you can implement better architectures and applications to meet their specific needs. It is important to note that users may change personalities, jobs, or analytical prowess and therefore may demonstrate characteristics of more than one community member. For example, a marketer may be a farmer in the morning, a miner or explorer after lunch, and a tourist at the end of the day. That means he needs multiple tools and environments to work in. We need to understand all of these communities to set up a flexible environment. We need to be able to anticipate their needs and be one step ahead of their desires.

access   The operation of seeking, reading, or writing data on a storage unit.

access method   A technique used to transfer a physical record from or to a mass storage device.

access mode   A technique in which a specific logical record is obtained from or placed onto a file assigned to a mass storage device.

access pattern   The general sequence in which the data structure is accessed (e.g., from tuple to tuple, from record to record, from segment to segment, etc.).

access plan   The control structure that is produced during program preparation and used by a data base manager to process SQL statements during application execution.

access time   The time interval between the instant an instruction initiates a request for data and the instant the first of the data satisfying the request is delivered. Note that there is a difference—sometimes large—between the time when data is first delivered and the time when *all* the data is delivered.

accuracy   A qualitative assessment of freedom from error or a quantitative measure of the magnitude of error, expressed as a function of relative error.

active data dictionary   A data dictionary that is the sole source for an application program insofar as meta data is concerned.

activity   1. The lowest-level function on an activity chart (sometimes called the "atomic level"). 2. A logical description of a function performed by an enterprise. 3. A procedure (automated or not) designed for the fulfillment of an activity.

activity ratio   The fraction of records in a data base that have activity or are otherwise accessed in a given period of time or in a given batch run.

address   An identification (e.g., number, name, storage location, byte offset, etc.) for a location where data is stored.

addressable memory   See *parallel search storage.*

addressing   The means of assigning data to storage locations, and locating the data upon subsequent retrieval, on the basis of the key of the data.

ad hoc processing   One time only, casual access and manipulation of data on parameters never before used.

Advanced Interactive Executive (AIE)   IBM's version of the UNIX operating system.

afterimage   The snapshot of data placed on a log upon the completion of a transaction.

agent of change   A motivating force large enough to not be denied, usually aging of systems, changes in technology, radical changes in requirements, and so forth.

algorithm   A set of statements organized to solve a problem in a finite number of steps.

alias   An alternative label used to refer to a data element.

alphabetic   A representation of data using letters—upper and/or lower case—only.

alphanumeric   A representation of data using numbers and/or letters, and punctuation.

analysis   The process of examining carefully and thoroughly both current requirements and the current operating environment.

analysis space   The space defined by the dimensions of an analysis.

analytical processing   The usage of the computer to produce an analysis for management decision, usually involving trend analysis, drill-down analysis, demographic analysis, profiling, and so on.

ANSI   American National Standards Institute.

anticipatory staging   The technique of moving blocks of data from one storage device to another with a shorter access time, in anticipation of their being needed by a program in execution or a program soon to go into execution.

API   Application Program Interface—the common set of parameters needed to connect the communications between programs.

application   A group of algorithms and data interlinked to support an organizational requirement.

application blocking of data   The grouping into the same physical unit of storage multiple occurrences of data controlled at the application level.

application data base   A collection of data organized to support a specific application.

archival data base   A collection of data containing data of a historical nature. As a rule, archival data cannot be updated. Each unit of archival data is relevant to a moment in time, now passed.

area   In network data bases, a named collection of records that can contain occurrences of one or more record types. A record type can occur in more than one area.

artifact   A design technique used to represent referential integrity in the DSS environment.

artificial intelligence   The capability of a system to perform functions typically associated with human intelligence and reasoning.

association   A relationship between two entities that is represented in a data model.

associative storage   1. A storage device whose records are identified by a specific part of their contents rather than their name or physical position in the data base. 2. Content.

atomic   1. Data stored in a data warehouse. 2. The lowest level of process analysis.

atomic data base   A data base made up of primarily atomic data; an enterprise data warehouse; a DSS foundation data base.

atomicity   The property in which a group of actions is invisible to other actions executing concurrently to yield the effect of serial execution. It is recoverable with successful completion (i.e., commit) or total backout (i.e., rollback) of previous changes associated with that group.

atomic-level data   Data with the lowest level of granularity. Atomic-level data sits in a data warehouse and is time variant (i.e., accurate as of some moment in time now passed).

attribute   A property that can assume values for entities or relationships. Entities can be assigned several attributes (e.g., a tuple in a relationship consists of values). Some systems also allow relationships to have attributes as well.

audit trail   Data that is available to trace activity, usually update activity.

authorization identifier   A character string that designates a set of privilege descriptors.

availability   A measure of the reliability of a system, indicating the fraction of time when the system is up and available divided by the amount of time the system should be up and available. Note that there is a difference between a piece of hardware being available and the systems running on the hardware also being available.

back end processor   A data base machine or an intelligent disk controller.

backup   A file serving as a basis for the activity of backing up a data base. Usually a snapshot of a data base as of some previous moment in time.

back up   To restore the data base to its state as of some previous moment in time.

Backus-Naur Form (BNF)   A metalanguage used to specify or describe the syntax of a language. In BNF, each symbol on the left side of the forms can be replaced by the symbol strings on the right to develop sentences in the grammar of the defined language. Synonymous with *Backus—Normal Form*.

backward recovery   A recovery technique that restores a data base to an earlier state by applying before images.

base relation   A relation that is not derivable from other relations in the data base.

batch   Computer environment in which programs (usually long running, sequentially oriented) access data exclusively, and user interaction is not allowed while the activity is occurring.

batch environment   A sequentially dominated mode of processing; in batch, input is collected and stored for.

batch window   The time at which the online system is available for batch or sequential processing. The batch window occurs during nonpeak processing hours.

before image   A snapshot of a record prior to update, usually placed on an activity log.

behavior   The recurring, predictable response to a stimuli by some object.

bill of materials   A listing of the parts used in a manufacturing process along with the relation of one product to another insofar as assembly of the final product is concerned. The bill of materials is a classical recursive structure.

(b)inary digi(t) (bit)   The lowest level of storage. A bit can be in a 1 state or a 0 state.

binary element   A constituent element of data that takes either of two values or states—either true or false, or one or zero.

binary search   A dichotomizing search with steps in which the sets of remaining items are partitioned into two equal parts.

bind   1. To assign a value to a data element, variable, or parameter. 2. The attachment of a data definition to a program prior to the execution of the program.

binding time   The moment in time when the data description known to the dictionary is assigned to or bound to the procedural code.

bit map   A specialized form of an index indicating the existence or nonexistence of a condition for a group of blocks or records. Bit maps are expensive to build and maintain, but provide very fast comparison and access facilities.

block   1. A basic unit of structuring storage. 2. The physical unit of transport and storage. A block usually contains one or more records (or contains the space for one or more records). In some DBMSs, a block is called a page.

blocking   The combining of two or more physical records so that they are physically colocated together. The result of their physical colocation is that they can be accessed and fetched by a single execution of a machine instruction.

block splitting   The data management activity in which a filled block is written into two unfilled blocks, leaving space for future insertions and updates in the two partially filled blocks.

B*tree   A binary storage structure and access method that maintains order in a data base by continually dividing possible choices into two equal parts and reestablishing pointers to the respective sets, but not allowing more than two levels of difference to exist concurrently.

buffer   An area of storage that holds data temporarily in main memory while data is being transmitted, received, read, or written. A buffer is often used to compensate for the differences in the timing of transmission and execution of devices. Buffers are used in terminals, peripheral devices, storage units, and CPUs.

bus   The hardware connection that allows data to flow from one component to another (e.g., from the CPU to the line printer).

business intelligence   The discipline of understanding the business abstractly and often from a distance. With business intelligence, you can see the forest and the trees.

byte   A basic unit of storage—made up of 8 bits.

C   A programming language.

cache   A buffer usually built and maintained at the device level. Retrieving data out of a cache is much quicker than retrieving data out of a cylinder.

call   To invoke the execution of a module.

canonical model   A data model that represents the inherent structure of data without regard to either individual use or hardware or software implementation.

cardinality (of a relation)   The number of tuples (i.e., rows) in a relation. See also *degree of a relation.*

CASE   Computer Aided Software Engineering.

catalog   A directory of all files available to the computer.

chain   An organization in which records or other items of data are strung together.

chain list   A list in which the items cannot be located in sequence, but in which each item contains an identifier (i.e., pointer) for finding the next item.

chain of beneficence   The path that exploration proceeds down.

channel   A subsystem for input and output to and from the computer. Data from storage units, for example, flows into the computer by way of a channel.

character   A member of the standard set of elements used to represent data in the data base.

character type   The characters that can represent the value of an attribute.

checkpoint   An identified snapshot of the database or a point at which the transactions against the data base have been frozen or have been quiesced.

checkpoint/restart   A means of restarting a program at some point other than the beginning (e.g., when a failure or interruption has occurred). "N" checkpoints may be used at intervals throughout an application program. At each of those points, sufficient information is stored to permit the program to be restored to the moment in time when the checkpoint has been taken.

child   A unit of data that exists in a 1:n relationship with another unit of data called a parent, in which the parent must exist before the child can exist, but the parent can exist even if no child unit of data exists.

CIO Chief information officer—an organizational position managing all of the information-processing functions.

circular file (queue) An organization of data in which a finite number of units of data are allocated. Data is then loaded into those units. Upon reaching the end of the allocated units, new data is written over older data at the start of the queue. Sometimes called a *wrap-around queue*.

claimed block A second or subsequent physical block of data designated to store table data when the originally allocated block has run out of space.

class (of entities) All possible entities held by a given proposition.

"CLDS" The facetiously named system development life cycle for analytical, DSS systems. CLDS is so named because, in fact, it is the reverse of the classical systems development life cycle, SDLC.

Cluster 1. In Teradata, a group of physical devices controlled by the same AMP. 2. In DB2 and Oracle, the practice of physically colocating data in the same block based on the content of data.

cluster key The key around which data is clustered in a block (DB2/Oracle).

coalesce To combine two or more sets of items into any single set.

COBOL Common Business Oriented Language—a computer language for the business world. A very common language.

CODASYL model A network data base model that was originally defined by the Data Base Task Group (DBTG) of the Conference on Data System Language (CODASYL) organization.

code 1. To represent data or a computer program in a form that can be accepted by a data processor. 2. To transform data so that it cannot be understood by anyone who does not have the algorithm used to decode the data prior to presentation (sometimes called *encode*).

collision The event that occurs when two or more records of data are assigned the same physical location. Collisions are associated with randomizers or hashers.

column A vertical table in which values are selected from the same domain. A row is made up of one or more columns.

command 1. The specification of an activity by the programmer. 2. The actual execution of the specification.

commit A condition raised by the programmer signalling to the DBMS that all update activity done by the program be executed against a data base. Prior to the commit, all update activity can be rolled back or cancelled with no ill effects on the contents of the data base.

commit protocol An algorithm to ensure that a transaction is successfully completed.

commonality of data   Similar or identical data that occurs in different applications or systems. The recognition and management of commonality of data is one of the foundations of conceptual and physical data base design.

communication network   The collection of transmission facilities, network processors, and so on, which provides for data movement among terminals and information processors.

compaction   A technique for reducing the number of bits required to represent data without losing the content of the data. With compaction, repetitive data is represented very concisely.

component   A data item or array of data items whose component type defines a collection of occurrences with the same data type.

compound index   An index over multiple columns.

concatenate   To link or connect two strings of characters, generally for the purpose of using them as a single value.

conceptual schema   A consistent collection of data structures expressing the data needs of the organization. This schema is a comprehensive, base-level, and logical description of the environment in which an organization exists, free of physical structure and application system considerations.

concurrent operations   Activities executed simultaneously, or during the same time interval.

condensation   The process of reducing the volume of data managed without reducing the logical consistency of the data. Condensation is essentially different than compaction.

connect   To forge a relationship between two entities, particularly in a network system.

connector   A symbol used to indicate that one occurrence of data has a relationship with another occurrence of data. Connectors are used in conceptual data base design and can be implemented hierarchically, relationally, in an inverted fashion, or by a network.

content addressable memory   Main storage that can be addressed by the contents of the data in the memory, as opposed to conventional location addressable memory.

contention   The condition that occurs when two or more programs try to access the same data at the same time.

continuous time span data   Data organized so that a continuous definition of data over a span of time is represented by one or more records.

control character   A character whose occurrence in a particular context initiates, modifies, or stops an operation.

control data base   A utilitarian data base containing data that is not directly related to the application being built. Typical control data bases are audit data bases, terminal data bases, security data bases, and so forth.

cooperative processing   The ability to distribute resources (programs, files, and data bases) across the network.

coordinate system   The set of related dimensions emanating from a point of origin.

coordinator   The two-phase commit protocol defines one DBMS as coordinator for the commit process. The coordinator is responsible to communicate with the other data base manager involved in a unit of work.

corporate information factory (CIF)   The architectural framework that houses the ODS, data warehouse, data marts, IT interface, and the operational environment. The CIF is held together logically by meta data and physically by a network such as the Internet.

CPU   Central processing unit.

CPU-bound   The state of processing in which the computer can produce no more output because the CPU portion of the processor is being used at 100 percent capacity. When the computer is CPU-bound, typically the memory- and storage-processing units are less than 100 percent utilized. With modern DBMS, it is much more likely that the computer be I/O-bound, rather than CPU-bound.

Cross System Product (CSP)   An IBM application generator.

CUA   Common User Access—Specifies the ways in which the user interface to systems is to be constructed.

current-value data   Data whose accuracy is valid as of the moment of execution—as opposed to time-variant data.

cursor   1. An indicator that designates a current position on a screen. 2. A system facility that allows the programmer to thumb from one record to the next when the system has retrieved a set of records.

cursor stability   An option that allows data to move under the cursor. Once the program is through using the data examined by the cursor, it is released. As opposed to repeatable read.

Customer Information Control System (CICS)   An IBM teleprocessing monitor.

cylinder   The area of storage of DASD that can be read without the movement of the arm. The term originated with disk files, in which a cylinder consisted of one track on each disk surface so that each of these tracks could have a read/write head positioned over it simultaneously.

DASD   See *direct-access storage device*.

data   A recording of facts, concepts, or instructions on a storage medium for communication, retrieval, and processing by automatic means and presentation as information that is understandable by human beings.

data administrator (DA)   The individual or organization that is responsible for the specification, acquisition, and maintenance of data management software and the design, validation, and security of files or data bases. The data model and the data dictionary are classically the charge of the DA.

data aggregate   A collection of data items.

data base   A collection of interrelated data stored (often with controlled, limited redundancy) according to a schema. A data base can serve a single or multiple applications.

data base administrator (DBA)   The organizational function charged with the day-to-day monitoring and care of the data bases. The DBA function is more closely associated with physical data base design than the DA is.

data base key   A unique value that exists for each record in a data base. The value is often indexed, although it can be randomized or hashed.

data base machine   A dedicated-purpose computer that provides data access and management through total control of the access method, physical storage, and data organization. Often called a back-end *processor.* Data is usually managed in parallel by a data base machine.

data base management system (DBMS)   A computer-based software system used to establish and manage data.

data base record   A physical root and all of its dependents (in IMS).

data cleansing (data scrubbing)   The process of editing data and converting data for the purpose of improving its accuracy and usability.

data cube   A three-dimensional object composed of columns and rows of cells. The edges of the cube are the dimensions of the analysis space.

data definition   The specification of the data entities, their attributes, and their relationships in a coherent data base structure to create a schema.

data definition language (DDL) (also called a data description language)   The language used to define the data base schema and additional data features that allow the DBMS to generate and manage the internal tables, indexes, buffers, and storage necessary for data base processing.

data description language   See *data definition language.*

data dictionary   A software tool for recording the definition of data, the relationship of one category of data to another, the attributes and keys of groups of data, and so forth.

data division (COBOL)   The section of a COBOL program that consists of entries used to define the nature and characteristics of the data to be processed by the program.

data-driven development   The approach to development that centers around identifying the commonality of data through a data model and building programs that have a broader scope than the immediate application. Data-driven development differs from classical application-oriented development.

data-driven process   A process whose resource consumption depends on the data on which it operates. For example, a hierarchical root has a dependent. For one occurrence there are two dependents for the root. For another occurrence of the root there are 1000 occurrences of the dependent. The same program that accesses the root and all its dependents will use very different amounts of resources when operating against the two roots although the code will be exactly the same.

data element   1. An attribute of an entity. 2. A uniquely named and well-defined category of data that consists of data items and that is included in a record of an activity.

data engineering (see information engineering)   The planning and building of data structures according to accepted mathematical models, on the basis of the inherent characteristics of the data itself, and independent of hardware and software systems.

data extraction   The process of selecting data from a source and moving it to a target.

data independence   The property of being able to modify the overall logical and physical structure of data without changing any of the application code supporting the data.

data integration   The process of merging multiple sources of data and converting the data so that a single, integrated store of data results.

data item   A discrete representation having the properties that define the data element to which it belongs. See also *data element*.

data item set (DIS)   A grouping of data items, each of which directly relates to the key of the grouping of data in which the data items reside. The data item set is found in the midlevel model.

data manipulation language (DML)   1. A programming language that is supported by a DBMS and used to access a data base. 2. Language constructs added to a higher-order language (e.g., COBOL) for the purpose of data base manipulation.

data mart   A department-specific data warehouse. There are two types of data marts: independent and dependent. An independent data mart is fed data directly from the legacy environment. A dependent data mart is fed data from the enterprise data warehouse. In the long run, dependent data marts are architecturally much more stable than independent data marts.

data miner   A person who engages in data mining.

data mining   The process of finding patterns, trends, associations, and relationships from data (usually transaction data).

data model   1. The logical data structures, including operations and constraints provided by a DBMS for effective data base processing. 2. The system used for the representation of data (e.g., the ERD or relational model).

data record   An identifiable set of data values treated as a unit, an occurrence of a schema in a data base, or a collection of atomic data items describing a specific object, event, or tuple.

data security   The protection of the data in a data base against unauthorized disclosure, alteration, or destruction. There are different levels of security.

data set   A named collection of logically related data items, arranged in a prescribed manner, and described by control information to which the programming systems has access.

data storage description language (DSDL)   A language to define the organization of stored data in terms of an operating system and device-independent storage environment. See also *device media control language.*

data structure   A logical relationship among data elements that is designed to support specific data manipulation functions (e.g., trees, lists, and tables).

data transformation   The process of converting, reformatting, and restructuring data.

data type   The definition of a set of representable values that is primitive and without meaningful logical subdivision.

data view   See *user view.*

data volatility   The rate of change of the content of data.

data warehouse   A collection of integrated, subject-oriented data bases designed to support the DSS function, where each unit of data is relevant to some moment in time. The data warehouse contains atomic data and lightly summarized data. A data warehouse is a subject-oriented, integrated, nonvolatile, time-variant collection of data designed to support management DSS needs.

data warehouse administrator (DWA)   The organization function designed to create and maintain the data warehouse. The DWA combines several disciplines, such as the DA, DBA, end user, and so on.

DB2   A data base management system by IBM.

DB/DC   Data base/data communications.

DBMS language interface (DB I/O module)   Software that applications invoke to access a data base. The module in turn has direct access with the DBMS. Standards enforcement and standard error checking are often features of an I/O module.

deadlock   See *deadly embrace.*

deadly embrace   The event that occurs when transaction A desires to access data currently protected by transaction B, while at the same time, transaction B desires to access data that is currently being protected by transaction A. The deadly embrace condition is a serious impediment to performance.

decision support system (DSS)   A system used to support managerial decisions. Usually DSS involves the analysis of many units of data in a heuristic fashion. As a rule, DSS processing does not involve the update of data.

decompaction   The opposite of compaction: once data is stored in a compacted form, it must be decompacted to be used.

decryption   The opposite of encryption: once data is stored in an encrypted fashion, it must be decrypted to be used.

definition   The result of identifying the salient and unique characteristics of an object.

degree (of a relation)   The number of attributes or columns of a relation. See also *cardinality of a relation.*

delimiter   A flag, symbol, or convention used to mark the boundaries of a record, field, or other unit of storage.

demand staging   The movement of blocks of data from one storage device to another device with a shorter access time when programs request the blocks and the blocks are not already in the faster access storage.

denormalization   The technique of placing normalized data in a physical location that optimizes the performance of the system.

derived data   Data whose existence depends on two or more occurrences of a major subject of the enterprise.

derived data element   A data element that is not necessarily stored but that can be generated when needed (e.g., age given current date and date of birth).

derived relation   A relation that can be obtained from previously defined relations by applying some sequence of retrieval and derivation operator (e.g., a table that is the join of others plus some projections.) See also *virtual relation.*

design review   The quality assurance process in which all aspects of a system are reviewed publicly prior to the striking of code.

development spiral   The process of iteratively and heuristically creating one or more components of the CIF in a continuous manner.

device media control language (DMCL)   A language used to define the mapping of the data onto the physical storage media. See also *data storage description language.*

dicing   The analytical process of the constriction of the analysis space across multiple dimensions.

dimension   The axes of a coordinate system that bind the space defined by the coordinate system.

dimension table   The table that is joined to a fact table in a star join. The dimension table is the structure that represents the nonpopulous occurrences of data in a data mart.

direct access   Retrieval or storage of data by reference to its location on a volume. The access mechanism goes directly to the data in question, as is generally required with online use of data. Also called *random access* or *hashed access.*

direct-access storage device (DASD)   A data storage unit on which data can be accessed directly without having to progress through a serial file such as a magnetic tape file. A disk unit is a direct-access storage device.

directory   A table specifying the relationships between items of data. Sometimes a table or index giving the addresses of data.

distributed catalog A distributed catalog is needed to achieve site autonomy. The catalog at each site maintains information about objects in the local data bases. The distributed catalog keeps information on replicated and distributed tables stored at that site and information on remote tables located at another site that cannot be accessed locally.

distributed data base A data base controlled by a central DBMS, but in which the storage devices are geographically dispersed or not attached to the same processor. See also *parallel I/O.*

distributed data warehouse Where more than one enterprise data warehouse is built, the combination is called a distributed data warehouse.

distributed environment A set of related data-processing systems, where each system has its own capacity to operate autonomously, but with some applications that execute at multiple sites. Some of the systems may be connected with teleprocessing links into a network in which each system is a node.

distributed free space Space left empty at intervals in a data layout to permit insertion of new data.

distributed meta data Distributed meta data is data about data that resides in different architectural entities, such as data marts, enterprise data warehouses, ODS, and so forth.

distributed request A transaction across multiple nodes.

distributed unit of work The work done by a transaction that operates against multiple nodes.

division An operation that partitions a relation on the basis of the contents of data found in the relation.

DL/1 IBM's Data Language One—for describing logical and physical data structures.

domain The set of legal values from which actual values are derived for an attribute or a data element.

dormant data Data loaded into a data warehouse that has a future probability of access of zero.

download The stripping of data from one data base to another based on the content of data found in the first data base.

drill-down analysis The type of analysis where examination of a summary number leads to the exploration of the components of the sum.

dual data base The practice of separating high-performance, transaction-oriented data from decision support data.

dual data base management systems The practice of using multiple data base management systems to control different aspects of the data base environment.

dumb terminal A device used to interact directly with the end user in which all processing is done on a remote computer. A dumb terminal acts as a device that gathers data and displays data only.

dynamic meta data Meta data whose state is constantly in flux.

dynamic SQL SQL statements that are prepared and executed within a program while the program is executing. In dynamic SQL, the SQL source is contained in host language variables rather than being coded into the application program.

dynamic storage allocation A technique in which the storage areas assigned to computer programs are determined during processing.

dynamic subset of data A subset of data that is selected by a program and operated on only by the program, and released by the program once the program ceases execution.

EDI Electronic Data Interchange.

EIS Executive Information Systems—systems designed for the top executive, featuring drill-down analysis and trend analysis.

embedded pointer A record pointer (i.e., a means of internally linking related records) that is not available to an external index or directory. Embedded pointers are used to reduce search time, but require maintenance overhead.

encoding A shortening or abbreviation of the physical representation of a data value (e.g., male = "M," female = "F").

encryption The transformation of data from a recognizable form to a form that is unrecognizable without the algorithm used for the encryption. Encryption is usually done for the purposes of security.

enterprise The generic term for the company, corporation, agency, or business unit. Usually associated with data modeling.

enterprise data warehouse A data warehouse holding the most atomic data that the corporation has. Two or more enterprise data warehouses may be combined to create a distributed data warehouse.

entity A person, place, or thing of interest to the data modeler at the highest level of abstraction.

entity relationship attribute (ERA) model A data model that defines entities, the relationship between the entities, and the attributes that have values to describe the properties of entities and/or relationships.

entity relationship diagram (ERD) A high-level data model. The schematic showing all the entities within the scope of integration and the direct relationship between those entities.

evaluation The process of determining whether past goals have been met and what future goals should be.

event A signal that an activity of significance has occurred. An event is noted by the information system.

event-discrete data Data relating to the measurement or description of an event.

expert system A system that captures and automates the usage of human experience and intelligence.

exploration warehouse   A special kind of warehouse that is designed to optimize the process of exploration. Typically, exploration warehouses can handle huge amounts of data in main memory and can do set processing very efficiently.

explorer   A DSS end user who operates on a random basis looking at large amounts of detailed data for patterns, associations, and other previously unnoticed relationships.

extent   1. A list of unsigned integers that specifies an array. 2. A physical unit of disk storage attached to a data set after the initial allocation of data has been made.

external data   1. Data originating from other than the operational systems of a corporation. 2. Data residing outside the central processing complex.

external schema   A logical description of a user's method of organizing and structuring data. Some attributes or relationships can be omitted from the corresponding conceptual schema or can be renamed or otherwise transformed. See also *view*.

extract   The process of selecting data from one environment and transporting it to another environment.

extraction log   A record of the extracts that have occurred.

fact table   The central component of the star join. The fact table is the structure where the vast majority of the occurrences of data in the data mart reside.

farmer   A DSS user who repetitively looks at small amounts of data and who often finds what he or she is looking for.

field   See *data item*.

file   A set of related records that is treated as a unit and stored under a single logical file name.

firewall   The barrier constructed in front of a server to keep unwanted users outside of the server and to allow wanted users into the server.

first in first out (FIFO)   A fundamental ordering of processing in a queue.

first in last out (FILO)   A standard order of processing in a stack.

flag   An indicator or character that signals the occurrence of some condition.

flat file   A collection of records containing no data aggregates, nested repeated data items, or groups of data items.

floppy disk   A device for storing data on a personal computer.

foreign key   An attribute that is not a primary key in a relational system, but whose values are the values of the primary key of another relation.

format   The arrangement or layout of data in or on a data medium or in a program definition.

forward recovery   A recovery technique that restores a data base by reapplying all transactions using a before image from a specified point in time to a copy of the data base taken at that moment in time.

fourth-generation language   Language or technology that is designed to allow the end user unfettered access to data.

functional decomposition   The division of operations into hierarchical functions (i.e., activities) that form the basis for procedures.

future, later processing   Once collected, the batch input is transacted sequentially against one or more data bases.

gigabyte   A measurement of data between a megabyte and a terabyte—1×10^9 bytes of data.

global data warehouse   A data warehouse that is distributed around the world. In a global data warehouse, the system of record resides in the local site.

granularity   The level of detail contained in a unit of data. The more detail there is, the lower the level of granularity. The less detail there is, the higher the level of granularity.

graphic   A symbol produced on a screen that represents an object or a process in the real world.

hash   To convert the value of the key of a record into a location on DASD.

hash total   A total of the values of one or more fields, used for the purposes of auditability and control.

header record or header table   A record containing common, constant, or identifying information for a group of records that follow.

heuristic   The mode of analysis in which the next step is determined by the results of the current step of analysis. Used for decision support processing.

hierarchical model   A data model providing a tree structure for relating data elements or groups of data elements. Each node in the structure represents a group of data elements or a record type. There can be only one root node at the start of the hierarchical structure.

hit   An occurrence of data that satisfies some search criteria.

hit ratio   A measure of the number of records in a file expected to be accessed in a given run. Usually expressed as a percentage – number of input transactions/number of records in the file $\times$ 100 = hit ratio.

homonyms   Identical names that refer to different attributes.

horizontal distribution   The splitting of a table across different sites by rows. With horizontal distribution, rows of a single table reside at different sites in a distributed data base network.

host   The processor receiving and processing a transaction.

Huffman code   A code for data compaction in which frequently used characters are encoded with fewer bits than infrequently used characters.

hypercube   An object of greater than four dimensions, composed of columns and rows.

IDMS   A network DBMS from CA.

IEEE   Institute of Electrical and Electronics Engineers.

image copy   A procedure in which a data base is physically copied to another medium for the purposes of backup.

IMS   Information Management System—an operational DBMS by IBM.

index   The portion of the storage structure maintained to provide efficient access to a record when its index key item is known.

index chains   Chains of data within an index.

index point   A hardware reference mark on a disk or drum; used for timing purposes.

index sequential access method (ISAM)   A file structure and access method in which records can be processed sequentially (e.g., in order, by key) or by directly looking up their locations on a table, thus making it unnecessary to process previously inserted records.

indirect addressing   Any method of specifying or locating a record through calculation (e.g., locating a record through the scan of an index).

information   Data that human beings assimilate and evaluate to solve a problem or make a decision.

information center   The organizational unit charged with identifying and accessing information needed in DSS processing.

information engineering (IE)   The discipline of creating a data-driven development environment.

Informix   A leading data warehouse vendor.

input/output (I/O)   The means by which data is stored and/or retrieved on DASD. I/O is measured in milliseconds (i.e., mechanical speeds) whereas computer processing is measured in nanoseconds (i.e., electronic speeds).

instance   A set of values representing a specific entity belonging to a particular entity type. A single value is also the instance of a data item.

integration/transformation (I/T) program   A program designed to convert and move data from the legacy environment to the data warehouse environment. I/T programs are notoriously unstable and require constant maintenance.

integrity   The property of a data base that ensures that the data contained in the data base is as accurate and consistent as possible.

intelligent data base   A data base that contains shared logic as well as shared data and automatically invokes that logic when the data is accessed. Logic, constraints, and controls relating to the use of the data are represented in an intelligent data model.

interactive   A mode of processing that combines some of the characteristics of online transaction processing and batch processing. In interactive processing, the end user interacts with data over which he or she has exclusive control. In addition, the end user can initiate background activity to be run against the data.

interleaved data   Data from different tables mixed into a simple table space where there is commonality of physical colocation based on a common key value.

internal schema   The schema that describes logical structures of the data and the physical media over which physical storage is mapped.

internet   A network that connects many public users.

interpretive   A mode of data manipulation in which the commands to the DBMS are translated as the user enters them (as opposed to the programed mode of process manipulation).

intersection data   Data that is associated with the junction of two or more record types or entities, but which has no meaning when disassociated with any records or entities forming the junction.

intranet   A network that connects many private users.

inverted file   A file structure that uses an inverted index, where entries are grouped according to the content of the key being referenced. Inverted files provide for the fast spontaneous searching of files.

inverted index   An index structure organized by means of a nonunique key to speed the search for data by content.

inverted list   A list organized around a secondary index instead of around a primary key.

I/O   Input/output operation—Input/output operations are the key to performance because they operate at mechanical speeds, not at electronic speeds.

I/O bound   The point after which no more processing can be done because the I/O subsystem is saturated.

ISAM   See *Indexed Sequential Access Method.*

"is a type of"   An analytical tool used in abstracting data during the process of conceptual data base design (e.g., a cocker spaniel is a type of dog).

ISDN   Integrated Services Digital Network—telecommunications technology that enables companies to transfer data and voice through the same phone lines.

ISO   International Standards Organization.

item   See *data item.*

item type   A classification of an item according to its domain, generally in a gross sense.

iterative analysis   The mode of processing in which the next step of processing depends on the results obtained by the existing step in execution; heuristic processing.

JAD   Joint application design—an organization of people, usually end users, to create and refine application system requirements.

join   An operation that takes two relations as operands and produces a new relation by concatenating the tuples and matching the corresponding columns when a stated condition holds between the two.

judgment sample   A sample of data where data is accepted or rejected for the sample based on one or more parameters.

junction   From the network environment, an occurrence of data that has two or more parent segments. For example, an order for supplies must have a supplier parent and a part parent.

justify   To adjust the value representation in a character field to the right or to the left, ignoring blanks encountered.

keeplist   A sequence of data base keys maintained by the DBMS for the duration of the session.

key   A data item or combination of data items used to identify or locate a record instance (or other similar data groupings).

key, primary   A unique attribute used to identify a single record in a data base.

key, secondary   A nonunique attribute used to identify a class of records in a data base.

key compression   A technique for reducing the number of bits in keys; used in making indexes occupy less space.

label   A set of symbols used to identify or describe an item, record, message, or file. Occasionally, a label may be the same as the address of the record in storage.

language   A set of characters, conventions, and rules used to convey information and consisting of syntax and semantics.

latency   The time taken by a DASD device to position the read arm over the physical storage medium. For general purposes, average latency time is used.

least frequently used (LFU)   A replacement strategy in which new data must replace existing data in an area of storage; the least frequently used items are replaced.

least recently used (LRU)   A replacement strategy in which new data must replace existing data in an area of storage; the least recently used items are replaced.

legacy environment   The transaction-oriented, application-based environment.

level of abstraction   The level of abstraction appropriate to a dimension. The level of abstraction that is appropriate is entirely dependent on the ultimate user of the system.

line   The hardware by which data flows to or from the processor. Lines typically go to terminals, printers, and other processors.

line polling   The activity of the teleprocessing monitor in which different lines are queried to determine whether they have data and/or transactions that need to be transmitted.

line time   The length of time required for a transaction to go from either the terminal to the processor or the processor to the terminal. Typically, line time is the single largest component of online response time.

linkage   The ability to relate one unit of data to another.

linked list   Set of records in which each record contains a pointer to the next record on the list. See also *chain*.

list   An ordered set of data items.

living sample   A representative data base typically used for heuristic statistical analytical processing in place of a large data base. Periodically, the very large data base is selectively stripped of data so that the resulting living sample data base represents a cross section of the very large data base as of some moment in time.

load   To insert data values into a data base that was previously empty.

locality of processing   In distributed data base, the design of processing so that remote access of data is eliminated or reduced substantively.

local site support   Within a distributed unit of work, a local site update allows a process to perform SQL update statements referring to the local site.

local transaction   In a distributed DBMS, a transaction that requires reference only to data that is stored at the site where the transaction originated.

lockup   The event that occurs when update is done against a data base record and the transaction has not yet reached a commit point. The online transaction needs to prevent other transactions from accessing the data while update is occurring.

log   A journal of activity.

logging   The automatic recording of data with regard to the access of the data, the updates to the data, and so on.

logical representation   A data view or description that does not depend on a physical storage device or a computer program.

loss of identity   When data is brought in from an external source and the identity of the external source is discarded, loss of identity occurs. A common practice with microprocessor data.

LU6.2   Logical Unit Type 6.2—peer-to-peer data stream with network operating system for program to program communication. LU6.2 allows midrange machines to talk to one another without the involvement of the mainframe.

machine learning   The ability of a machine to improve its performance automatically based on past performance.

magnetic tape   1. The storage medium most closely associated with sequential processing. 2. A large ribbon on which magnetic images are stored and retrieved.

main storage data base (MSDB)   A data base that resides entirely in main storage. Such data bases are very fast to access, but require special handling at the time of update. Another limitation of MSDBs are that they can only manage small amounts of data.

master file   A file that holds the system of record for a given set of data (usually bound by an application).

maximum transaction arrival rate (MTAR)   The rate of arrival of transactions at the moment of peak period processing.

megabyte   A measurement of data—1×10^6 bytes of data.

message 1. The data input by the user in the online environment that is used to drive a transaction. 2. The output of a transaction.

meta data 1. Data about data. 2. The description of the structure, content, keys, indexes, and so on, of data.

metalanguage A language used to specify other languages.

microprocessor A small processor serving the needs of a single user.

migration The process by which frequently used items of data are moved to more readily accessible areas of storage and infrequently used items of data are moved to less readily accessible areas of storage.

mips Million instructions per second—the standard measurement of processor speed for minicomputers and mainframe computers.

mode of operation A classification for systems that execute in a similar fashion and share distinctive operational characteristics. Some modes of operation are operational, DSS, online, interactive, and so on.

modulo An arithmetic term describing the remainder of a division process. 10 modulo 7 is 3. *Modulo* is usually associated with the randomization process.

multidimensional processing Processing of data where data can be drilled down to lower levels of detail.

multilist organization A chained file organization in which the chains are divided into fragments and each fragment is indexed. This organization of data permits faster access to the data.

multiple key retrieval That requires searches of data on the basis of the values of several key fields (some or all of which are secondary keys).

MVS Multiple Virtual Storage—IBM's mainline operating system for mainframe processors. There are several extensions of MVS.

Named Pipes Program-to-program protocol with Microsoft's LAN manager. The Named Pipes API supports intra- and intermachine process-to-process communications:

- Natural forms

- First normal form—data that has been organized into two dimensional flat files without repeating groups

- Second normal form—data that functionally depends on the entire candidate key

- Third normal form—data that has had all transitive dependencies on data items other than the candidate key removed.

- Fourth normal form—data whose candidate key is related to all data items in the record and that contains no more than one nontrivial multivalued dependency on the candidate key.

natural join A join in which the redundant logic components generated by the join are removed.

natural language   A language generally spoken, whose rules are based on current usage and not explicitly defined by a grammar.

navigate   To steer a course through a data base, from record to record, by means of an algorithm which examines the content of data.

network   A computer network consists of a collection of circuits, data-switching elements, and computing systems. The switching devices in the network are called communication processors. A network provides a configuration for computer systems and communication facilities within which data can be stored and accessed and within which DBMS can operate.

network model   A data model that provides data relationships on the basis of records, and groups of records (i.e., sets) in which one record is designated as the set owner, and a single member record can belong to one or more sets.

nine's complement   Transformation of a numeric field calculated by subtracting the initial value from a filed consisting of all nines.

node   A point in the network at which data is switched.

nonprocedural language   Syntax that directs the computer as to what to do, not how to do it. Typical nonprocedural languages include RAMIS, FOCUS, NOMAD, and SQL.

nonvolatile data   Data whose content does not change frequently.

normalize   To decompose complex data structures into natural structures.

NT   An operating system built by Microsoft.

null   An item or record for which no value currently exists or possibly may ever exist.

numeric   A representation using only numbers and the decimal point.

object   Discrete entities represented by tangible occurrences of data.

object class   A grouping of objects based on a set of common attributes and behaviors.

object-oriented analysis   The practice of conceiving of the environment in terms of objects and their associated behaviors.

object-oriented design   The practice of creating the architecture of a system based on objects and their associated behaviors.

object superclass   An object classification that contains lower classes of objects.

occurrence   See *instance*.

ODS   The architectural entity that shares properties of a data warehouse and operational processing. An operational data store is the following:

- Subject oriented
- Integrated
- Volatile (able to be updated)
- Containing current data

The ODS serves the corporate clerical community.

offset pointer   An indirect pointer. An offset pointer exists inside a block and the index points to the offset. If data must be moved, only the offset pointer in the block must be altered; the index entry remains untouched.

OLAP   Online analytical processing—the infrastructure designed for accessing and analyzing data. Synonomous with multidimensional processing.

online storage   Storage devices and storage medium where data can be accessed in a direct fashion.

operating system   Software that enables a computer to supervise its own operations and automatically call in programs, routines, languages, and data as needed for continuous operation throughout the execution of different types of jobs.

operational application   See *legacy application.*

operational data   Data used to support the daily processing a company does.

operational data store (ODS)   The form that data warehouse takes in the operational environment. Operational data stores can be updated to provide rapid and consistent response time, and contain only a limited amount of historical data.

operations   The department charged with the running of the computer.

optical disk   A storage medium using lasers as opposed to magnetic devices. Optical disk is typically write only, is much less expensive per byte than magnetic storage, and is highly reliable.

ORACLE   A DBMS by ORACLE Corp.

order   To place items in an arrangement specified by such rules as numeric or alphabetic order. See also *sort.*

OS/2   The operating system for IBM's Personal System/2.

OSF   Open Software Foundation.

OSI   Open Systems Interconnection.

overflow   1. The condition in which a record or a segment cannot be stored in its home address because the address is already occupied. In this case the data is placed in another location referred to as overflow. 2. The area of DASD where data is sent when the overflow condition is triggered.

ownership   The responsibility for update for operational data.

padding   A technique used to fill a field, record, or block with default data (e.g., blanks or zeros).

page   1. A basic unit of data on DASD. 2. A basic unit of storage in main memory.

page fault   A program interruption that occurs when a page that is referred to is not in main memory and must be read in from external storage.

page fixed   The state in which programs or data cannot be removed from main storage. Only a limited amount of storage can be page fixed.

paging   In virtual storage systems, the technique of making memory appear to be larger than it really is by transferring blocks (pages) of data or programs into external memory.

parallel data organization   An arrangement of data in which the data is spread over independent storage devices and is managed independently.

parallel I/O   The process of accessing or storing data on multiple physical data devices.

parallel search storage   A storage device in which one or more parts of all storage locations are queried simultaneously for a certain condition or under certain parameters. See also *associative storage*.

parameter   An elementary data value used as a criteria for qualification, usually of searches of data or in the control of modules.

parent   A unit of data in a 1:*n* relationship with another unit of data called a child, where the parent can exist independently, but the child cannot exist unless there is a parent.

parsing   The algorithm that translates syntax into meaningful machine instructions. Parsing determines the meaning of statements issued in the data manipulation language.

partition   A segmentation technique in which data is divided into physically different units. Partitioning can be done at the application or the system level.

path length   The number of instructions executed for a given program or instruction.

peak period   The time when the most transactions arrive at the computer with the expectation of execution.

performance   The length of time from the moment a request is issued until the first of the results of the request are received.

periodic discrete data   A measurement or description of data taken at a regular time interval.

physical representation   1. The representation and storage of data on a medium such as magnetic storage. 2. The description of data that depends on such physical factors as length of elements, records, pointers, and so on.

pipes   Vehicles for passing data from one application to another.

plex or network structure   A relationship between records or other groupings of data in which a child record can have more than one parent record.

plug-compatible manufacturer (PCM)   A manufacturer of equipment that functionally is identical to that of another manufacturer (usually IBM).

pointer   The address of a record or other groupings of data contained in another record so that a program may access the former record when it has retrieved the latter record. The address can be absolute, relative, or symbolic, and hence the pointer is referred to as absolute, relative, or symbolic.

point of origin   The point at which all axes of a coordinate system meet or appear to meet.

pools   The buffers made available to the online controller.

populate   To place occurrences of data values in a previously empty data base. See also *load*.

precision   The degree of discrimination with which a quantity is stated. For example, a three-digit numeral discriminates among 1000 possibilities, from 000 to 999.

precompilation   The processing of source text prior to compilation. In an SQL environment, SQL statements are replaced with statements that will be recognized by the host language compiler.

prefix data   Data in a segment or a record used exclusively for system control, usually unavailable to the user.

primary key   An attribute that contains values that uniquely identify the record in which the key exists.

primitive data   Data whose existence depends on only a single occurrence of a major subject area of the enterprise.

privacy   The prevention of unauthorized access and manipulation of data.

privilege descriptor   A persistent object used by a DBMS to enforce constraints on operations.

problems data base   The component of a DSS application where previously defined decision parameters are stored. A problems data base is consulted to review characteristics of past decisions and to determine ways to meet current decision making needs.

processor   The hardware at the center of execution of computer programs. Generally speaking, processors are divided into three categories—mainframes, minicomputers, and microcomputers.

processor cycles   The hardware's internal cycles that drive the computer (e.g., initiate I/O, perform logic, move data, perform arithmetic functions).

production environment   The environment where operational, high-performance processing is run.

program area   The portion of main memory in which application programs are executed.

progressive overflow   A method of handling overflow in a randomly organized file that does not require the use of pointers. An overflow record is stored in the first available space and is retrieved by a forward serial search from the home address.

projection   An operation that takes one relation as an operand and returns a second relation that consists of only the selected attributes or columns, with duplicate rows eliminated.

proposition   A statement about entities that asserts or denies that some condition holds for those entities.

protocol   The call format used by a teleprocessing monitor.

punched cards   An early storage medium on which data and input were stored. Today, punched cards are rare.

purge data   The data on or after which a storage area may be overwritten. Used in conjunction with a file label, it is a means of protecting file data until an agreed upon release date is reached.

query language   A language that enables an end user to interact directly with a DBMS to retrieve and possibly modify data managed under the DBMS.

record   An aggregation of values of data organized by their relation to a common key.

record-at-a-time processing   The access of data a record at a time, a tuple at a time, and so on.

recovery   The restoration of the data base to an original position or condition, often after major damage to the physical medium.

Red Brick   A DSS data base management system by Red Brick Corp.

redundancy   The practice of storing more than one occurrence of data. In the case where data can be updated, redundancy poses serious problems. In the case where data is not updated, redundancy is often a valuable and necessary design tool.

referential integrity   The facility of a DBMS to ensure the validity of a predefined relationship.

reorganization   The process of unloading data in a poorly organized state and reloading the data in a well-organized state. Reorganization in some DBMS is used to restructure data. Reorganization is often called "reorg," or an "unload/reload" process.

repeating groups   A collection of data that can occur several times within a given record occurrence.

repository   A central gathering place for meta data.

rolling summary   A form of storing archival data where the most recent data has the lowest level of detail stored and the older data has higher levels of detail stored.

roll up   The summarization and/or aggregation of data at a higher level of detail than that currently being considered.

scope of integration   The formal definition of the boundaries of the system being modeled.

SDLC   System development life cycle—the classical operational system development life cycle that typically includes requirements gathering, analysis, design, programming, testing, integration, and implementation. Sometimes called a "waterfall" development life cycle.

sequential file   A file in which records are ordered according to the values of one or more key fields. The records can be processed in this sequence starting from the first record in the file, continuing to the last record in the file.

serial file   A sequential file in which the records are physically adjacent, in sequential order.

set-at-a-time processing   Access of data by groups, each member of which satisfies some selection criteria.

slicing   A constriction of the analysis space that includes only a subset of the data in the original space.

snapshot A data base dump or the archiving of data as of some one moment in time.

snowflake structure The grouping together of two or more star joins.

spiral development methodology An iterative methodology where small parts of the system are produced quickly and heuristically. The requirements for processing are not known when the system development process commences.

spreadsheet An analytical tool for individual decision support analysis.

star join A denormalized form of organizing data optimal for the access of a group of people, usually a department. Star joins are usually associated with data marts. Star joins were popularized by Ralph Kimball.

static meta data Nonchanging data about data. As opposed to dynamic meta data.

storage hierarchy Storage units linked to form a storage subsystem, in which some units are fast to access and consume small amounts of storage, but which are expensive, and other units are slow to access and are large, but are inexpensive to store.

subject data base A data base organized around a major subject of the corporation. Classical subject data bases are for customer, transaction, product, part, vendor, and so forth.

surrogate keys Keys generated by the system for usage of identification inside the warehouse.

Sybase A data base management system by Sybase Corp.

synthetic keys See *surrogate keys*.

system log An audit trail of relevant system events (for example, transaction entries, database changes).

system of record The definitive and singular source of operational data or meta data. If data element abc has a value of 25 in a data base record but a value of 45 in the system of record, by definition the first value must be incorrect. The system of record is useful for the management of redundancy of data. For metadata, at any one moment in time, each unit of metadata is owned by one and only one organizational unit.

table A relation that consists of a set of columns with a heading and a set of rows (i.e., tuples).

terabyte A measurement of a large amount of data, 1×10^{12} bytes.

Teradata A data base management system by NCR.

time stamping The practice of tagging each record with some moment in time, usually when the record was created or when the record was passed from one environment to another.

time-variant data Data whose accuracy is relevant to some one moment in time. The three common forms of time variant data are continuous time span data, event discrete data, and periodic discrete data. See also *current value data*.

tourist An individual who knows how to quickly cover a wide breadth of territory.

transaction processing   The activity of executing many short, fast-running programs, providing the end user with consistent two- to three-second response time.

transition data   Data possessing both primitive and derived characteristics; usually very sensitive to the running of the business. Typical transition data include interest rates for a bank, policy rates for an insurance company, retail sale prices for a manufacturer/distributor, and so on.

trend analysis   The process of looking at homogeneous data over a spectrum of time.

true archival data   Data at the lowest level of granularity in the current level detail data base.

Unix   A popular operating system for data warehouses.

update   To change, add, delete, or replace values in all or selected entries, groups, or attributes stored in a database.

user   A person or process issuing commands or messages and receiving stimuli from the information system.

waterfall development   The development practice of completing one phase of design before the next phase of design starts. The waterfall approach to system design came about because of structured analysis and design.

Zachman framework   A specification for organizing blueprints for information systems, popularized by the the great John Zachman.